I0470449

TALES FROM THE OLDEST PROFESSION

As Told by a Very Common Lawyer

KEVIN O'DONNELL

BALBOA
PRESS
A DIVISION OF HAY HOUSE

Balboa Press books may be ordered through booksellers or by contacting:

Balboa Press
A Division of Hay House
1663 Liberty Drive
Bloomington, IN 47403
www.balboapress.com.au
1 (877) 407-4847

Printed in the United States of America.

ISBN: 978-1-4525-1387-4 (sc)
ISBN: 978-1-4525-1388-1 (e)

Balboa Press rev. date: 05/30/2014

CONTENTS

Chapter 12 – More Lawyers and a Little Funny Business 108

Chapter 17 – From a Different Angle   161

INTRODUCTION

If you are expecting that this book is about the law, I'm sorry. It's not. It's about people. Specifically about the people I came across in over forty years of legal practice. It might contain some germs about the way the law works in practice, but it's mainly about the different (some weird) characters that inhabit the world that lawyers walk in.

When I set out to start writing a few rambling recollections, I expected to have a few thousand words in me. As it turned out, the process, from my point of view at least, has been both fascinating and truly enjoyable.

Once I began writing, more and more often would a story, buried deep in my memory, come to the surface (sometimes in the middle of the night, and even while out riding my bicycle). It became common for me to reach for my phone to jot down a couple of words, so as not to forget the anecdote in question.

Often, in conversation with some old friends, when I mentioned what I was doing, they would assist with a laugh and "You remember what happened with so and so" and another tale or two would be added.

Some of the stories are inherently improbable, BUT - they are all true! I'm sure that some people will look at a few of them and say - "No. that's impossible. That could not have ever happened". My response is - "You're right. It couldn't have happened…. But it did!"

By the way, when I use the expression 'lawyer', I do so in a generic sense, and generally avoid the expression 'solicitor'. All those who practise law are lawyers. some specialise as tax lawyers, corporate lawyers, mergers and acquisitions lawyers, commercial lawyers or whatever - and then there are those who specialise in appearance work in the superior courts. We refer to them as 'barristers'.

I should also point out that, with the exception of a few public figures, the names of the many characters (and some times and places) have been changed to protect the innocent (and also, hopefully, to ensure that the author does not finish up defending a defamation claim).

I'd hasten to add that I have generally treated the characters fairly - and where I might have been a little harsh, I'll rely on the defence that the anecdotes are true, and delivered without malice.

I hope the reader gains some of the enjoyment from reading my ramblings that I have gained from writing them.

CHAPTER 1

SOME CONFRONTATIONS, AND THE MANLY ART OF SELF DEFENCE

Gus and Me

Way back in the 1970's I used to do some legal work for the collection of unpaid debts. I knew quite a few lawyers who did some of this work, although some of the more pretentious of them said they worked in "commercial litigation".

One of my first debt collection experiences, following my admission to practice in 1970, involved the legendary boxing referee, actor and raconteur Gus Mercurio.

As a very young lawyer, one of my duties was to attend the County Court whenever a judgment debtor was due to appear to give evidence as to their income and assets, in relation to money they owed under a judgment.

So, each month, for about five months, I would be at the County Court, when the name August Eugene Mercurio would be called, followed shortly by the statement "No appearance, Your Honour".

The procedure was that the judgment debtor would be served with a subpoena requiring them to attend. In Gus's case, the subpoena was, each time, returned to the court with the notation "Unable to serve, whereabouts unknown".

At the time, each of Melbourne's three commercial television channels, 7, 9 and 0 (before it became channel 10) had a live boxing program on weeknights. So, after the day's work which included attending the County Court, I'd go home that night and watch the boxing on channel 0. As I recall, the referee for every bout, as large as life, was Gus.

At no time in my attendances at the County Court was Gus ever served with a subpoena. I figured that the process servers weren't brave enough to track Gus down at the TV studio and serve him. Gus had a reputation for being a tough man, and I doubt that I would have served the subpoena in their position.

After a while, the matter was no longer listed. I concluded that Gus's finances had improved and that he ultimately paid the debt.

A couple of years later, I was watching Division 4, a police drama (each of Melbourne's commercial channels had one of these too), on channel 9.

In this particular episode, the main characters, played by Gerard Kennedy and Terrence Donovan (Jason Donovan's father) were approaching the front door of a house, where they were trying to track down a suspect. The front door burst open, and out came Gus, swinging like a rusty gate.

In the show, the police characters quickly overpowered the aggressor, and demanded to know why he was attacking policemen - to which Gus's character replied, in his raspy voice "Oh, police? I thought you was process servers!"

Sometimes the writers of fiction don't know how closely their work reflects real life.

The Man Who Shouldn't Have Been in Prison

At that time there was a piece of legislation called the Imprisonment of Fraudulent Debtors Act. The way it worked was that a person who hadn't paid a judgement debt would be required to attend court to give evidence about their income and assets. If the magistrate found that they could afford to pay the debt (e.g. by instalments), they would be ordered to pay it off, at a specified rate, in default a number of days imprisonment.

One of these cases involved a man we'll call Trevor, who owed money to my client, a finance company. After telling the court about his finances, Trevor was ordered to pay the debt and costs by fortnightly instalments, in default ten days imprisonment. He made a couple of payments and then stopped paying. Acting on the client's instructions, we applied for a warrant, which the court issued, and the police (in those days, police executed all warrants) picked up Trevor and carted him off to jail.

First thing the next morning, I received a phone call from a very capable young lawyer I knew, Peter Ryan, who much later became deputy premier of Victoria. Peter was one of a number of lawyers on a roster system to give legal advice to those who'd been recently been taken into custody. He told me that Trevor's story was that he'd actually gone back to the finance company and that they'd re-written his loan.

I immediately called the finance company who confirmed Trevor's story, and added "Oh, didn't we tell you?" (Gee thanks, fellas!)

I called Peter back and confirmed the position with him. Then I raced down to the court to apply to have Trevor released. The magistrate noted the injustice of Trevor being locked up, but said he couldn't order his release as the imprisonment order was not defective in any way. It was a proper order of the court, executed properly.

The magistrate instructed the clerk of courts to make some phone calls, and see if anyone in the department could find a way through this.

About an hour later, I received a phone call from a gentleman who introduced himself as "Booth, Director-General of Social Welfare". He quizzed me about the case and the circumstances. I was able, in my capacity as solicitor on the record for the judgement creditor, to confirm that Trevor should not have been in prison. Mr Booth, as it happened, had an overarching discretion to order the release of a prisoner when he was satisfied that justice so required.

In the circumstances, and as I verbally confirmed that Trevor should not be in prison, Mr Booth ordered his release. Trevor walked free that afternoon.

Trevor would have had a strong case to claim damages from the finance company for wrongful imprisonment. It's possible that the company made a payment to him, or at least gave him a discount on his loan. If they did, they certainly didn't tell me about it.

"Come Outside and Say That"

The reader might think that lawyers, as people who engage in a combative process, would often be challenged to a fistfight. Actually, it's very rare, although it did happen to me once, when I was quite a young lawyer.

One day when I was working in Morwell, fairly late in the afternoon, I heard a man's raised voice at reception. I arrived there in time to hear a middle aged man yelling at the teenage girl who was at reception at the time. He was roundly abusing her, and calling her some very unpleasant names. She found the abuse more than she could handle and collapsed in tears.

He had apparently, just that afternoon, been served with a summons for a debt he owed to one of our clients. I suspect he had been drinking, and he was certainly in a foul mood.

I demanded to know what he thought he was doing, and suggested that it didn't reflect well on his manhood to be abusing a young girl. He asked if I was calling him a coward, and I replied that his conduct was certainly cowardly.

At that, he challenged me to step outside and repeat the comment. So, we both stepped out onto the footpath. He was still angry, telling me that his son was a policeman, and that he knew what "you lot" were like.

He then shaped up to me, saying "You called me a coward. Now prove it." I have never been a fighter and had no intention of taking a swing at him. My strength was in the use of words (some might call it sledging), so I responded "I don't need to. You've already proved it for me."

He asked "What do you mean?" I replied "A real man wouldn't talk to a girl like that."

He was still angry and menacing. I was a fair bit younger than he was, and light on my feet, so I figured I could keep out of his way if he took a swing at me. He didn't, but he kept repeating that I had called him a coward and should prove it. I kept responding that I didn't need to; he'd already proved it beyond doubt.

After a few minutes of this, and still muttering, he eventually gave up and wandered away.

I never came across him again, but I noted that the debt and the costs were paid the next week.

Another Confrontation

A few years later, when I was a sole practitioner, I acted on a number of occasions for a couple, Manny and Eva who were, over a few years' time, involved in various businesses.

Manny and Eva were slow to pay their bills, which would mount up over some months, but whenever they sold an asset, I would deduct what they owed me from the proceeds of the sale.

The last time I acted for them, I had been waiting longer than usual, and the money owed had grown significantly. There was finally another sale, and I duly deducted the total debt from the sale proceeds as usual, and sent them a statement setting out how it was all worked out.

A few days later, Manny rang, demanding to know why I had "stolen" his money. I explained that I had only taken what they owed me, as I had done previously, and that I was entitled to be paid.

At this time, I was starting work at 5.30 am. I would work till about 7.45 or so, go home for a shower and breakfast, and return to the office by 9.00.

One morning, as I opened the door to leave the office, at about 7.45, Manny and Eva and their adult son brushed past me and stepped inside the office.

Manny told me that they were there to collect the money that I had withheld from their last cheque.

Over the next twenty minutes or so, Manny continued to demand the money, with what I took to be an implied threat of violence.

I explained to them that:

- I had no intention of paying him anything,
- The office did not carry cash,
- I was not proficient in the accounts system,
- If I did give him a cheque, I'd call the bank and stop payment on it before he had a chance to cash it, and
- He was committing a criminal act which could cost him his freedom and/or a lot more than the money we were talking about.

While all this was going on Linda, one of my employees, arrived for work. She regularly started work at 8.00 and I was normally gone home for breakfast/shower by then. She raised an eyebrow at what she saw, but I told her things were under control, and she went into her office.

After a bit more time had passed, Manny and Eva seemed to realise that their plan was seriously flawed, and they left. I never saw them or heard from them again. Good riddance.

Yet Again

Some years later, when I was working with a law firm in Geelong, I represented Rod, a young man who was defending a claim which related to the use of his car.

I thought we achieved a good result for Rod, and he initially seemed very happy with the outcome, but he did not pay the bill. Eventually we sued him, and obtained judgement for the amount of our bill and the further costs of the new summons.

When Rod still did not pay, we applied to the court and obtained a warrant for the Sheriff to seize and sell his assets (specifically his car) to pay the debt.

A month or so later, the Sheriff sent in a report on the warrant, saying that Rod claimed he owned nothing, and that the car was not his. He said (as did his father) that, although the car was registered in his name, it was really the father's car and was only in his name for family reasons.

We didn't buy this argument, and responded that the Sheriff should proceed to seize and sell the car to satisfy the judgement debt.

About a week later, Rod and a friend of his came to the office. They marched past reception without a word, and stormed into my office in quite a threatening manner.

Rod demanded that the firm withdraw the warrant. I told him that

- It was no longer up to me,
- There was a committee of the partners of the firm that was in charge of these matters, and
- They would be very unlikely to write off the debt.

I also pointed out that what he and his mate were doing constituted a serious criminal offence, and that they should leave before things got out of hand.

After a bit of muttering, they seemed to accept what I had said, and left somewhat sheepishly.

A few days later, we received payment in full.

Garnishees

One of the steps we used to take to enforce a judgement debt was called a garnishee. This involved serving notice on their employer requiring money to be taken out of the debtor's wage or salary.

In the Latrobe Valley, by far the biggest employer in those times was the State Electricity Commission (SEC). In some quarters it was referred to as the slow easy and comfortable. I heard it said that, in the local administration offices you might be talking to a person in the morning, and see that they had a piece of paper in hand. Many hours later, they'd still be clutching the same piece of paper.

Each Friday morning, my first duty was to drive to the administration office and deliver a handful of garnishee orders to the SEC.

Of course, there were also many contractors who worked in the power construction projects for the SEC. The boss of one of these companies was George Cole, a large, overweight impatient, irascible man who liked to drive his Rolls Royce around construction sites and yell at people. I had heard that George had an inflated idea of his own importance.

On one occasion, we served a subpoena on George's company, requiring it to deduct money from the pay packet of one of his employees. George responded with an irate letter accusing us of wasting his time, telling us to keep out of his business, and not to bother him again. He said he would ignore the notice, and had thrown it in his rubbish bin.

I wrote back to George, apologising for annoying him, detailing the relevant legislation under which the garnishee had been issued, explaining that he was obliged to act in accordance with the order, and setting out the penalties for failing to comply with it.

We didn't hear from George again, but a cheque came in the next week.

Other Objections

On another occasion, we were seeking to enforce a judgement against a person who lived in the Gippsland lakes area. We applied for, and the court issued a warrant for the seizure and sale of the debtor's assets, and sent it off to the local police for execution (the police handled all such warrants in those days).

A couple of weeks later, we received a letter from the local police sergeant, who said he personally knew the defendant and would vouch for his honesty. He outlined the debtor's position that he did not actually owe the debt claimed, and that in fact the judgement creditor was the one who owed money to the debtor. He finished by saying "...In view of his obvious truthfulness, I have declined to execute the warrant."

I sent a letter in reply, pointing out that it wasn't the police officer's function to determine the question of liability - the court had already done that. I also noted that the warrant was an order of the court, and that he was duty bound to carry it out. I added that he was subject to potential disciplinary action from both the court and the Chief Commissioner of Police if he refused to do his duty.

He didn't reply, but soon afterwards, he executed the warrant and we received payment for the full judgement debt.

Better Memory Than Barry Jones?

As a young lawyer, I had a file where Barry Jones was on the other side. This was after Barry had become famous as a quiz king, but before he entered politics.

Curiously, I was in a position to correct Barry's memory of a very minor incident. What happened was that Barry rang one day when I was in court. He asked who was handling the file, and was given my name. Apparently he requested a copy of a document, and was told it would be posted to him.

The person who took the call made a note for the file, but did not detail the request. A few days later, he called, not happy that I had not done what I had promised. I told him that we had not, in fact spoken. While my memory might not be in his class, it was nevertheless very good, and I would not have forgotten a call from the famous Mr Jones.

When I outlined that I had been in court when he rang, he accepted my version of events. I then sent him the copy that he wanted, and the case settled not long after.

So, for a little while, I boasted (well, half jokingly) about having a better memory than Barry Jones.

It was a big deal to me, but I'm sure Barry has long ago put such a minor incident out of his mind!

CHAPTER 2

STUDENTS AND THE LAW

Raiding the Kitchen - Who Gets the Blame?

This story didn't happen in my time as a lawyer, but it involves a man who became very prominent in the profession.

In my undergraduate days, I was privileged to have a number of years as a resident of one of the colleges at the University of Melbourne. We who lived in college were very fortunate. We were in the thick of whatever was happening at the university, and were largely able to come and go as we pleased.

Occasionally, late at night, we might feel a little hungry. How to deal with this in the days before cafes and stores opened late? Well, the college had a big kitchen, didn't it?

A few of us became very adept at raiding the kitchen in the wee hours, and having a nice little feast. The college rector was unimpressed, but we were never caught.

As it happened, we weren't the only ones who liked a late feed. It seems that Gareth and some of his mates had similar needs. Anyway, on one occasion, Gareth was apprehended and brought before the rector, who threw the book at him. Gareth only very narrowly avoided being expelled.

After that incident, whenever the kitchen was raided (and no-one caught red-handed), the rector would call Gareth in and go through him. The routine was the same every time; the rector would go off and Gareth would protest his innocence - arguing once that he was not even in college when it happened.

The rector was very unhappy with Gareth, but couldn't expel him in the absence of any further evidence.

We were aware of all this going on and had great entertainment at poor Gareth's expense.

One of my mates, Walsh, who had a great historical perspective, started referring to Gareth as 'Trotsky'.

None of us ever let on who the villains were, and I'm not sure whether, to this day, Gareth (who much later became the senior partner of a substantial law firm) knows who we were, or why some people used to refer to him (and some still do) as 'Trotsky'.

A Student Encounter With the Police

Way back in the 1960's, university student life was lively and entertaining - and we even had the option of going to lectures if we wanted.

There were occasions of anti-conscription demonstrations, flour-bombing lecturers, raiding women's colleges (they were single-sex in those days), and all sorts of shenanigans. I hasten to deny that I was involved in anything like this.

Many students in those times lived in shared accommodation in Carlton and surrounding suburbs - in the days before those areas became uber-trendy.

Often there'd be a party on a Saturday night at someone's lodgings, and a crowd would arrive, each with their own preferred drinks, some with other substances.

On one of these occasions, Walsh and I left the party at about midnight with a couple of fine young women. We were feeling a bit peckish, and found a Lygon Street cafe still open (it was not a 24/7 precinct in those days), with a few tables of elderly Italian men engaged in some form of gambling.

We went in, found a table and ordered some food. After a while a few plainclothes policemen came in. I made the mistake of picking up a small breadbasket and holding it over my face (yes, I had had a couple of drinks).

Two of the cops came and stood over me, demanding to know if I was trying to take a rise out of them. "Not me sir" I replied, still sitting down. "Well what do you think you're doing" was the response. I shot back with "Are you accusing me of breaching the Crimes Act or the Police Offences Act?"

A sharp shove in the chest, and I was on my back on the floor. Attempting to restore some dignity, I stood up, picked up my chair and set it back to the table as they continued to glower at me.

A few seconds of silence, then I told them "Excuse me, but I only stand up in the presence of gentlemen." and sat down. Half a second later, I was on my back on the floor again. I picked up the chair and sat down again, this time in silence.

At this stage, I was concentrating on not doing anything more to provoke them. I reckoned they would like me to take a swing at them so they could react, beat me up, and lock me up for assault and resisting arrest. One sobers up very quickly in that scenario. This was not the time to continue being a cheeky, smart-arse student. I had already overplayed that role!

After a couple of minutes, they backed off a little. I went over to the tables of gamblers, and asked if they would back me up if I lodged a complaint. They told me they were worried that they'd get into trouble if they did. Their attitude was that they'd have to say that they saw nothing.

We left soon after, but the story ran on for some time.

Jack Galbally QC and the Bread Knife Case

As law students, PJ and I thought it might be a good idea to check out a few cases in the courts. We sat in on a number of Magistrates

Court hearings, and then decided to observe a Supreme Court murder trial.

We found a case, where Jack Galbally QC was listed as defending a man accused of murder, so we took up our position in the court.

We saw the jury selected, and watched as the Crown Prosecutor began outlining the evidence that he would call. He was only speaking for about five minutes when he was interrupted by one of the jurors. This man must have read about the case when the accused was committed for trial, and had heard that a bread knife was involved. Unable to restrain himself, he interrupted the Crown Prosecutor, yelling out "But Your Honour, what about the bread knife?"

The judge and most people in the court sat up straight, and it was quickly decided to discharge this jury and start again.

So, it all went back to the start, and this time there were no interruptions. There was no argument over the facts. The defence was that the accused was in an alcoholic psychosis at the time, and was incapable of forming a criminal intent at the time he stabbed the victim.

Jack Galbally was a Labor Party member of the Victorian Parliament at the time (Opposition Leader in the upper house, the Legislative Council) and was leading a campaign against capital punishment. In this case, he led evidence as to the accused's condition and state of mind at the time of the victim's death.

The most important witness was Dr Allen Bartholomew, who was a leading forensic psychiatrist in Victoria for many years. He told the court that, in his opinion, the accused was so damaged by his psychosis that he would have been incapable of forming an intention to harm the accused, and could not have understood the consequences of what he was doing.

The end result was that the jury, unsurprisingly, returned a verdict of not guilty on the grounds of insanity.

CHAPTER 3

ODD LAWYER TALES

Fast Fred and the Axe (Also Known as Fred's Folly)

Fast Fred was a bright young lawyer who did his articles (the year after university that must be completed and certified before being admitted to practice) with the firm I worked with, which was a strong, established firm with an excellent reputation.

Fred was an ambitious and impatient young man, who wanted to be seen by his community as making good and heading for the top.

My firm offered him a good job as a first year lawyer. If he had accepted it he could have looked forward to being well trained, tutored and mentored in the legal profession. He would have progressed through the firm in the conventional way.

Depending on his efforts and achievements, he would have gone through the usual steps. This would have led him, over a number of years, to promotion to associate and ultimately partner.

Instead, Fred moved to a smaller, 3 partner firm, where he had expectations of a more rapid rise to partnership. This prospect, with the enhanced status he was looking forward to, was important to him.

A few of us who knew Fred (and had had dealings with his new firm) had some misgivings, but he presented the move as a done deal, and was highly excited about it.

In later years, I became a regular, official mentor to articled clerks and young lawyers. In those times, I made a point of saying to them:

"If at any time, you're planning to leave this firm, come and have a talk to me first. I won't tell anyone you don't want me to tell, but I might be able to help you not to do something you'll regret. I know many lawyers and firms. There are some I know little about, some I'd be in favour of, and some I'd advise you not to touch with a barge pole".

Anyway, Fred moved to his new firm and was duly appointed an associate six months later. He was very impressed with how he was going.

The new firm was one where each lawyer largely looked after their own clients. In a sense, each was a sole practitioner, so there was little scope for anyone to develop any specialist area of practice. Whatever need each client had, their lawyer personally attended to it.

There was also very little in the way of assistance, support, supervision or counselling, which one would normally expect in a good firm. This was a firm to which the *'barge pole'* prohibition might well have applied.

As part of Fred's practice, he appeared in the Magistrates' Court from time to time on assorted traffic and criminal matters. One of the magistrates was known as 'the Axe' - he was sharp but fair - but could sniff out a scam and could cut you off at the knees if you tried to put anything over him.

Anyway, Fred had a client who was facing some dishonesty charges, but was very unwilling to present himself at court. Fred had obtained a few adjournments for him, but the Axe had warned Fred not to bother asking for any more adjournments. The next time, the case would proceed - no matter what.

So, on the next hearing day, the Axe was waiting for Fred and his client. When there was no sign of the client, a displeased Axe wanted to know where he was.

Fred responded that the client was in Queensland, and was too ill to travel. The Axe asked if Fred had a medical certificate to confirm the illness, and was unimpressed to hear that he did not. He asked Fred when he became aware that the client would not be appearing.

Fred told him that he had only learned of the position that morning, when he received a letter from the client, telling him of the illness, and begging him to have the case adjourned one more time.

The Axe asked for the letter and Fred handed it up to him. On reading it, the Axe commented on it being typed, and proceeded to cross-examine Fred about it. Fred confirmed that it had arrived in the mail that morning, in a standard sized, stamped envelope, but no, he had not brought the envelope to court with him.

The Axe pointed out that there were no crease marks in the letter, that it had not been folded. He also wondered aloud how that could be if it had come in a standard sized envelope. After a moment's silence, and under the Axe's withering stare, Fred conceded that he had himself prepared the letter.

After suggesting that a lawyer should leave crime to the criminals (some of whom are much better at it), the Axe went on to tell Fred that he was standing the matter down till after lunch. At that time Fred would be required to present himself before the court with all the firm's partners.

In the meantime, the Axe would reflect on possible courses of action, including punishment for contempt of court and deliberately misleading the court, as well as referring the proceedings to the appropriate authorities for action to revoke Fred's entitlement to practise law.

When the case came on after lunch, the firm's partners were present with Fred, who provided a grovelling apology, which the Axe accepted. On Fred's undertaking to the court to immediately resign from the firm, to leave the city, and not to appear before him again, the Axe agreed to take no further action in respect of Fred's freedom - or to refer the matter to the other authorities.

So, Fred left town. He took up a position with a firm in a rural area for many years. I caught up with him much later. He is still practising law, but never achieved the heights to which he once aspired.

In the long run, Fred was a lucky man. He was ultimately at the mercy of the Axe. Not many occupants of the bench would have been as forgiving as the Axe turned out to be!

But how silly can you get?

Sunny

Sunny was one of the local characters, and a great personality. He was of Indian extraction, loved his cricket and was always looking for the funny side of a situation.

Sunny and Greg were often opposed to each other but were great mates, and used to sledge each other mercilessly, in a way that only good friends can. If they weren't such good mates, some of their comments would have been unacceptable.

Sunny and his wife used to throw good parties. One of them was legendary. They served a wide variety of finger food, the highlight being the most magnificent (and a little spicy) meatballs. Everyone loved them, and after having one, would need to take a good swig of a nice cold drink.

With this as a starting point, it developed into a very memorable party indeed.

Greg

Greg was a big man with a big personality. After a very brief career in league footy, he started working with a Latrobe Valley law firm. He enjoyed a beer, a smoke and a day at the races.

On one occasion Mark, one of Greg's partners appeared at court in one of Greg's cases, asking for an adjournment. He told the court that Greg had had to go to an important meeting in Kilmore that day. I suspected that all might not have been as it appeared. Outside the court a few minutes later, I winked at Mark and asked him what the meeting was. He replied "The only meeting I know of in Kilmore today is a race meeting."

Greg and I were often opposed to each other in the local Magistrates' Court. Often, we'd be waiting with our clients for a case to come on. The clients sometimes found it hard to understand that Greg and I would be chatting away in a friendly manner outside the court. I made a point of explaining that we were friends, but that we'd go hard at each other in court.

Sure enough, we'd give each other heaps in court, and, at the end of the day, go to the pub for a couple of beers.

Greg and I would always catch up with each other at our annual law convention. On one of them, we were playing golf in a foursome. Greg had a fairly cavalier attitude to the rules and conventions of golf. If he had a putt of about a metre, he'd say "That's a gimme" and pick it up. For most of us, a 'gimme' was no more than 10 centimetres.

At another convention, he challenged me to a game of tennis. In the first game, I passed him with what for me was an unusually good backhand. It landed just over the service line, and over a metre in from the tramlines. Greg called "Bad luck mate" and headed back to serve for the next point. I was so stunned, I just shook my head and said nothing. Greg won that game.

Greg's tennis game was built upon hitting every shot as hard as he could. After the first game, I changed my game plan. Instead of trying to pass Greg, I started hitting the ball directly to him, generally at his feet - real junk shots.

Having to hit low balls, from the middle of the court, without any pace on them, Greg's game fell apart. He kept on hammering every ball, and most of them hit the net or landed well outside the court. I finished up winning the set 6-1.

That night, on the way in to dinner, Mark came up to me, saying "I saw you having a game of tennis with Greg today. How'd you go?" I told him that I'd won 6-1. "You must be good" he declared "He cheats!"

After any big night out, Greg would complain that the moose got him. "I was feeing good when I went to bed" he'd say "But the moose came in, kicked me in the head and took a shit in my mouth."

Serge

While Christopher (even with his foibles) was a good person and well regarded, Serge, whom I came across some years later, was a very different type of person and lawyer. I don't know if he ever had any friends. If he did, I doubt any of them would have been lawyers. He was *always* difficult, abrupt, rude and unpleasant. Often he was just plain nasty.

You might gather that Serge was a sole practitioner. I can't imagine any other lawyer being prepared to work with him. He also had a lot of staff turnover.

There was never a straightforward matter when Serge was on the other side, whether it was a commercial transaction, a simple sale of a vacant block of land, a family law settlement, or any other matter.

Even where the parties had agreed on all the terms, you would still have to negotiate every single condition or warranty in excruciating detail. It was often difficult to explain to the client why you would have spent so much time on what, to them, was very simple - not to mention why the bill was so high!

My good friend Rocky used to talk about lawyers who made the 'honour board' behind his left ear. He would say that he had a long memory, and while it took a lot to get on the board, it took a lot more to get off it. His view was that it might take years, but the wheel would turn, and eventually he'd exact revenge.

Many lawyers I knew had Serge at the top of their honour board. For the same reason that Christopher's clients sometimes missed out, Serge's did too - only much more so. Not many lawyers would take hard technical points against Christopher, or each other, but

Serge's conduct guaranteed that his opponents would, whenever the situation arose, use every available trick (some of them quite underhanded) against him.

As it happened, Serge (through his family trust, as I recall) owned the building from which he conducted his practice. He put it up for sale, with a long term lease back to himself.

I used to get referrals for various commercial transactions from a number of accountants for their business and investor clients. One day Jimmy, an accountant, came to me for advice for one of his clients on a contract and lease-back that Serge had prepared for the sale of the building.

After going through the documents, and advising on quite a number of clauses that unduly favoured the vendor (in the contract) and the tenant (in the lease), I asked Jimmy about his client, the investor.

It turned out that neither Jimmy nor his client knew anything about Serge. The investor was looking for a steady, risk-free, drama free investment for the long term, and having a lawyer for a tenant sounded good.

My view was that he could expect to always be in dispute with Serge, and the investment would turn into a nightmare. I told Jimmy what I knew of Serge. Jimmy passed this information on to the investor, and the deal did not proceed.

I don't know if Serge succeeded in selling the building, but I felt some satisfaction in saving this investor from having to deal with him. Most likely, Serge was never aware of what had transpired.

In the movie 'The Sting', when the Paul Newman and Robert Redford characters set out to take down the 'mark' (the Robert Shaw character), they did it in such a way that he didn't even know they had ripped him off. I felt a bit like that with Serge. It's quite possible he never knew I had cost him a sale. While a part of me would have liked to tell him, I was nevertheless content without telling him.

Some years later, another lawyer brought to my notice a case in the law reports, where Serge, as the lawyer, had lost a case where a company which he controlled had behaved badly. It lost heavily, and had serious orders made against it. The judge also made some adverse comments about Serge.

We agreed that this could not have happened to a more deserving lawyer.

Arthur

Here was a lawyer who had a different approach to practising law.

Arthur developed what he regarded as a specialist practice for senior citizens. He would make their wills free of charge.

Of course, he wasn't the first and won't be the last to prepare free wills. The State Trustee does free wills, but only where it is appointed as executor and trustee to administer the estate, so it will show a profit when the person (the testator) dies.

Some lawyers prepare simple wills free, so long as they are appointed to act for the deceased estate in due course. This is very risky, as there is a temptation to trot out a simple precedent, without taking the care necessary to make sure it is a good fit with the client's individual circumstances.

Arthur's approach was quite novel. He would seek out persons of dubious mental capacity, become their new best friend, and prepare wills in which they left a good slice (if not all) of their estate to him.

After a while, Arthur decided to refine his approach. He became a regular visitor to a number of aged care facilities, and initially was welcomed as a volunteer, coming to visit the elderly. However, suspicions were aroused when he would be seen bringing paperwork in, for residents to sign - especially when he would ask the staff to witness the new wills.

The management of one facility eventually warned Arthur off, and notified a number of authorities. There was a subsequent investigation, resulting in Arthur losing his certificate to practise law.

As a result of his conduct, Arthur was responsible for changes to the law, and to the rules of legal practice. For a clause in a will leaving anything to a lawyer to now be upheld, the will should be prepared by another lawyer, who is obliged to provide independent advice. It is also strongly recommended, if the person is elderly, that mental evidence of their medical capacity be provided at the time.

Another Very Naughty Lawyer

Simon was a very stylish lawyer who proudly wore expensive Italian mohair suits. He was proud of who he was and of his position in the local community. He lived the high life, and spent freely on the good things of life.

Unfortunately, Simon did not see himself as bound by the rules that applied to other mortals. He handled money for a number of his clients, but eventually, could not keep his hands off some of it.

In my latter days as a mentor of young lawyers, I would repeat a number of mantras to them. One of these was the simple rule "Trust account money is the clients' money. IT IS NOT YOUR MONEY!!!"

Simon seems to have overlooked that simple dictum. Anyway, he used nearly $300,000 of his clients' money to purchase a flock of emus. Presumably it was his plan to make a quick profit on the emus, and return the clients' money. This was a time when fearless salespeople were assuring gullible people that there was enormous money to be made from breeding emus.

The bad news was that a virus went through the emu flock, and they all died. Simon suddenly had a problem, which ultimately led to him losing his ticket to practise, and having a holiday at public expense.

At the same time, Simon was in the throes of an affair with a lady real estate agent in the same town. On a regular basis, at pre-arranged times, each of them would leave their office and head out. In the lady's case, she would say she was going on an 'inspection'.

In Simon's case, he was off to see a 'client'. He and the lady would rendezvous at a home that the lady had on her list of properties for sale, so they would engage in their 'inspection' while the owners were at work.

Imagine how you'd feel if you discovered that people you trusted with your house were having 'inspections' in your bedroom or en-suite while you were at work.

In due course, Simon's wife learned of his assignations with the lady agent, and she went ballistic. He arrived home one evening to find a pile of his possessions on the nature strip, and the locks changed.

Simon hurriedly found somewhere else to live, but noticed that his Italian mohair suits were not in the pile he'd collected from the nature strip. After a couple of days, he was able to speak to his wife, and asked her for his suits. She told him she'd taken them down to the Salvation Army's op shop.

Simon rushed down to the op shop, enquiring about the mohair suits, only to be told, "Oh, we don't have any demand for them around here. We sent them off to Melbourne."

In any event, Simon wouldn't be able to wear them where he was going.

== CHAPTER 4 ==

CHRISTOPHER

Christopher the Saintly Lawyer?

Over the years, I came across a large number of lawyers. I know that the general public has a poor view of lawyers, but there are so many lawyers with such widely varying personalities, political views, behaviours, methods and manner that it is impossible to group them under one heading.

In my Morwell days, Christopher was one of the leading lawyers in the area. Christopher was a prominent man in the Catholic Church and in the wider community. His hero was St Thomas More, who was tried for treason and beheaded by Henry VIII, for refusing to recognise the king as head of the church. He seemed to see himself as a man of similar principle.

Christopher and his large family always occupied the same pew at mass every Sunday morning. He was known as a strong and committed Catholic and a genuinely good man, who worked hard and did his best for his clients.

But Christopher had a weakness as a lawyer. He assumed that his own 'holiness' applied to his clients as much as it did to himself. He could not understand that his clients could be imperfect, or ever do anything wrong. He would spread the cloak of his holiness over them and 'tut tut' about how bad, evil and generally dishonest the other party always was.

All the other lawyers in town would sigh with resignation when they realised that Christopher was on the other side in any kind of dispute. He was much more difficult to deal with, or talk settlement with, than almost any other lawyer I came across.

No matter how much we tried, we could not get Christopher to understand that, over time, we would all get our share of good, honest, reasonable clients, dishonest, evil ones, and those in between.

In the long run, this attitude disadvantaged Christopher and his clients, as reasonable compromises could not be reached when he was on the other side. You had no alternative than to fight to the bitter end, with the result being often worse, and always more expensive, than could have been achieved.

Many readers will not understand the concept of shorthand. Christopher was one of those lawyers who began practice before the ascent of the dictaphone, when a lawyer verbally dictated correspondence and documents to a secretary (called a 'stenographer') who would record it on a pad by means of symbols, and then type it up - on a typewriter!

Christopher would pace up and down his office, dictating and amending. When he wanted to hear how it sounded, he would ask the secretary to "Read that back", before declaring whether he was happy with it.

Christopher and Another Pedant

As I said at the outset, Christopher was a good and honourable man. He was conservative in a number of ways, and hated what he saw as the bastardisation of English grammar, especially when a lawyer was doing it.

One thing which he and I spoke of from time to time was the way many lawyers would use "I" when "me" was called for. For instance, a simple sentence such as "Tom bought a drink for Tracey and me" would come out as "Tom bought a drink for Tracey and

I". Christopher would exclaim "It's like saying 'Tom bought a drink for I'. How can they be so uneducated?"

Christopher was particularly outraged when a barrister, whom he had briefed, was heard using sentences such as "Can you please pass that document to I", or, even worse "What did you say to he?". He assured me he would never brief that barrister again!

Christopher lamented the growth of such instances, and so, we formed the Society for the Preservation of the Accusative Case. It was a very small group of pedants who made small, occasional, efforts to reverse the decline. I doubt that we made any difference.

We also lamented the modern practice of referring to noon as 12 pm. In our (yes, pedantic) view, and applying the true Latin expressions, am indicated 'before midday' (therefore midnight) and pm indicated 'after midday' (therefore also midnight). Thus, the correct expression was 12 noon or 12 midnight.

Another 'pedantic' observation we made was the misuse of the apostrophe. We would wince when we came across the hot bread shop called "Charle's Bake House" or the tradesman's van with the owner's name, followed by "The name say's it all".

Such episodes would make us groan, and we would regularly share our observations. For Pete's sake - if you don't understand the apostrophe, please don't use it!

Christopher the Tourist

As a sole practitioner for several years, Christopher had no other lawyer to rely on to look after his clients when he was not there. Apart from a very short break each Christmas, he took no holidays for years.

Eventually, he felt able to trust an employee lawyer enough to take a European holiday with his wife Maureen. They had a wonderful time, going to the opera in Paris and Milan, and visiting his forebears' home in Ireland.

He denied kissing the Blarney Stone, but told me that, when they arrived in England, they went to Covent Garden. Even though (or maybe because) there was no-one else around, he couldn't resist breaking into a couple of bars from Mozart's *The Marriage of Figaro*. Just so he could say he had sung at Covent Garden!

Christopher's Risque Wit

Christopher was regarded as being fairly strait-laced in his sense of humour, and kept well clear of anything colourful or sex-related.

One time, Christopher was attending a weekend law conference with many other leading lawyers. On the Sunday morning, he was in fine form at breakfast. As each couple arrived, he'd ask in cheerful voice "How are the Smiths this morning?" or "How are the Youngs this morning?"

He confided in me later "I had to rephrase the question when Professor and Mrs Ball came down".

Quite unexpected from Christopher!

CHAPTER 5

CHARLIE

Charlie was another sole practitioner (having had a few years with Seamus - see below) who was more than a tad pretentious on occasions, and very tight when it came to spending money on alcohol (or in fact on anything).

Charlie the Fussy Beer Drinker

One Saturday night, we were at a party at Greg's, when Charlie and his wife arrived - a little late, but that's OK. Everybody brought their own drinks, but Charlie was empty-handed. He apologised, saying "Sorry Greg, but I only drink Crown Lager, and they didn't have any at your local bottle shop".

Charlie then got stuck into everyone else's Fosters and VB and was one of the last to leave.

Charlie's middle name was Ernest, but he changed it to Michael, which he felt was more dignified and suited him better.

One Sunday, the local lawyers organised a tennis day. We started about 10.00 am, at the local tennis courts, and had a good social time for two or three hours. The deal was we'd repair to Charlie's for a BBQ lunch, and bring our own food and drinks.

Charlie arrived at the courts a little while after everyone else, dressed in the most fashionable tennis gear. I heard later that he had expected to dazzle us all with his impeccable tennis, but no-one took much notice of him and he struggled to hold his own.

When we all rocked up to his house, his wife Lucy (who was truly lovely and liked by all) told us Charlie had had to rush off to see a client (not likely, most of us thought!). We went ahead and cooked and ate our lunch, and Charlie eventually appeared over an hour later, in a bad mood. Some were unkind enough to say that he was miffed about not winning at tennis, and had in fact been sulking.

Anyway, the beer in those days all came in longneck bottles with crown seals. Not long after he appeared, Charlie announced that the bottle opener (apparently the only one he had) had disappeared, so we couldn't open any more bottles.

This caused some consternation among the stayers (of whom there were a few), but by this stage, some people were starting to drift off home anyway.

Charlie consoled the stayers by saying "I'm sure Lucy will find it when she cleans up after everyone leaves."

Greg and Sam had a better idea. They went out to their cars, and one of them found a bottle opener in his glovebox. They then made a point of staying till all the beer was gone.

One year, for Lucy's birthday, her father gave her a cheque for $100 (in those days $100 was quite a deal of money). Not to be outdone, Charlie presented her with a cheque for $101. Interestingly, his cheque was drawn on their joint account, and then deposited back into the same account.

Charlie and Christopher both had their banking arrangements with the same bank. One year, the local bank manager took them out for lunch just before Christmas. As usual, Charlie arrived about half an hour late, apologising for being so busy. Christopher responded "Oh, did you have a meeting with your December client?"

Charlie, Max and the Swimming Pool

On one occasion, Lucy asked my wife and me to come around to visit her and Charlie on a Sunday afternoon. We duly arrived, early afternoon, and were warmly welcomed by Lucy.

No sign of Charlie. Lucy told us that he was over the road visiting Max, and suggested I go over. So, across I went, and Charlie introduced me to Max, an estate agent who had recently arrived in town. I shouldn't have been surprised, but Charlie was 'brown-nosing' Max quite shamelessly.

Max was setting up a new above-ground pool in his back yard, and Charlie had generously volunteered my labour as well as his own to help put it together (without bothering to tell me first).

I still recall toiling away all afternoon in the hot sun to get Max's pool finished, and not a cold beer in sight.

A few weeks later, I ran into Max in the course of business. He thrust out his hand to me, saying "My name's Max. Don't think I've had the pleasure."

Not long afterwards, I was recounting this story to Greg and Rocky, who noted how typical this was of Charlie - and how Max had the pleasure every time he jumped into his pool. A pleasure I never had!

Charlie and Waste Disposal

Charlie also seemed to have a thing about where he was or was not prepared to be seen. Such as the local tip.

On an occasional weekend, I'd do some work in the garden. As a result, there'd be a trailer load of garden rubbish (and perhaps some other rubbish) to take to the tip.

Doing this one day, I was emptying a trailer load, and looked up to see Christopher doing the same, about 10 metres away. We exchanged cheerful sledges and then went our separate ways.

Another time, I noticed Charlie in similar circumstances, but he refused to make eye contact and hurried away as quickly as he could. Greg told me that Charlie would never acknowledge that he went to somewhere as common as the tip.

Very much 'up himself'!

CHAPTER 6

SEAMUS

In the course of legal practice, you come across a huge variety of people, all of them very different. Seamus was probably the most unusual of them all. He was born and raised in Ireland and never lost his Irish origins or accent. He was forever the fierce ginger haired (and bearded) leprechaun. who drank and behaved accordingly. He and the issues that flowed from his behaviour are worth their own chapter.

Seamus in Fiji

Before coming to Australia, the young lawyer Seamus had been appointed by the British Colonial Office as Chief Magistrate of Fiji (which at that stage was still a British colony).

In this capacity, he had a short but colourful career, dispensing justice in his own style, and not always to the liking of his colonial masters. His rebellious Irish nature quickly came to the fore. He would find particularly creative ways to acquit any defendant who dissented from British rule - and became close friends with a couple of the defence lawyers who regularly appeared in his court.

Things came to a head when he joined a group of locals who were campaigning for Fijian independence, and was part of a demonstration calling for the end to British rule. It was altogether too much for his colonial masters to see photos of him carrying protest placards against the regime that had appointed him.

One of his lawyer friends got wind of treason charges that were being prepared against him, and bundled Seamus and his family onto the first plane to Australia. He avoided arrest by a couple of hours only.

Seamus in Australia

After a few years in partnership with a couple of more conventional types, who found him impossible to deal with, Seamus found himself running his own practice. He had a number of employee lawyers and other staff go through the firm, but none stayed long with him. He could be pleasant (charming in fact) when he wanted, but was very volatile and was often extremely hurtful and downright nasty.

Seamus built a strong practice, including in the personal injuries area. For several years, his office had the bulk of the personal injuries cases at the local County Court sittings. He delegated the running of the files to his employee lawyers, but kept a close eye on them to ensure that his cash continued to flow.

He also bought one of the pubs in town, and was often in it as much as at his practice. From time to time trust account auditors would be sent down from the Law Institute of Victoria to go through his trust account records. Seamus was very smart and could be exceptionally charming. More than once he was seen enjoying a long drinking session with the auditors at his pub. None of them ever filed an adverse report!

Seamus and the Expensive Yearling

At one stage, as someone who liked to gamble, he decided to get into the horse-racing business. Off he went to the bloodstock sales in Sydney, and was featured in the TV news, sitting alongside one of Australia's leading racehorse trainers as he set a then Australian record price for a yearling.

That same afternoon, Seamus telephoned his office, to ensure that the settlement money from a couple of injury cases had been received in his trust account. When the answer was yes, he instructed his employees to immediately transfer the costs to his office account, so his bank would honour his cheque for the yearling. Not many lawyers have purchased a racehorse with an office account cheque!

Seamus and the famed trainer hit it off well initially, but not for long. Seamus had the view that he was an old style gentleman and that the trainer was working class. He demanded that the trainer call him 'Mr' and that he would call the trainer simply by his surname. He behaved quite objectionably and the relationship quickly fell apart.

Sadly for Seamus, the horse (named 'His Honour') was a dud. After a number of starts, it won a maiden event on a country track, but chalked up several bad defeats. For a short while, it was kept for his children to ride, and then it vanished, never to be mentioned again.

Seamus the Showman

Seamus (some of us would refer to him as 'Shameless') also enjoyed making a big splash at casinos. Back in the days when Hobart has the only casino in Australia, he would regularly fly over for a session on the tables.

We would hear stories of him having a few good wins and many bad losses (as well as copious amounts to drink), and being escorted from the premises as he hurled insults at the staff. On one occasion, as he was being assisted to the door, he told the security guards "You're very efficient. I could use you in one of my corporations back home". We wondered how his law practice survived.

What Seamus had going for him was a strong group of clients with money to invest, whom he looked after (and to whom he applied his considerable charm). In those days, law practices in country towns were often measured by the strength of their mortgage fund. Seamus had one of the best, and generally had borrowers queueing up for loans if they couldn't get funding from the banks.

Seamus enjoyed the power that this gave him, and he often held court in his pub, boasting that he had more people begging him for loans than all the other lawyers in Gippsland combined.

Late Night Drinking

Seamus was generally unpopular with the police, although he was known to sometimes shout drinks for a small number of them when he was looking for a favour.

Many Irish people have a love of strong drink - and Seamus's was greater than most. Often, the gathering in his pub would continue after closing time.

A few of the police became aware of this trend, and decided to notch up Seamus's scalp. This would be a real feather in their caps, so they decided to raid the pub after hours, and catch him in the act.

One night a team of police burst in to find (unsurprisingly) Seamus and some of his mates enjoying a drink and a spot of banter. When they started asking questions, Seamus would loudly demand that the guests "Tell the dummies nothing!"

The police were jubilant - they had him cold for trading outside hours!

But Seamus wasn't a smart lawyer for nothing. The subsequent cross-examination of the police (by his barrister, of course) went along theses lines:

Q. "Officer X, did you see money change hands?"
A. "No, but there were several people drinking in the premises."
Q. "Were the doors open?"
A. "No."
Q. "Were people coming and going?"
A. "No."

The short answer - no case to answer! This was a private party, and the accused was having a drink with his friends, not selling liquor to members of the public.

Just another instance of Seamus having fun thumbing his nose at the police.

More Taunting the Police

Seamus refused to lead a boring life. He delighted in stirring up some action or controversy wherever he could.

After the last episode, some of the police were determined to nail Seamus. They knew that he was a heavy drinker, and that he lived on some acres a few kilometres out of town. Obviously, he was a drinking driver! So a few local coppers were looking for an opportunity to take him down.

Being aware of this, Seamus decided one night (about 1.30 am) to have a bit of fun. He called the police station, announcing that he'd been drinking all night, was well and truly under the weather, and would soon be heading home.

The person who took the call notified the officers on duty, who leapt into their squad car, and began cruising around the vicinity of the pub, checking out where his car was parked and waiting for him to appear.

After nearly another hour, Seamus was back on the phone. "I'm heading for the car now" he blustered. "To make it easy for you, I'll come by the pig sty. Make sure you're ready for me. Jeez I'm pissed."

About half an hour later, he was on the phone again. "Leaving just now. I'll be coming down the pig sty drive, right past the front door. Make sure you're ready for me. I'm coming through, I'm coming through."

Sure enough, his car shortly appeared, driving slowly down the drive in the police yard. And there was Seamus, grinning and waving in the passenger seat, as one of his mates drove through, and exited through the back gate.

Was This a Con?

A couple of Seamus's children became lawyers, and a daughter set up in a neighbouring town, building up a moderate practice over a couple of years. She didn't appear to have much to do with her father, and strongly maintained that she was independent of him.

Walkers was a prominent and well regarded East Gippsland firm, with strong commercial relationships with other local businesses. Together they were affectionately known as the 'Main Street Mafia'.

Walkers decided to expand into the Latrobe Valley, and Seamus became aware of this. All of a sudden, Seamus announced that he had sold his practice to Walkers. He set up the transaction so that settlement would take place four months later. He said this was to allow him time to unravel his personal affairs from those of the firm.

Shortly after this announcement, I began to hear rumours that some of Seamus's wealthy investor clients were considering moving their business to his daughter after he departed.

A few weeks later, Walkers announced that it had acquired the daughter's practice. The parties settled the purchase quickly, and Walkers moved in about two months before the settlement date for Seamus's practice.

Barry, one of Walkers' brightest young stars, moved down from East Gippsland to take over the daughter's practice, and to supervise the settlement of the purchase of Seamus's.

However, at the eleventh hour, Seamus announced that he'd changed his mind, and wasn't going anywhere. We all held our breath and waited to see if Walkers would take action to enforce its contract with him, or just let it ride. After thinking it over for a couple of days, they opted to let him be.

Some of us who knew Seamus wondered whether he had plotted for this outcome all along.

CHAPTER 7

SOME OTHER CHARACTERS

Barney

There are some lawyers, when you see them in court, who make you think "If I couldn't do a better job than that, I'd give up." Barney was not one of those. He was a very sharp advocate, and a good man. His one flaw was that he drank too much.

In court, on a good day, there was none better than Barney. He was very nimble, and one of the very best in dealing with whatever unexpected evidence came out.

One day, he was defending a man on a few charges arising from a big night out (fortunately there was no driving involved). The client insisted on pleading not guilty, but hadn't given Barney anything to work with. His story was that he couldn't remember what had happened, so he couldn't plead guilty to it. It also meant that he couldn't deny anything the police said.

The police evidence was that Barney's client was staggering all over the place, his eyes were bloodshot, and that he was badly slurring his words. Barney innocently asked if the witness thought the accused had been drinking. "Oh yes" was the reply "He was drunk, off the scale". To the next question, the witness responded that he had never seen anyone so drunk.

The prosecution had played right into Barney's hands. He quickly secured an acquittal, based on the rules in *O'Connor's* case.

His client had been so drunk that he was incapable of forming an intention to do what he was accused of doing. Most criminal cases depend on the accused having a *mens rea* (guilty mind), so Barney's client walked.

I have seen many other attempts to use the *O'Connor* defence. None have ever succeeded.

Bert

The police in the Latrobe Valley used to describe Bert as the FBI (fat bald and ignorant). Fat and bald he certainly was, but he was not a man to be underestimated. I preferred to regard him as fierce. blustering and implacable

When I arrived in the valley, Bert was my first and greatest enemy. His beef was that his debt recovery work had been taken from him, and it finished up with me (I was an innocent abroad at that stage and unaware of what had led to all this - I later learned that there was a perception that Bert was more sympathetic to the debtors than the creditors).

In my first appearance in court in the area, Bert appeared on behalf of the debtor, carrying on about what a travesty of justice it was for the person to be hauled before the court.

The irony was that the application to bring the debtor to court had been certified by Bert in an affidavit which he had sworn!

I quickly learned that the only way to handle Bert was to come back at him as hard as he came at me. Over a few years, we had quite a few 'no holds barred' tussles, and developed a kind of mutual regard.

They don't make lawyers like Bert any more. He hated paperwork and loved nothing more than a real old-fashioned courtroom brawl. There was not much subtlety about Bert. He tackled everything head on.

More than once I received a (very short) letter from Bert, that had smudges of tomato sauce or egg on it. His letters were always very short and to the point. They looked as though he typed them himself.

He had a very small office that finished up as an exhibit in the Old Gippstown Folk Museum at Moe, and looked like it was put together in the 1850s. Later, Bert worked from his home.

One day, at the County Court in Morwell, Bert and a few other lawyers were waiting at one end of the bar table, while the crown prosecutor was presenting his final argument to the jury in a criminal trial. The address was being recorded through the microphones on the bar table.

Bored with the proceedings, in which he was not involved, Bert was entertaining the other waiting lawyers, in his best stage whisper, about how he got back at whatever miscreants had been stealing from the beer fridge he kept on his back porch. "I fixed the bastards" he croaked, "I pissed in a few bottles, put new crown seals on them, and left them in the fridge. They won't come back now."

The defence counsel had kept one ear on Bert's story, and knew where it coincided with the prosecutor's summing up. With an innocent face, he queried the prosecutor's comments on *mens rea* (the question whether the accused had a 'guilty mind'), and asked the judge to play back that section. This was done, to the amusement of the jury and most of those in court, but to the judge's immense displeasure.

As well as sometimes entertaining us, Bert could sometimes be very irritating as well. More than once, at the beginning of a busy day in the Magistrates' Court, Bert would say "I've only got this little matter. It'll take no more than five minutes. Put me on first, and I'll be out of the way." Come mid afternoon, he'd still be going, and the waiting lawyers would be fuming. It was ridiculous that he got away with it as much as he did.

Ferdi the WIP Rustler

Most law firms wrestle with the question of how to most effectively charge their clients for the work they do. In a few areas of law, firms charge (by negotiation with their clients) a range of fixed fees.

In most areas of legal work, however, the hourly rate has for some time been the basis of charging. From time to time, each firm will determine the hourly rates charged by each of its fee earners.

Each practitioner has a time sheet, to be completed each day, and broken down into six minute segments (called 'units'), making up ten units per hour. They are required to record at least sixty (in some cases seventy, eighty or more) units of chargeable time per day.

Most firms then bill their clients on a monthly basis for the work done during that month. The value of that work is referred to as 'Work in Progress' or WIP.

Time spent on training, mentoring, general research, supervision, administration, policy, marketing, etc. is not included. So, a lawyer may need to be at work for ten, twelve or more hours a day to achieve sixty (or whatever the required number is) chargeable units. Bear in mind that lawyers are paid in accordance with their level of billings, so there's pressure to keep recording time.

In addition to the pressure and depression that results from it, the burden (the tyranny in some cases) of the chargeable hour can occasionally lead to creative practices. A minority of lawyers have earned themselves a reputation as WIP rustlers.

At the end of the month, you might be reviewing the bills to be rendered, and note that (on a file only you have worked on) another lawyer might have recorded a few hundred dollars of time. Sometimes this might be a simple matter of the wrong file number being entered, and is easily remedied. Sometimes, you have a sneaking suspicion that some WIP rustling has been going on.

Ferdi was a regular suspect in the WIP rustling area. It was said (only half in jest) that you should never leave your files on your desk in an unlocked office. If you did, Ferdi would casually wander in at lunch time, write down a few file numbers on a piece of paper, and presto, they'd be on his time sheet.

Ferdi and the GST

Our firm was engaged by the Commonwealth government to roll out some thousands of seminars throughout the country in 2000 to educate various business and community groups on how the GST would work. The idea was to enable the business community to hit the ground running, with as few problems as possible.

As a result, Garry, one of the tax partners (and a former Commissioner of State Revenue) became a real guru of GST. We also developed numerous clauses to cover just about every conceivable scenario relating to GST.

It became second nature for us, when preparing the documentation for any business transaction, to take a step back and ask ourselves - "OK, now how does the GST affect this?" and make sure our clients were always covered.

Ferdi and I worked alongside each other acting for a number of clients in commercial transactions. After a time, he left the firm to set up his own practice, and I took over many of his files.

On one of them, I noticed a serious problem. A good client was selling a couple of properties, in a scenario where GST was payable. The contract of sale had not passed on the GST liability to the purchaser in the way one would normally expect. This left the firm liable to cover the client's GST liability.

We did a quick assessment of the position, and concluded that we could minimise the problem by opting to use the margin scheme. We contacted a valuer who assessed the value of the properties as at 1 July 2000 as being the same as the price at which they were sold.

No margin between the two, therefore no GST.

Phew, all it cost the firm was the valuer's fee and writing off the lawyer time involved. A great result!

The 'Cricketer' and the Load Test

At another time, Seamus had a young, bumptious employee lawyer who had an elevated (and unjustified) opinion of his own talents, and had a very plummy speaking voice. Greg nicknamed him the 'Cricketer', because he talked "like he had a cricket stump up his arse".

I was opposed to the Cricketer in a building case. My client the builder, a man of German origins, was building a house for a young couple. The young couple had asked the wife's uncle, a man of Dutch heritage, to supervise the construction. They called him their 'clerk of works'.

The Dutchman was not otherwise employed, and made a point of being on site most of the time. He was a considerable annoyance to my client, and his workers, and kept getting in their way. He and my client developed a very strong mutual hostility.

The 'clerk of works' picked fault with everything that happened with the house, and particularly with the elevated slab, which he maintained would fail. Nevertheless, my client continued with the construction, till the house was practically completed.

At that stage, the Cricketer had issued proceedings in the County Court, seeking an order to have the house demolished, and damages. We counterclaimed for the money owed under the building contract.

When the case came up at the next County Court sittings, it became apparent that the judge on circuit did not want to hear the case. He ordered it to be sent off to arbitration, to be conducted by a building arbitrator. The Cricketer queried whether that was the right course, and received a severe dressing down from the bench.

The arbitrator was an experienced builder, who ultimately dismissed most of the complaints. However the Cricketer and his clients were insisting that the slab, and therefore the house, would collapse, and all would end in disaster.

My client had no doubt that the slab was sound. As the land was sloped, the slab was not laid on the ground, but suspended on stumps and rafters. He produced engineering plans, specifications and calculations, and I provided copies to the arbitrator and the cricketer.

I could never warm to the Cricketer. With most lawyers, you could have a sensible conversation to sort out the issues, but not with the Cricketer. He wanted to fight every single issue, even when it was economic madness to do so.

In any event, the arbitrator cut through the minor issues, and arranged for a load test to be conducted, using bags of cement to provide weight, based on an engineering formula which he worked out. My client was confident that there was nothing to be concerned about, and he was proved right. The slab passed the load test with flying colours.

So, we won the case on all relevant points, my client was paid in full, and we had our costs.

The Cricketer left town not long afterwards. I later heard that his client was very unhappy with him. My own view was that his client's uncle was the main problem, but that the cricketer had not had the experience or judgement to rein him in, and introduce some reality into the picture.

Physical Fred

In the roll call of Seamus's employees, Fred is another sad case. Fred married one of Seamus's daughters (this one was not a lawyer) and soon afterwards was working for Seamus.

Seamus had a cruel streak, and he bestowed the ironical nickname 'Physical Fred' on one of the least physical men you'd ever meet. Fred was a skinny young man of below average height, with ginger hair and pale skin, and no presence whatsoever.

After tiring of being Seamus's gopher for a couple of years, Fred opened up his own practice down the street. Although he wasn't a bad lawyer, he was no businessman, and went out backwards. The

Law Institute took over his practice and sold it off cheaply to another firm in town.

The next I heard of Fred, he was in hospital, in plaster, with many broken bones and a leg up in traction. He'd been up on the roof at his wife's behest, trying to adjust the TV antenna.

Fred's wife was very high maintenance. While he was laid up, she took up with another fellow. She continued to visit Fred in hospital for a while, but (not unlike her father) was quite cruel to him. On one occasion, she kept taunting him about his injuries, and challenging him with "Come on. Fuck me, Fred". A difficult task for a man in traction.

A couple of years later Ray, a sole practitioner in another Gippsland town, lost his practising certificate for two years for grossly overcharging his clients. Lo and behold, the practice was transferred to Fred during those two years, with Ray being notionally employed there as a consultant, not providing any legal services or giving legal advice.

Yes, I believe that, too.......

At the end of the two years, when Ray recovered his right to practise, it was all transferred back to Ray, and Physical Fred went his own way.

Ray

Ray (mentioned above in the tale of Physical Fred) was another lawyer who had a healthy ego, and could never admit he was wrong. A recurring theme was that some (unidentified) people made a habit of stealing his car. They never kept it for long, and didn't drive it far. Each time, they'd return it to somewhere not too far from where they stole it. Surprisingly, it was never damaged in any way, and none of the contents was stolen.

When someone would suggest he'd just forgotten where he left the car, Ray would reject the idea out of hand. He's not that stupid, he would protest. He knew where he parked it and it simply wasn't there. There was simply no possibility that he could have been mistaken.

Ray was driving me back from a meeting one day when he was pulled over for speeding. I expected him to remain low key, be polite and friendly to the police, and maybe get the offence downgraded to a lower category. That was the strategy that I would use.

Not Ray! He fairly bristled with aggression to the unfortunate coppers, and insisted that they were in the wrong in pulling him over. He remained confrontational and abrupt right through the episode.

I remained dumfounded at his lack of diplomacy/negotiating skill. Unsurprisingly, the coppers charged him with a few extra offences, and there was certainly no downgrade.

Colum

I had known Colum from my school days. He was a few years older than me, and did law ahead of me. He was one of the young lawyers at the firm where I did my articles, and was a good friend and mentor to me there.

Colum had married his childhood sweetheart Jessie. As a good Catholic couple, they soon started having children. The first (Aidan) arrived about a year after their wedding, followed by another in less than twelve months, and another in the next year.

Then, within the next year, they had twins. This left them with five children before Aidan had turned three.

Jessie was a remarkable woman, who seemed to cruise through all of this with no fuss. She was calm, capable and unflappable.

Now, you might expect that they'd work out what was causing this, but they continued on, and finished up with ten children in all.

While all this was going on, Colum was very much out and about. He was a popular person around town, and busily built up a strong personal following. He'd be playing cards one night a week, at the races regularly, at community and school activities and meetings. He seemed able to survive and thrive on very little sleep.

When I moved on at the end of my articles, Colum stayed on for another year. By then, he'd become impatient about his prospects with that firm. He'd call me to discuss his plans, and stayed with us one night, while he was having interviews.

Colum soon took a position with a strong suburban firm, and shortly was made partner. I still saw him from time to time, and noted that nothing had changed. He was still out and about, driving himself hard at work and building up his contacts. He had a great love of life, and enjoyed everything he was doing.

Sadly, Colum had a massive heart attack at age thirty-eight and died, leaving Jessie and ten children. By that time, the eldest few were teenagers. A few years later, Jessie remarried. Her new husband was a widower with seven children of his own. Their family car was a bus, and they didn't have bedrooms, they had dormitories.

Several years later, I met up with Aidan, who was carving out an excellent career as a lawyer, working for the government. He told me that he had no intention of going into private practice, as that was what had killed his father.

My own view was that it wasn't just private practice that killed Colum, It was his whole lifestyle. Sadly missed!

Jeff the Quiz King

One of my employees was a young man called Jeff. Jeff was a pleasant young man who was good company, funny and was (as with many lawyers, including myself) a smart-arse, know-all type.

My son still cannot believe that, in one conversation with him, Jeff referred to one of the Star Wars movies as 'Revenge of the Jedi". But I digress.

After we had worked together for some time, I sold my practice, and we both moved on to other parts of Victoria.

A couple of years later, Jeff turned up on my TV screen in one of the popular quiz programs. I was not surprised to see him go through and win everything. He became an instant celebrity.

Soon afterwards, Jeff became a partner of the firm he was working with. And then came the disaster. Jeff became embroiled in some shady business which culminated in the disappearance of a client's money, and Jeff spending time in prison.

Always remember..... it's the client's money!

Some time later, when I couldn't locate Jeff, I tracked down his brother and left a message for Jeff to contact me. However, I have not been able to get in touch with him.

Jeff, we have much to talk about. If you read this, please contact the publisher. I'd love to catch up with you.

Sam the Busy Family Lawyer

Sam was always a keen observer of family law issues, and took on family law as soon as the *Family Law Act* 1975 became law.

It was Sam who once drily noted that there's someone for everyone, so long as you're not too fussy. He used also to joke about the three great lies of all time:

- Your cheque is in the mail,
- I'm from the government and I'm here to help you, and
- Of course I'll still respect you in the morning.

Over the years, Sam developed a busy family law practice, representing mainly females. He always had a good share of the list whenever the family court came to town on circuit.

Sam was always available for his clients, and always strove to develop a rapport with them. In turn, they found him sympathetic and easy to relate to. They were able to feel comfortable that he understood their concerns and would fight for their rights in court.

Those of us who knew Sam would stir him about his female clientele, some of whom were quite attractive. He would reply by analysing the different types of women he represented.

There were those, he said, who might be OK for a one-night stand, but the problem would be trying to have a conversation the next morning. On the other hand, he'd point out some who'd be suitable for a long-term relationship.

Sam was happily married with an attractive wife, Jill, and two children, and it was a real shock when two of his female clients (at the same time) accused him of rape. They were friends, and Sam had acted for both of them in their divorce proceedings. Sam at all times denied the accusations.

The allegations were very similar, and the police (quite properly) took them very seriously. They brought a number of charges against Sam, and the Magistrates' Court held a committal hearing.

The purpose of a committal hearing is to hear what evidence there is against the accused, and to determine if, on hearing that evidence, there is a reasonable prospect that a jury would convict the accused. The committal hearing often does not hear any evidence from the accused, and it does not decide guilt or innocence. It is simply a question of determining if the matter should go to trial.

In Sam's case (and as with many accused persons), he did not give evidence at the committal. His counsel simply cross examined the two complainants to establish precisely what they claimed Sam had done.

At the end of the hearing, the court committed Sam to stand trial on both sets of charges in the County Court at a date to be determined.

What happened next was that the Office of Public Prosecutions analysed the case against Sam. They noted that there was nothing to corroborate the evidence of either of the women. Accordingly, at trial, it would come down to Sam's word against one woman in the first case, and against the second woman in the other.

For a jury to convict Sam it would need to be satisfied beyond reasonable doubt that he had raped the women. On this basis, the OPP concluded that, as it was simply a matter of one person's word against another's, there was no reasonable prospect of a conviction. It therefore elected to take the prosecution no further, and formally entered a 'Nolle Prosequi' which is a Latin phrase, meaning the prosecution would not be proceeding.

Sam was duly acquitted, and continued to practise for a few more years. He was, of course, legally innocent of the charges, but his reputation had taken a severe blow in the process.

Sam died recently after suffering from cancer for the last few years. While the exact causes of cancer are very difficult to detect, I strongly suspect that the stress and difficulty of the allegations against him were partly responsible for his death.

Amos

Earlier I wrote about Serge, a sole practitioner who would never be able to find a partner in his firm. Amos is another, but for slightly different reasons.

Many lawyers have big egos. Few would have one bigger than Amos's. He has long had his own practice, but has had more employees than you could count. The roll call of his former employees is a who's who of law firms in his area.

When I was planning to move to the area, I had interviews (on the same day) with Keith and Amos. Keith's firm impressed me, whereas I had some reservations as to what it would be like working for Amos.

Amos has a talent for self promotion, what we might call a 'Finder' - he finds plenty of work. But he needs the other characteristics, the 'Minder' to consolidate (and keep working on) the client relationship, and the 'Grinder' in the back office to churn out the work.

The trouble for Amos was that he was very insecure. He had to be the one running the show. While he was happy to (and indeed needed to) delegate the actual legal work, he was never confident enough to delegate any authority to his employees, or to trust them to do what was needed. A very self-limiting way to practice.

I worked with a number of lawyers who had worked for Amos, and they all had similar stories about him.

Many firms would (and do) provide drinks for their staff at, say, 5.00 pm on Fridays. Not Amos. On one hot Friday, one of his employees dashed out at lunchtime to buy a six-pack of cold beers for after work, and popped them in the office fridge to keep them cold. As he was enjoying one of them about 6.00, Amos gave him a hard time about putting them in his fridge!

Another story came from one of Amos's hard working Grinders, who had been working consistently long days, starting at 5.30 am, and churning out the work. He incurred Amos's wrath when he asked if he could leave at 4.00 pm to visit his sick mother.

In each case the lawyer soon left Amos and found a position where they were much more appreciated, and went on to have a successful career.

Rex

I worked with Rex for a few years. He is one of the best people and best general commercial lawyers I have met.

Rex was a very precise lawyer - he took great pains to make sure that his advice and documents were absolutely tight. He and I would often check with each other for a second opinion, just to be on the safe side.

When it came to costing his files and sending bills, Rex always erred on the light side. We would talk about the permitted loading for 'care skill and responsibility'. Rex used to refer to this as 'Scare kill…' but he never charged the amounts I felt he was entitled to.

Rex has many friends in the legal profession and in the wider community. One of these was a sole practitioner, Grant. Sadly, Grant died unexpectedly from a heart attack. Rex took a call from Elaine, Grant's wife, telling him of Grant's death, and asking for his help.

Rex notified the Law Institute of Victoria, who appointed a receiver to Grant's practice, and he helped them find a lawyer who managed Grant's practice temporarily, and ultimately purchased it from his estate.

The larger and more immediate issue, however, was the funeral. As a number of people do, Grant had said to his family "When I die, don't worry about getting any undertakers. Save the money and just give me a quick cremation."

A silly thing to say, because Elaine was sufficiently naive and misguided as to take this seriously, and was determined to give effect to Grant's wishes.

So she called Rex, and dumped all this on him. Being the terrific person that he is, Rex took it on. I wouldn't have done it for all the money in the world, but Rex felt obliged to look after his deceased friend.

He asked me how he should go about it. My advice was to open a file with the firm and record the time he spent on it, and **not** to touch the body (I wasn't sure if it was a problem, but I had heard that dead bodies could contain various toxins).

Rex called in a favour from another friend, who worked in the funeral industry, and was able to obtain a body bag, some gloves, and a bottom of the range coffin. The two of them managed, with great difficulty, to get the body in the bag, then into the coffin, and thus into the back of Grant's station wagon.

The next stop was the crematorium. Rex had spoken to the crematorium operators and arranged a time with them to bring the body and run it through. Only Elaine and her children were present with Rex to say farewell to Grant, whose many friends were denied the opportunity to say goodbye.

After all this, Rex was ready to move on with the probate file and deal with Grant's estate - the more routine (and less unpleasant) part of the affair.

A few days later, Rex was mortified (sorry, bad pun, but accurate in the circumstances) to receive a letter from another law firm in the town. They said that they had been instructed to take over the file and the estate, and enclosed an authority, signed by Elaine, for Rex to deliver his file to them.

This was one of the most insulting things a client could ever do to a lawyer - after Rex had done the really dirty, unpleasant part! I suggested that he allow his liver to play a role in preparing his bill, but Rex was too much of a gentleman for that.

Nigel and 'Lurch'

Over many years working in the city, I had the privilege of working with Nigel, one of nature's gentlemen, and remarkably well known around Melbourne. If you happened to be in the street with Nigel, you would make very slow progress, due to the number of people who stopped to say hello to him.

Nigel's children all went to one of Melbourne's more prominent public schools. During his school years, Stewart, one of Nigel's sons, met up with Sandra, a delightful girl who happened to be the daughter of a colourful and controversial character known as 'Lurch'.

It was said that Lurch was a significant player in Melbourne's underworld, which was constantly in the news around town, as several of its leading characters declared war on each other.

From the beginning, Stewart and Sandra were sweethearts. They were inseparable through school and university, and became engaged shortly after they both graduated.

As Melbourne's gangland wars escalated, Stewart and Sandra took some good advice and left the country. They were determined to be married in Melbourne, and made all the arrangements from afar, with the help of supportive family networks.

Stewart and Sandra flew in a few days before the wedding, and left again a couple of days after the big day. At that time, the word was out that 'Lurch' was a 'dead man walking', and the wedding day was notable for the presence of a substantial number of armed security guards.

Despite the presence of the armed guards, the wedding was a great success, and enjoyed by all who attended. Nigel later commented that he was introduced to a number of well-known underworld names, and noted how charming some of them were.

Sadly, however, the happiness of the families was destroyed within six months, when 'Lurch' was gunned down at his home.

CHAPTER 8

KEITH AND HIS FIRM

Keith

Keith was a strong personality and the senior partner of one of the firms where I worked. He was an excellent technical lawyer, and one of very few who was expert in dealing with 'general law' or 'old law' land, going back to the times before certificates of title, where ownership of land was proved by the production of a chain of documents tracing the proprietorship right back to the original crown grant. If there was a defective link in the chain, Keith would find it!

The firm's partners had car parks at the rear of the four-level building which we occupied. The partners' car spots were clearly marked out, but occasionally a member of the public would decide to use one of them in preference to using a metered park around the front.

One day when Keith returned to the office after a difficult and unsuccessful mediation meeting, he was very displeased to find someone had parked in his spot. He parked his 4WD very close behind the offending car, and left a note on its windscreen.

A couple of hours later the owners of the car returned, read Keith's note, saw that their car was blocked in, and presented themselves at reception, asking to be let out. Keith was still annoyed and made them wait nearly an hour before sending one of his assistants to move his vehicle and let them go.

Sharon the Drama Queen

I had been employed by Keith's firm to fill a vacancy which was left by the departure of another lawyer. Nothing unusual about that. After starting with the firm, I heard a few tales about Sharon, the previous occupant of the office I had been allocated. I was told that Sharon was a very capable lawyer, but quite volatile. It seems that she had a love-hate relationship with Keith, with voices often raised between them.

About a year after I started there, Sharon returned to work with us. I first met her a couple of weeks before she started back, at a small party at Rick's home. Rick was one of the other partners.

At the party, I laughingly thanked Sharon for leaving when she had, and creating the vacancy for me. We chatted a while, and I told her I was looking forward to working with her.

When Sharon started back, Rick was on leave. Before leaving, he had authorised his assistant Brenda to use his car parking space in his absence. This was his custom, and no-one had a problem with it. No-one, that is, except Sharon, who was carrying on like a real 'prima donna'. She had it in her mind that what Rick had done was a personal slight against her.

Sharon stormed around the office, ranting at Brenda, telling others how offended she was, wailing and collapsing in tears.

Sharon's return lasted less than a week. Cyclone Sharon was gone on the Wednesday, leaving us all wondering 'what was that all about?'

Nobby the Practice Manager

Nobby became the practice manager of Keith's firm at quite a young age. He was a very capable young lawyer, and was viewed as having special administrative abilities.

He was appointed partner and given responsibility to manage the firm, leaving the other partners with less to do in terms of the day-to-day running of the firm, so they could concentrate more on their strengths as lawyers.

At about this time, the firm was looking to expand, and it opened a new branch office. I was asked to run the new office, and happily obliged. This involved getting out and about, introducing myself and the firm to the community and potential sources and referrers of work.

This succeeded to the extent that, six years later, we had five lawyers and two law clerks working there, not to mention other support staff. But I digress.

Nobby and the 'Advertorials'

One of the things we did to raise our profile was to write articles for the local newspaper. These were called 'advertorials' and we published one each second week. I wrote most of them, and submitted them for publication.

Nobby insisted that he would write a few, but I was able to ensure that he channeled them through me. Thank goodness! I tried to develop a casual, folksy style, avoiding jargon and long sentences.

Nobby was the other extreme. his average sentences ran to over 50 words - you'd have to re-read it a few times to try and work out what he was saying. So I did quite a deal of editing and rewriting his work to make it readable.

Nobby and the Carpet

When we were setting up the new branch office, it included a significant carpeting job. As it turned out, my brother-in-law Tom had a carpet business, and I asked him to quote. Tom and his family business were good clients of the firm, and always paid their bills promptly. Tom laid most of his carpets himself and was highly qualified as a carpet layer.

Tom told me that his quote was very competitive, and he expected to get the job. However Nobby rang him to say that he'd given the job to another firm. Tom asked if the other quote was lower. Nobby replied no, in fact it was higher, but he'd given the job to the other man because he owed the firm money, and this was the best way to get it.

Tom responded "Are you telling me that you gave the business to a person whose quote was higher than mine, who has been a client of your firm who hasn't paid his bill, in preference to a client with a lower quote, who pays his bills on time? That I'm being penalised for bringing work to your firm and being a prompt payer? If that's how you do business, and if that's how you treat good clients, then you've lost me!"

An object lesson in how not to handle a client!

How *Not* to Pick Up New Business

Nobby's next effort for the new branch office was also a clanger. It came about when I received a letter at the firm from a substantial non-government organisation (NGO) in the area, looking for a local firm to do its work. I called Nobby, and we made an appointment to visit the NGO's CEO.

Nobby picked me up and we called on the CEO. He showed us around his impressive premises and talked about the volume of commercial and other legal work that his organisation required.

He specified that he did not want to use a major city firm, and was adamant that he wanted it done at the *local level.*

To this end, he had sent the same letter to a number of local firms, but we were the only one so far to respond to him. We were in the box seat.

I had a really good feeling about the meeting, and believed that the CEO and I had established a very good rapport, that we'd be able to work together for his benefit and ultimately to ours.

In discussing the meeting, Nobby and I were very optimistic. I suggested that we confirm that all the contact be made through me, and that, if and when necessary, I could refer to head office for backup in specialist areas.

Nobby agreed with this and said he'd write to the CEO, thanking him for the meeting, and confirming our availability and willingness to act for the NGO. I asked him to let me have a draft of the letter before he sent it - of course he would!

A couple of weeks later, I asked him about the letter (I'd been following him up since just after the meeting, as I wanted to have it sent while we were still 'front-of-mind' with the CEO). "Oh", said Nobby, "I sent if off last week". He then sent me a copy.

The letter started off well enough, thanking the CEO for seeing us, setting out what we could do for him, and extolling the virtues of the firm. It then went on to talk about the head office (completely ignoring the branch office which was where the CEO wanted to have the work done!), and finished up by inviting the CEO *to come to head office for a coffee whenever he was in town.....*

I could have cried!

Not surprisingly, we never heard from that NGO again.

I might be a slow learner, but I eventually came to the conclusion that Nobby loved the sound of his own voice, and *never listened!*

The Jim Carrey Comparison

Those of us at the branch office didn't take long to fall out of love with Nobby.

At one stage, he told us that he'd be there all day every Tuesday to be available for us to talk to, so we should bring forward our ideas on what we should do to continue with our (already impressive) growth.

Good idea! We were strongly in favour of this. We had always felt a little neglected and on our own, and had become used to doing our own business development without waiting for Nobby and head office.

On the very first Tuesday, we saw him for about half an hour. OK, that'll settle down, won't it? It never did. It became standard for Nobby to rush in at about 11.30 am. George and I would have a list of things to discuss with him; he'd take or make three calls on his mobile phone and then rush off without hearing anything we had to say.

The position never improved. One of the lawyers there started to refer to Nobby as 'Jim Carrey' after his role as a lawyer in the movie 'Liar Liar'.

Keith, Wills and Plain English

When I joined Keith's firm, I had a close look at the precedent documents that they used. Keith was very old school in his documentation, and loved what I regarded as outdated language. He favoured intricate, complex sentences that sometimes seemed to go on forever.

As for me, I tried to write my letters and documents so they could be easily read and understood. Keith had a problem with this, and particularly liked his beloved wills precedents to be given full play.

It was nothing for one of Keith's wills to have one sentence go on for ages, occasionally for more than a page at a time.

While I appreciated the need to use precise language, I was comfortable that precision need not be sacrificed in writing more briefly. That, after all, is where the skill lies in drafting. Anyone can use words that go on ad nauseam, but it takes skill to phrase a concept in shorter form.

At Keith's insistence, I started off with his style. So I sent out a draft will, using his precedents. The client rang a couple of days later, asking me to translate the will into English for him. I then re-drew the will, using the same words, but breaking it down into shorter (bite-size) sub-paragraphs. The client was much happier, and signed up the amended version, understanding what his will said.

Keith was not happy with this approach, and he and I had a running battle over some years about the wording of wills.

At one stage, we both attended an all day conference, at which one of the speakers was a lady from the Law Reform Commission. She was very strong on plain English and short sentences. She told us that we should never write a sentence of more than fifteen words.

This drew an intake of breath from several in the audience. She responded by saying that our limit was fifteen words, because most of us looked over thirty. She said she'd spoken to a group of under thirties the week before. She gave them a limit of ten words per sentence.

In the process, the speaker showed us an old style (Keith style) will, and a plain English version of the same thing. The contrast was stark. One was beautifully clear, concise and easy to understand. The other was completely dense and indecipherable.

I could not understand how anyone could disagree with her, but Keith was adamant. Plain English, in his view, was a fad and would quickly pass. Good drafting (by which he meant his style of drafting) would always triumph!

No, Keith, I maintain that the law is about communication. If the people we are writing to, or for, can't understand what we've written, we have failed!

The alert reader will have noted that I don't always keep within that fifteen word limit. Correct, I don't. But I am aware of it and try to keep it in mind.

Keith and the Branch Office

One of the problems with running a branch office is that its needs are mostly subsumed by those of head office. We became used to it being treated as a 'spare parts' store for head office.

On a number of occasions, we'd be told that person X or Y was coming from head office to join us. It was apparent in each case that the person in question was surplus to requirements at head office. Sending them to us was the equivalent of positioning them in the departure lounge.

Several times this happened. Each time, with a more collegiate (dare I say caring, team-based and supportive) atmosphere, the person responded, to be very successful, and grew the office's business.

What would then happen was that the person would then be hauled back (not always happily) to head office, as a newly valued practitioner.

While all this was going on, George suggested to me that he and I might get together and buy out the firm, to run the office as our own independent practice. I had some reservations about this, (having had a problem with some partners previously) so it never happened.

I note, however that, some years later, George bought them out on his own behalf.

All the while, I had taken very little in holidays, and had substantial annual leave owing. One January, I took three weeks leave, for a holiday with my family.

While I was away, Keith came down to the branch office to 'look after' my files. He did so with exceedingly bad grace, and each time was grumpy and unpleasant to the staff. He made no friends there, criticising everything about the place, and demanding to know why particular precedents were being used. This bemused everyone there, as these were precedents that he had developed and which he and I regularly discussed.

On my return, the staff came to me en masse, and told me very sternly that I was never to take another holiday!

As it turned out, I was soon persuaded (the persuasion was actually more brutal than the word might suggest) to fill a vacancy at head office. I was very sad to say goodbye to 'my' people at the branch office. After little more than a year at head office (and not enjoying working with Keith and Nobby), I moved on, to a great city firm, where I was very happy for the rest of my years as a lawyer.

Paula

I first met Paula when I was with Keith's firm and running the branch office. She was employed only for a couple of weeks as a summer clerk, but made a big impression on everyone. She was one of those youngsters who had energy and enthusiasm bursting out of them.

When you gave Paula something to do, she would race off and do it at a hundred miles an hour, and in no time, be back looking for the next job. She made a big impression on those of us who worked with her.

Down the track, Paula saw a newspaper advertisement from Keith's firm for articled clerks for the following year, and specifying the date on which applications closed.

Paula had a small delay in obtaining her written academic record from her university, but was able to get it in time to lodge her application a few days before the closing date. She was very unhappy to receive a letter from the firm (Nobby in fact), telling her she was too late, and that applications had closed.

Ultimately, Paula was unable to secure articles with another firm, and she took the substitute course with the Leo Cussen Institute. At about the time she completed this course, she saw an advertisement for a job at my new firm (I had left Keith's firm a couple of months earlier).

Paula started on the application, and rang Keith's firm, asking for me, so I could give her a reference. She spoke to Jenny, who told her that I no longer worked there, but was forbidden to tell her where I was (standard procedure, so their clients didn't follow me).

When Paula told her the reason she was looking for me, Jenny started laughing. She took Paula's number, rang me, told me the story, and gave me Paula's number.

So, I called Paula. Long story short, she got the job, and has moved from success to greater success. She quickly became a partner of another, very well respected firm, acting for some of the highest profile business people in Melbourne.

A Big Night Out

One year, after successfully bedding down a merger, and as a reward for everyone's hard work for Keith's firm, it was decided to celebrate with a slap-up dinner at a very fancy restaurant in Williamstown.

The firm provided buses for all who preferred not to drive, so we all rocked up ready to eat, drink and make merry - and particularly looking forward to a lovely dinner. We were told that (apart from a few with special dietary needs) it was a set menu. No problem with that!

Well, so much for that idea! After a miniscule entree (the property lawyers were suggesting we should charge a search fee for trying to find it on the plate), we were served with the 'main course'. "Where is it?" The plates were huge, but where was the food?

"Wait a minute, there's a small dollop of something in the middle of the plate." And there it was, no bigger than a 50 cent piece.

I don't know how much the firm paid for the food, but it was a rip-off. We all had a few drinks to get something out of the night, but they would not have been cheap.

On the way home, one of the buses stopped off at a certain fast food joint, so the starving masses could assuage their hunger. I'm not a fan of that establishment, so I waited and raided the fridge when I got home.

Funnily enough, that Williamstown restaurant is no longer there. I wonder why!

Leaving Keith's Firm

Not long before I resigned from Keith's firm, I had undergone a preliminary bowel scan (a number of family members had had bowel cancer, and one of them died from it). As a result, my doctor recommended I undergo a colonoscopy. I was booked in for this, and told HR that I'd need to take a day's sick leave for the procedure.

A couple of days before the colonoscopy, the HR manager came into my office, looking very sheepish. She asked me not to be angry with her, not to "shoot the messenger". She had been told to ask me if the procedure I was going in for was "elective".

I took a couple of deep breaths to contemplate this, and replied: "Well I suppose you could call it elective, because I'm electing to have the colonoscopy as opposed to putting my head in the sand and taking the risk that I might have bowel cancer." I reminded her that I'd had relatives who had died from bowel cancer, and others who had gone close, and now survived only by having had most of their bowel removed.

I had a full head of steam up by now, and went on: "If they think that it doesn't constitute a sickie, they should remember that:

1. I haven't taken a sickie in the last ten years,
2. For quite a few of those years I was working six days a week, when we opened the new branch office, and

3. When I leave here in two weeks time, I'll be leaving behind over a hundred days worth of sick leave that I haven't taken. As my free gift to the firm!"

She smiled apologetically and left. No-one ever mentioned it again.

When I gave my notice, I had asked not to be given any new files, so I could devote my time to leaving my existing files in the best shape I could. No chance! I was still being allocated new files on the day I left - so much so that I was still going after 9.30 that night. By that time, I was the last out of the office, leaving my keys on the reception desk.

By the way, the colonoscopy came up clear, but I was laid low about six months later with another health problem, and had to take six weeks off (I was a little annoyed to not have my over a hundred days sick leave to claim any more). My new firm looked after me very well and supported me fantastically through that time.

The Phone Call From Keith's Firm

About five months after I left Keith's firm, I took a very brusque call from a young lawyer there (Griff), about a file I had handled in the few months before I left. I had never met young Griff, who had started after my departure, but he had me in the gun.

He reminded me of the file, and I confirmed that I remembered it. I recalled taking instructions, discussing the position with the clients, and preparing and sending out the documents for them to sign and return.

Griff pounced on me here, full of aggression, but not much subtlety. "Well, they signed the documents, and they're still in the file. What's your excuse for that?"

I asked what he meant, and he told me that the clients had signed and dated the documents and returned them, and that they were still in the file. There was also a cheque in payment of the stamp duty. As some time had passed, the clients would be up for penalty duty, and this was all my fault. When the documents and the cheque came in I had obviously just put them in the file and left them there…..

"Hmm" I asked "When did they return the documents to the office?". "Can't say" Griff shot back. "You didn't make a note on the file"

"OK then, what date is on the documents and the cheque?" I enquired. "5 August" he replied, "What are you going to do about it?"

I asked him "Do you know that my last day there was 20 July?" "No, I didn't". "And, given that the clients appear to have signed the documents and made out the cheque on 5 August, would you conclude that the clients returned the documents on or after 5 August?" "Err yes, quite possibly."

"So, it would appear that the clients brought them in after I had left, and that someone else put the documents in the file and left them there, and that you shouldn't be trying to point the finger at me?"

"Err yes" and he hung up. No apology.

I hope Griff learned to get his facts straight in future before getting his foot so far into his mouth. I never actually learnt who put him up to making that call, but I have my suspicions. Most of the good people there would have had more sense!

Nobby and the National Firm

Some years after I left Keith's firm, it made a big push to become a national firm. Nobby established relationships with about a dozen other firms around the country, each with similar style practices.

The firms announced their intention to merge and to seek a Stock Exchange listing, not the same as the way Slater & Gordon did it, but with some similarities. They signed a preliminary agreement for the merger, began exchanging financial information, and set up a new company to be the umbrella organisation, in which the existing firms (or more precisely their partners) would hold shares.

Nobby resigned from Keith's firm, and was appointed CEO of the new company, working hard and long to set up the structures of the new business.

However, at this stage, differences began to appear between the various firms. It became apparent that they each had different profitability ratios, and some of the individual shareholders began to worry about potentially having reduced incomes.

Gradually the whole deal fell apart and each of the firms went back to their own practices.

One of the losers out of this was Nobby, who had already resigned from Keith's firm (and been replaced), and had no new position to go to. He was quickly snapped up by another professional services firm in a similar position as he had held for years with Keith's firm, so he still landed on his feet.

Rick

Rick is a fine man and an excellent tax lawyer. I've never seen anyone become so excited about tax law. Most of us are very 'ho hum' about tax legislation, but not Rick.

He was very talented, and had a reputation for being one of the best at helping his clients set up their businesses in the most tax effective way.

Rick knew everything about Section 260ZZX of the Income Tax Assessment Act, and would regale us about the intricacies of the section. On one occasion, he told us of an inspiration he'd had in the shower, and how he rushed out, with water going everywhere, while he searched for a pen to write down his thoughts.

One of my colleagues commented that Rick was the only lawyer he knew who could 'cream his jeans' over Section 260ZZX.

Some years later, Randy (more of him later) joined the firm and worked a lot with Rick. He found Rick wonderful to work with in most respects, but frustrating in others.

Rick has had a high profile for many years, and clients come to him for tax and business structuring advice. Rick analyses their business, or the business they are proposing to get into, and works out the best structure for them. He quotes what his advice and the tax structure will cost them, and then also gives a quote for handling the commercial transactions and documents that are necessary to give effect to his advice.

Randy's problem with this is that Rick knows what his advice and setting up the structures will cost, but he always seriously underquotes what he (mistakenly) sees as the less exciting and less exacting process of documenting the transaction. The way Randy complains about it, Rick gets the cream and Randy gets the shaft.

CHAPTER 9

RANDY

After over 13 years, I left Keith's firm and joined a city firm where I worked happily for many years. That's where I met many fine people, including Randy. After a few years, Randy left. Interestingly, he finished up with Keith's firm, where he worked closely with Rick.

Randy got his law degree in Tasmania, and did his articles with a small firm in Hobart. He told us about his old style principal who would correct his work with a red felt-tipped pen, and give him points out of ten for every single piece of work he produced.

Randy and the Office Manager

At one place where Randy had worked, after coming to the mainland, there was an office manager whose name was Amanda Hore. Amanda was absent for a couple of days when Randy started there.

At the end of Randy's first week, one of his co-workers took him along to the firm's Friday night drinks. Relieved at having survived his first week, Randy rapidly downed a few beers. After a while, the office manager arrived. She marched straight up to Randy, held out her right hand, and introduced herself as "Amanda Hore."

Randy swears that he looked her in the eye, shook her hand and responded "Randy solicitor. Pleased to meet you."

When Randy related this story, I exclaimed "Great call, but a bad career move." He agreed, adding that Amanda went on to make his life extremely miserable.

Tennis with Randy?

A few of us would occasionally have a game of tennis on the tennis court on the roof of the building where we worked. It was mostly mixed doubles, very ordinary tennis, high quality sledging, lots of fun.

Randy had once told me that he hadn't had much sporting success as he fell apart under pressure. Described himself as a choker. So, when he was serving to me in a tight game, I'd be calling out "pressure", and have one hand on my throat in a choking motion.

In turn when I was up on the net, Randy would belt his return of serve as hard as he possibly could, straight at me.

Randy and His Favourite Client

One of our clients was a company that offered tax deductible primary investment opportunities (especially in the month of June each year) to wealthy investors. Randy was appointed as the lawyer to manage the relationship and co-ordinate the various types of legal advice and work for the client.

One of our frustrations was the way the client tried to minimise its expenses. It would regularly embark on what appeared to be a cheap option, only for unforeseen consequences to arise, and the client was on the brink of disaster. This would cause a panic, and we'd have to drop everything and rectify the problem. We'd duly fix it all up, and then the client would complain about our fees. Our response was to suggest that if they'd consulted us in the first place, they'd be a lot better off.

In addition, the client was often slow to pay its bills to us. At one time, there was a large debt outstanding, running into some hundreds of thousands of dollars. It happened that we were acting for the client in some property sales. Following settlement, I called the client's financial controller to confirm the settlements. I told him I'd been instructed by the firm's finance committee that the outstanding fees were to be deducted from the proceeds.

When he replied that the client was expecting to receive the full proceeds of the sales, I asked him to come back to me about it within the next 24 hours, as my instructions were clear. I followed it up with an email the same day, saying the same thing, and adding that if I hadn't heard anything to the contrary within 48 hours, we'd be taking the amount of the debts and forwarding him a cheque for the balance.

We were not obliged to make this concession, but were simply being as fair as we could in the circumstances.

There was no reply, so, a few days later, we transferred the money, and sent him a cheque for the balance.

Many months later, and with not a murmur being heard in the meantime, I became aware of an uproar in the firm's boardroom. Randy and Allan (the firm's partner in charge of the client relationship) were being yelled at and being accused of theft by the client's CEO - all about the money we'd retained from the sales.

Allan buzzed me and I took the file in and showed them my handwritten note and the confirming email. The mood in the room quickly changed and the conversation moved on.

[Note here the importance of having a properly maintained file. If the relevant pieces of paper weren't complete, in order and in the file, the positions of the parties would have been very different.]

Randy and the Lingerie Model

The same client had originally been set up by a very prominent citizen, who was still at that stage involved with its business. More relevantly for Randy, the man's daughter Mia (while not a director) was the main contact for the day-to-day business between the client and the firm.

By co-incidence (and of interest to a number of Randy's co-workers), Mia was a very attractive young lady who had at one stage been a lingerie model. Whenever Mia made an appointment to come and see Randy, Kim and a couple of others would make a point of hanging around the reception area in the hope of running into her.

I should add that Randy always behaved quite properly and professionally in his dealings with Mia. The general attitude in the firm was that young romeos like Kim and Justin should be kept at a distance. There was not the same confidence that they would have behaved with the same propriety as Randy did.

Anyway Mia one day reported, in great distress, that her car had been stolen. Her greatest concern was that it contained a portfolio of photos from her lingerie modelling days - and that they might turn up on the internet, or some other place. This would cause her a great deal of embarrassment.

There was never any report of the photos turning up anywhere, even though Kim spent countless hours searching for them on the internet.

Randy and the Weekends Away

Some time later, Randy married his sweetheart Liz, a lovely lady. After they'd been married a little over a year, they decided it was time to start a family.

Their strategy was to take a long weekend away when the likelihood of conception was at its highest. So, one weekend a month, Randy and Liz would head down the coast for what became known as 'fertility weekends' or 'conception weekends'.

We had much fun ribbing Randy about this, giving him loads of gratuitous advice, wondering aloud how he'd perform under pressure, telling him not to choke, and all sorts of other unhelpful comments.

Anyway, the plan worked and Randy is now the proud father of a tribe of kids.

Randy and the Tax Breakfasts

Amongst other roles, Randy was a member of the firm's tax group in the early 2000s.

He regularly gave presentations and updates on various tax topics. Every Wednesday morning, the tax group had an 8.00 am meeting where breakfast was provided. At these meetings, Randy would provide a ten minute summary of recent developments in tax law.

At one of these meetings, Crystal, one of the articled clerks, made the mistake of dozing off. Word of this quickly spread around the firm, with Randy and Crystal the butt of many jokes.

My Business Proposition

Randy's tax talk led to me preparing an email and sending it to the articled clerks and a few of Randy's mates. The text was as follows:

"I've hit on a plan to get rich! You might want to subscribe for some shares in the new venture - it will be a sure-fire winner.

It's based on solid market research that shows there are thousands of insomniacs out there.

All we need is a proven cure for insomnia (which we have) and the money to run an advertising campaign on late night radio and TV. I've taken out all the necessary patents on the cure, and am ready to proceed with the next phase.

The plan now is to (surreptitiously or otherwise) tape Randy's next tax talk, take out a 1900 phone number and charge customers a modest fee of, say, $1.00 per minute to ring up for a cure. We'd put Randy's talk on a continuous loop and let it run all day and all night.

I've discounted putting it on the web, as people would have to be standing or sitting to access it, and they might hurt themselves when they fall over (beside, we might have to put Randy's photo on the website, and this would frighten their children). For the same reason, it wouldn't be accessible from a car-phone (think of all the fatalities if drivers dialled it up).

The real beauty of the scheme is that when someone rings in, they'll immediately drop off to sleep WITHOUT HANGING UP! The phone will still be off the hook (and running up dollars for us) when they finally wake up many hours later. It would probably be a good marketing move, after about a month or two, to make a big announcement that we'll automatically hang up on anyone who is still on the line, say, thirty minutes after they are connected - as we know they are asleep by then. By that stage, we'd expect to have strong cash flow, and such an announcement would be great for goodwill. It would also give us an opportunity to publicise our success rate.

Our advertising won't specifically give a guarantee, but will show that our product has been proven in clinical trials. We already have testimonials from a number of persons as to how effective it is. I don't expect any difficulties from the ACCC under TPA, Sec. 52, as we'll be relying on the sheer quality of our product - we won't need to make any outrageous claims, as it speaks for itself (no pun intended).

We'd expect to enjoy very rapid growth, as the product's effectiveness is recognised, so that we might want to go public after a couple of years, with great profits for the original investors. Soon after that there would, naturally, be enormous performance bonuses for key directors. We might even consider paying a very small royalty to Randy for his contribution.

Please let me know if you want to get in on the ground floor."

The email produced several entertaining responses, including one from Randy, who declared that my email was far too well conceived and written to have been prepared by me.

He noted that, in my role as mentor/teacher/trainer of articled clerks, I would regularly delegate work to them. He often referred to me as a muppet, and suggested that the email had been written by the articled clerk Samantha, as "she does all your best work".

Randy added that a royalty of 20% would be appropriate.

Over a couple of beers the next Friday night, we decided that the plan had wider application, such as:

- in the child care industry - imagine how easy it would be if you could get the kids to sleep the whole time they were in your care, and
- in the military - you'd just have to project Randy's tax talk into a country, and just walk in and take it over. Conquering without violence!

We had a very enjoyable, if somewhat adolescent, time rambling on over different scenarios for Randy's tax talks.

CHAPTER 10

A Few .05 Tales (and an Overdose)

The Magistrates' Courts spend a great deal of their time dealing with driving offences. It can be very sobering just to sit in court and watch errant drivers come up and get dealt with.

If I had my way, I wouldn't issue a driving licence to anyone until they had spent at least a full day sitting in the public gallery in the Magistrates' Court watching bad drivers lose their licences.

Another thing I noted was that most drink drivers are detected because they have done something else wrong. They might be pulled over for a less serious offence, such as crossing double lines, or failing to indicate, or some other relatively minor infraction. The policeman might then ask "Have you been drinking?" and bingo, all of a sudden, no more licence.

The Christmas Day Reading

The highest reading I ever saw in court was recorded by a dairy farmer who must have had a huge Christmas Eve. On Christmas morning, he woke up early as usual, milked his cows, changed into his better clothes and was heading into town, when he turned a corner without indicating. A policeman saw him and pulled him over.

After noticing the smell of alcohol, the policeman took the driver for a breath test, which showed a reading of 0.380%. A reading that high would normally have the driver close to death, but there was no obvious sign that he was affected by alcohol. He must have been a very seasoned drinker!

The breathalyser operator and the arresting officer were both so shocked that they thought the machine was malfunctioning, so they recalibrated it and repeated the test with the same result.

It was frightening to think of what his reading would have been when he went to bed the night before.

My Team-Mate Jim

In one of the sporting teams I played in, Jim was one of the most loved players. He was generous to a fault and a happy, outgoing friend to all.

One day, Jim was picked up with a reading of 0.08%. On the appointed day, we appeared at the Magistrates' Court, before the 'Chief' (more of him later). The trick from our point of view was to persuade the Chief that he should not take Jim's licence. He had a discretion, in appropriate cases, not to take the licence where the reading was less than 0.10%

After hearing the charge, and some excellent character evidence, the Chief let Jim keep his licence.

One of our mates, when Jim told him the result, turned to me and exclaimed "Gee, you must be good. He drinks like a fish." As well as being a little inaccurate, this was unfair to Jim.

I suppose it proves that you just can't keep a good sledger down, even when he's targeting one of his mates.

The Footy Coach and His Drinks

Occasionally, some buffoon thinks it is really hilarious and amazingly clever to spike another person's drinks. On this occasion, the victim was my client Ken, a football coach.

The team had played an away game at a town nearly two hours drive from home. Ken was a playing coach, and had arranged for the players to drive themselves to the game. Afterwards, they stayed for a counter meal and a couple of drinks.

Ken was a responsible person, who made it clear to his players that those who were driving home should be careful how much they drank.

Ken restricted himself to two standard beers, and left as soon as he'd had his meal. Not far down the road, the local police had set up a breath testing station. Ken was surprised when told he had a reading of 0.85%. He asked for another test, which came out the same.

At the next training session, Ken told the players what had happened, and one of them shamefacedly admitted spiking Ken's drinks.

The one saving feature was that the reading was less than 0.10%, so the magistrate would have a discretion not to take Ken's driving licence. If the reading had been over 0.10, there would have been no discretion, and Ken would have no chance.

The 'spiker' came along to the court and gave evidence confirming what he had done. We also had excellent character witnesses for Ken, so in the end he kept his licence. The magistrate commended the 'spiker' for coming forward, but pointed out that this did not excuse his stupidity at the pub.

As well as putting the coach at risk of losing his licence the idiot had placed him (and other road users) in serious danger. The magistrate was, very properly, scathing of such conduct.

Drinking Problem - What Problem?

One of our clients, Wally, was a regular drink driving offender. This time he was up for his sixth .05 charge, as well as his third of driving while disqualified. He knew he wouldn't be walking free out of the court, and that he'd need to bring his toothbrush.

Wally worked a regular early shift, 7.00 am to 3.00 pm on weekdays. This was years ago, when pubs were closed on Sundays.

After establishing that Wally drank every day, mainly at his local pub, the conversation about his drinking went like this:

Q - "What time do you go to the pub on weekdays?"
A - "When I finish work."
Q - "What time do you go home?"
A - "When it closes."
Q - "How much do you have to drink?"
A - "About ten to fifteen pots."
Q - "What about Saturdays?"
A - "I always go to the pub on Saturdays."
Q - "What time?"
A - "Before lunch-time."
Q - "When do you leave?"
A - "When it closes."
Q - "How much do you have to drink?"
A - "About twenty to twenty-five pots."
Q - "What about Sunday?"
A - "I always take a dozen bottles home for Sunday."

After this, the obvious question was whether he thought he had a drinking problem. His answer was that, no, he didn't have a problem at all.

What staggered us was the amount of money he was spending on beer to filter through his system and pour down the toilet. And that was his life…

A Technical Defence

Wes asked me to represent him on his third .05 charge. He assured me that he had only had three beers at the time, and that the 0.12% reading was incorrect. He had two witnesses who would give evidence to support his version of events, and would prove that the breathalyser reading could not be relied on.

I was not convinced about the story, or that Wes's mates would hold up under cross-examination, but those were my clear instructions, so off we went.

Curiously, he had not been given a copy of the .05 certificate. This made me wonder if there may be genuinely good grounds to dispute the reading.

Then, eight days before the hearing date, the police served Wes with another form of certificate as to the reading. This was interesting, as they were not allowed to rely on such a certificate unless it had been served at least ten clear days prior to the hearing.

At the hearing, I objected when the police tried to tender the certificate, and it was not admitted as evidence. When the police closed their case, I submitted that there was no case to answer. As there was no admissible evidence as to Wes's blood alcohol level, the charge was dismissed, and we did not need to call our witnesses. I was quite relieved about that.

The police were really dirty on losing the case, even though (if they had been able to think on their feet) they could have applied for an adjournment to overcome their difficulty, and had not done so.

I advised Wes to be particularly careful, because the police would be gunning for him after this case. Unfortunately, he was up again on a .05 case the following year, and that time, there was nothing anyone could do to save his licence.

You can give someone good advice, but that doesn't mean they'll follow it.

Larry

I mentioned before that Seamus had a poor record with keeping staff. The one exception was Larry, who had been a loyal, hard-working and long standing law clerk for Seamus for many years. Larry put up with a lot from Seamus. His health suffered and he began to drink more than he should.

One night, I received a phone call from Larry, about 11.00 pm. He was at the police station and was being asked to take a breathalyser test. He couldn't rely on Seamus. Could I come and help him?

I rushed to the police station (only a few minutes away) to confer with Larry. He was reluctant to take the test, but I told him that refusal would guarantee the loss of his driving licence anyway. He then decided to take the test, but told me that if it was adverse to him, he'd insist on a blood test as well.

Indeed, he didn't like the breathalyser result, and shortly after (having received his breath analysis paperwork) we presented at the hospital. My understanding was that blood tests generally gave a higher reading than breath tests, and this was borne out at the hospital.

Regrettably, I was unable to assist Larry, who duly lost his licence. Over the next few months, his health problems worsened, and he died less than a year later.

When Barry Came to Dinner

My wife and I made a point of welcoming any young new lawyers and their spouses to the Latrobe Valley, and giving them a start in getting to know the area and the people. Most of them would come to the area, as we had, with no family or other contacts in the area, so it was useful to have someone to help them settle in.

We had done this with Rocky and his wife Gail, and Matthew and his wife Sarah. Then, between us all, we were able to assist a few others to settle in.

So, a couple of months after my call out with Larry, we invited Barry and his wife Heather for dinner on a Friday night. The reader will recall that Barry was running the Walkers' practice that it had bought from Seamus's daughter. We also had Sam and his wife Jill, together with my old mate Dicko.

The evening was going along nicely, and we'd all had a few drinks when, after the main course, Barry decided he needed some smokes. He had recently given up, so he didn't bring any with him, and no-one else there was a smoker.

So Barry jumped in his car and headed off to buy some gaspers. Within five minutes, I was walking past the phone when it rang. It was Barry, at the police station. He hadn't been wearing his seatbelt (foolish) and this was spotted by a keen young copper.

The smart young cop soon noticed that Barry might have had a drink, and gave him a preliminary breath test. The test confirmed that he had some alcohol in his system. Thus, they were back at the station, and Barry was contemplating the breathalyser.

After my experience with Larry not long before, I'd been thinking about the process of alcohol getting into the blood. I knew that it took about an hour to find its way into the bloodstream, so Barry 's reading would be at its highest in about fifty to fifty-five minutes.

I tried to estimate how much Barry had drunk, and concluded that he would probably be over the legal limit of .05%, and might be close to 0.10%. This was a critical amount. If it was less than 0.10%, a court would have a discretion not to take away his driving licence. If it was over 0.10%, there was no discretion and he would certainly lose his licence.

So, it was important to get him on the machine as soon as possible, and certainly within the next fifty minutes.

All this calculation took only a few seconds, so I rang for a taxi, asking for one as a matter of urgency (there was no point in my being charged as well). Dicko twigged what was going on, and came out the front, while I was waiting for the cab. He told me he'd keep the conversation flowing and busy for me.

The cab was there in a minute and hurried me to the police station, where I rushed in, saying I was there for Barry. The officer on the desk told me "He's just being breathalysed. Take a seat and he'll be out soon." "No" I declared "I'm his lawyer and I must see him - NOW".

He took me in. Barry was with the young copper and Marty, a sergeant whom I knew fairly well, and who was regarded as a good man,

I took Barry into the next room and quickly told him what I thought. He agreed, so we went back and said "Let's do it, straight away."

Marty wanted to wait a while, saying it was for Barry's protection. We told him we waived that, and insisted that he take the test immediately. Marty shrugged his shoulders and Barry took the test.

In those days, it took a couple of minutes for the result to come up, so we had quite a friendly chat before Marty went back and looked at the machine. He turned to us and asked "What would you think of .045?". I recall responding "We'll take it" as Barry and I both let out a huge sigh of relief.

The young copper insisted on writing out a ticket for Barry for not wearing a seatbelt, and Marty gave him the breathalyser certificate. Barry was starting to relax now (he had been hyperventilating earlier) and said "Come on, you can drive me back to your place." "Bullshit" I replied, "You've got a certificate that says you're under .05. I haven't". So, we drove home, cigarettes forgotten.

The whole episode took little more than thirty minutes, so we weren't really missed. Apart from Dicko, no-one believed us, until Barry proudly produced his breathalyser certificate.

After that highlight, the drinks really flowed and we had a big, and late, night.

My wife had a visitors book at that stage. Many hours later, as they eventually readied to leave, Barry penned a short entry ".045% - what a lousy host!"

In the many years since, Barry has long since left the law, and set up his own winery, where he and his family produce some high quality, premium wines.

After the visitors had all left, I recall finally getting to bed at about 4.30 am. I received a call at about 10.30 am on the Saturday, to ask if I could play tennis that day. I was an emergency player with a local tennis club, and sometimes filled in if a regular player was away.

I remember stepping sluggishly onto the tennis court that afternoon wondering if I would still have been over .05% in charge of a tennis racquet.

Davo and the Overdose

Another short-term employee of Seamus was Davo, a very capable young lawyer who later went to the bar. Davo and his wife Marion weren't long in the area, and were living on ten acres out in the Gippsland hills.

Davo found Seamus and his unusual ways difficult to work for, and was very worried about some of the files which he inherited. He didn't want to be the last man standing when the music stopped.

Not long after they arrived in town we had Davo and Marion around for dinner with another young couple, Jeff and Julie.

One Saturday, a couple of months later, there was an all-day medico-legal conference at the local hospital. Several leading lawyers and surgeons were to present papers and discuss issues relevant to both professions.

As I was signing in for the conference, I received a message to call home. Marion had rung, and said Davo had taken an overdose of sleeping pills, and wouldn't go to hospital. Could I help?

I quickly headed out to see Davo and Marion. Davo was OK at that stage, but admitted to having taken a pile of sleeping pills. He didn't know how many, and resisted my attempts to get him to hospital. He was despondent about his work, and sure he'd get blamed for things that he wasn't responsible for.

The three of us talked through the issues, and I told him I couldn't see him being held responsible for anything he hadn't done, that there were ways of protecting himself, and that, if it was too much for him to deal with, resigning was a better solution than ending it all.

After a while, I was able to persuade him to start drinking lots of water, and to see if he could make himself vomit up some of the pills. Eventually, he allowed himself to be taken to the hospital, where he had his stomach pumped, and suffered no real effects from the pills.

I finally returned to the conference in time to see it being closed!

Soon afterwards, Davo resigned, and he and Marion left the area. Last I heard, after going to the bar in Melbourne, he was practising as a barrister interstate.

CHAPTER 11

SOME OF THE DIFFICULTIES OF BEING A LAWYER

The Basic Elements of Legal Practice

One of the basics of legal practice is to make sure your practice makes a profit. It matters not if you are a great advocate, or turn out the most fantastic documents for your clients, if you go broke in the process.

Lawyers have various ways of charging for their services. The fundamental points are to charge appropriately for your services, and to make sure you actually get paid.

Of course, an incompetent lawyer is always going to be a problem. The police were contemptuous of any lawyer who came along to court and didn't help their client's case. It would sometimes be said that a particular lawyer was as much help as two prior convictions.

Another problem is the common view that lawyers are very expensive. No doubt some are! And this in turn leads to many people finding great difficulty in accessing justice. Legal Aid, in its present guise, is no solution, as all governments are loath to provide anything like the level of funding for it to have a meaningful impact.

Free Legal Services

Many law firms have generous and extensive pro bono (free) programs, where they provide legal services for segments of the community who would otherwise remain unrepresented. Sadly, these services barely scratch the surface of the problem.

Many lawyers, in their own time, work as volunteers in various legal services around the metropolitan area, and indeed, in many regional areas. They do this for some hours, often one evening a week, as part of their commitment to assisting those who cannot afford to engage their own private lawyer.

There are limits to what one can do in this scenario, but many of their 'clients' at least have their problems listened to, and receive direction and advice as to their best options. In many cases, there is no solution. I can recall several instances where the 'client' was happy just to have had someone listen as they outlined the problem.

A significant number of the 'clients' present with family law problems. Some of these can be helped, some are more difficult.

Many years ago, a lady came to me at one of these evening services. She told me about her husband, who was an interstate truck driver, carrying loads across the Nullarbor between Melbourne and Perth. He had, quite sensibly, rented a cabin in a caravan park, as a 'sleeping' base in the west.

One day, she needed to get in touch with him (this was a long time before mobile phones). She rang the caravan park, to be told that he was not there. The helpful person at the other end went on to add 'I think his wife's there though. I can give her a message". Oops!

Access to Justice?

Several commentators have bemoaned the lack of access to justice, but the problem has not yet been solved.

Some firms have done away with the standard practice of billing in accordance with the time their lawyers have spent on the file. Instead, they negotiate and agree with the client, up front, on what the fee will be. This requires a high degree of skill and experience, as a miscalculation can mean that the firm loses money on the file.

Paolo

Laziness is also a worry. At one firm where I worked, a young lawyer, Paolo, was never able to meet deadlines for his work, or the financial targets which others regularly met. He seemed to be always out the back having a smoke, or wandering around distracting others from their work.

At his half-yearly review, these issues were put to Paolo. His response was a disarmingly frank "I'd work harder if you paid me more." He never got the fundamental point that if he worked harder and made money for the firm, he'd be paid more. It was no surprise when he departed the firm shortly afterwards.

Vivienne

Vivienne was a quite intelligent young lady, but she was the most nervous and insecure articled clerk I ever came across. On the phone, you'd hear her panicking and stammering away "..but I'm only an articled clerk. I don't know anything about this." and giving the impression of being totally useless.

Vivienne came in for some special training on how to be calm and present herself as being competent and able to look after a client's problem. One of my colleagues, Jenny, said one day that she wanted to slap Vivienne, and tell her to pull herself together.

Vivienne moved on after completing her articles, so I don't know if she ever got on top of this problem.

What Do You Pay a Lawyer For?

Overall, and more than anything else, lawyers are their clients' problem solvers. The client comes to us with a problem, and leaves the office happy, as they don't have the problem any more - we do. It's our job to solve the problem for them. Our success will depend on how well we do it.

Sometimes the problem can be solved by applying the law, sometimes the issues are practical, sometimes it needs an approach from left field. If we solve the problem, the client is happy, and often isn't interested in how we did it.

In my later years as a mentor/teacher/trainer of young lawyers and as an occasional *'quasi academic'* (more about that later), I would stress over and over the need to approach the profession as a business. They were generally able to deal with the law, but had no idea how it worked in practice.

Often, on receipt of new instructions, I'd ask the new lawyers (or students) to identify the first question we had to determine. They'd invariably start talking about the legal issues, until I pulled them back to the absolute basics.

The first question, I'd tell them, was to identify who the client was. Often, that's an easy question; sometimes it's not, particularly if there are several parties. Plus, it's easy to become confused between a company and its directors.

The next question was - how are we going to get paid? "Remember, if the firm doesn't make a profit, it will go broke and you'll be looking for a job."

Firms which operate on a 'no win, no fee' basis need to carefully assess the cases they take on. They need to be confident that a case will be a winner. If they back too many losers, they'll quickly go out backwards.

Once we had those issues sorted out, we could consider the legal aspects.

Getting Paid

One of the things I was taught as a young lawyer was that those clients you were defending in court had to pay up front. If they went off to jail, or did a runner, you wouldn't get paid.

In some circles, this was known as making sure you had your 'instructions' (of the folding variety) before you went to court.

The correct approach was best summarised by an old American lawyer from the deep south. He maintained that there are three principles of legal practice. These are:

1. Get the money up front,
2. When the client goes off to jail, the lawyer goes home for supper, and
3. Get the money up front!

Fast Fred, as you might recall, had forgotten about the second rule. Many lawyers have forgotten the other two.

Mae West"s View of the Law

Older readers might recall some of the droll sayings of the legendary movie star Mae West (she of the "Come up and see me some time" command).

One of Mae's quotes came as she was leaving the divorce court, dripping in diamonds, after a very satisfactory result, A young woman, dazzled by the diamonds, murmured "goodness!"

Mae turned to the young woman, drew her breath theatrically, and purred "Goodness had nuthin' to do with it, dear!"

The other tale was of Mae in the witness box, bored, chewing gum, and completely indifferent to what was going on.

The judge didn't appreciate her demeanour, and asked if she was trying to show her contempt for the court. She sighed, and took a few seconds to reply "Mattera fact, I was tryina hide it!"

The Client Who Knew Everything

One of our more significant clients had a number of subsidiaries, one of which found itself in dispute with the landlord of one of its retail premises. The manager of the business in those premises was Abel, the son of the general manager of the subsidiary company.

Abel (by name but not by nature) had a remarkable self-confidence. Sadly, it was not matched by his ability. He was in his early twenties, and had no real qualifications for the job. Indeed, the job was well in excess of his ability to carry it out. His greatest failing was that, as an inexperienced manager, he would not listen to any advice.

Abel was convinced that he knew more than any of the people trying to advise him, and kept on telling us that he had a brilliant and subtle strategy, including stopping payment of rent. It struck us as sheer idiocy, and played right into the hands of the landlord.

He ignored our advice that such action would result in a speedy eviction. When a tenant fails to pay the rent, the landlord can, in some circumstances (and those circumstances existed here) simply change the locks and end the tenancy. Abel insisted that we issue proceedings in VCAT to have the landlord punished, all the while without paying rent.

At this stage, we told him that we'd need $10,000 up front to pay for our continuing time, as well as barrister's fees. When a client won't take advice and insists on suing (often as a 'matter of principle'), that's the time to ask them to put some money on the table - particularly when they don't have a case! He then decided we weren't his cup of tea, and instructed another law firm to take over.

Not surprisingly, it didn't end well for Abel. I heard, a couple of months later, that he was no longer with the company. In the meantime, wiser heads took over and sensibly resolved things with the landlord.

Financial Issues

Running a legal practice is no bed of roses. There are significant set-up costs. Plus, a law firm is expensive to run, with library and IT requirements. Salaries and rents are generally high, and you have to do the work before you can be paid for it.

There are many good lawyers who have experienced financial difficulty or even bankruptcy.

One day, Rex and I noticed an advertisement in the commercial pages, relating to a law firm we knew, where the three partners owned their office building (subject, of course to the small question of how much they owed their bank).

The advertisement offered any interested party their choice of these three options:

- the sale of the building with a long term lease back to the firm,
- the sale of the building with vacant possession, or
- a long term lease of the building, with the firm as landlord and the new party as tenant.

How's that for telling the world your firm is in financial strife?

The Slack Worker and the Lawyer Who Wouldn't Listen

Some years ago, we had a new employee, Sharyn, who started her new job with gusto. She was full of enthusiasm, and got on top of her role very quickly. We had high hopes for her.

Unfortunately, Sharyn wasn't able to keep up the pace. Little by little, her performance slipped away, from very good to good to average, and ultimately to unacceptably poor. Her attendance record also slipped, and she quickly used up her quota of sick leave days, without any medical certificates.

Sharyn then resigned, and I never saw her or spoke to her again. Curiously though, I took several phone calls over the next few years as she took jobs with various legal firms and gave my name as referee. While I did not want to be unfair to Sharyn, I could hardly enthuse about what a wonderful employee she was. So I struggled through, not saying "don't employ her" but also not saying a great deal in her favour.

Almost every six months, I received another call from another firm. It seems that each of them gave her a job, and each time she started well and then faded. About the fifth of these was from a lawyer who had plainly decided that he was going to employ Sharyn. When I twice expressed some misgivings, he was already making excuses for her. Why he had bothered to call me I'll never know.

Inevitably, that job didn't last long. Less than six months later, I was called by yet another lawyer. This time, as I was struggling to be honest with him, without absolutely canning Sharyn, he caught my drift. He then cut to the chase and asked me the simple question (which prospective employers should always ask, but few do) - if I had a vacancy and Sharyn applied for it, would she get the job? "Sorry, no" I replied. "Thanks", he said, "That's all I need to know".

After that, I never had another call requesting a reference for Sharyn.

Plagiarism

One of the great sins of the academic and business worlds is plagiarism. There is the story of two young men in Queensland who, as students, were disciplined by their university for plagiarising the work of prominent academics.

This was bad enough, but then they failed to disclose the episode when they were applying to be admitted as lawyers. The Board of Examiners found out about it, and refused to certify them as suitable to join the legal profession.

The men applied to the Supreme Court, and lost. They were told that, while the plagiarism itself was serious, the failure to disclose it was worse. It indicated that they had insufficient respect for the law, and could not be regarded as fit and proper persons to practise as lawyers.

Devastating consequences for the men in question!

Plagiarism also comes in other forms, some of them quite surprising. When a form of words is found to work, to effectively protect the position of a particular party, others will analyse it and produce their own version.

It is generally not regarded as difficult to make enough changes to be different, and often there are many expressions which can achieve very similar meanings. Some lawyers use a thesaurus to help them out in this way.

On the other hand, there are some very shoddy lawyers who don't even try. There is a firm which practised in a town not far from where I worked, who were very obvious about it. We had noticed, on a few occasions, that some of our documents were being regularly reproduced by them for their own clients.

It was especially obvious with our commercial documents, which were painstakingly put together for particular purposes, and tailored to the needs of specific clients. One always has to tweak documents for the needs of each client. So, when such documents were being reproduced with nothing changed other than the client's details, that's where it becomes dangerous.

In one instance, it was clear that the document had simply been photocopied, except for the front page, which had been retyped in a slightly different font. What really amused us was that a couple of typos had been faithfully reproduced.

We thought about lodging a complaint, but decided not to. We figured that they weren't really operating in our market. In any event, the way they operated meant they'd get themselves in trouble anyway.

Lawyers and Blackmail

As a general rule, lawyers like their clients to have the law and justice on their side. Christopher, in particular, was one who could not accept that any of his clients ever did anything wrong. Any evidence to confirm the client's view is seized upon with great enthusiasm - particularly if the other party has broken the law in some way.

Some have been known to go overboard on this, and run the risk of getting themselves into trouble. Over the years, I had a few occasions where the opposing lawyer rang me, breathlessly telling me that they had strong evidence that my client had committed a particular crime.

They would go on to say that, unless my client agreed to their client's terms, they'd have no alternative than to report my client's conduct to the authorities.

My response would be to ask them if they realised what they were doing? "Yes, of course. We're demanding that you settle."

"Let me understand you" I'd say. "Are you threatening to report my client to the authorities if they don't agree to your terms? Because, if that's what you are saying, you are committing the crime of blackmail, and I'd have to report you. That's exactly the same as threatening to report a murder if the other party doesn't pay up."

Most of them backed off at this stage, and would come back later with a more modest proposition, but not all would get it.

I came across a more subtle (and sophisticated) approach from a lawyer I greatly respected. This was to outline what conduct my client was supposed to have done and to add "We have no intention of talking to any authorities, but thought you should have the opportunity of putting it to your client and not being ambushed by it."

Yes, I saw his point.

One of the less sophisticated approaches I had related to a client who was in litigation against a former customer of his, who was claiming misuse of funds entrusted to our client.

The other party was being represented quite aggressively by one of the major firms. While all this was going on, our client was charged with fraud in relation to the same matters. Remarkably, he was referred, by a 'friend', to a criminal law specialist working with the same major firm.

We spoke to the specialist, pointing out the conflict of interest. "Oh no" he said, "We have strong Chinese walls. There is no chance of any information going between my section and the other one." (more about 'Chinese walls' later).

Within two days, we received another aggressive fax from the other section of the same firm, telling us that they had just become aware that our client had been charged, and setting out information that could only have come from the other file. We protested and ultimately, they had to surrender both files - each to a quite unrelated firm.

As to 'Chinese walls' don't give me the pious argument that each section is sealed, and there can't be any cross-over! You're joking aren't you?

Seriously, if someone in a firm knows something, the whole firm knows it. Just as one example, management has access to both sections, and it is not possible to assume complete confidentiality.

Plus, it's not as though there aren't plenty of capable law firms around!

Undertakings

Another thing that lawyers get wrong is the giving of undertakings. A lawyer's undertaking is a solemn promise that ***must*** be honoured.

Undertakings help to make the practice of the law workable. To breach an undertaking is an act of professional misconduct, and will generally lead to the loss of entitlement to practise - for maybe two years.

An undertaking might be given at the settlement of a commercial transaction. It might be that one of the lawyers has neglected to bring a necessary document. Rather than put off settlement (and cause considerable inconvenience to all the parties) the lawyer might undertake to deliver the document to another party within 24 hours.

If the document is not delivered, that's a breach, and the authorities will deal with it - severely.

In a recent case, a lawyer had been charged with a lesser form of misconduct, and fined $30,000 (without losing his certificate to practise). He was unable to pay immediately, so the court accepted his undertaking to pay it off by regular monthly instalments. He made the initial two instalments but missed the next four.

He was hauled back before the court, on a charge of professional misconduct. The breach of the undertaking was in fact more serious than his first offence, and he was suspended from practice for two years.

Sackings - My Responsibility

From time to time, and no matter how much you dislike it and try to avoid it, you cannot avoid having to terminate someone's employment. There are those who have trouble working regular hours, occasionally someone is dishonest, and we even had an employee who blabbed about a client's business.

Sacking someone is a thankless task. I treated it the same as swallowing unpleasant medicine, and found I was able to do it relatively gently and sensitively. Generally, a staff member would know, having been given warnings, that they were in the 'departure lounge'. We never felt good about putting a person in the dole queue, but decided that it was better them than us.

When I was one of three partners, it seemed to fall to me to deliver the bad news. It had to be done, so I did it. I recall one occasion, when the three of us concluded on a Friday morning that a certain employee had to go. One of the other partners suggested that I wait till the Monday, so as not to spoil her weekend. I thought about it for a few minutes, and decided to do it immediately - and avoid spoiling *my* weekend!

At the same time, we had a crusty old woman (Mavis) working as our receptionist. Mavis was very idiosyncratic, and could be very blunt, and sometimes quite rude. We'd spoken to her about it, but nothing ever changed. One partner insisted that we'd have to get rid of her, to which I'd respond "Yes, but we must have a good receptionist to replace her." He demanded that, when the time came, he'd give Mavis the bad news. OK, fine by me.

A few months later, Mavis transgressed again. At precisely the same time, we secured the services of Moya, a charming lady, to become receptionist. Time to show Mavis the door. OK pardner, your turn, you insisted that you'd do it. Guess whose enthusiasm for the task had run out?

Once again, it was left to me!

By the way, Moya was a great success in the position, and became a very good friend as well.

Mavis v Bobby

Mavis was not out of a job for long. Within a couple of weeks, she was working as electorate secretary for Bobby, the local member of state parliament. We'd had a bit to do with Bobby on behalf of a couple of clients, and he had had a couple of dealings with Mavis.

It didn't seem to bother either of them that Bobby was a left wing Labor Party MP, while Mavis was a fan of Sir Joh Bjelke-Petersen, the then National Party premier of Queensland. Politically, a million miles apart!

After a while, Bobby began to realise that he and Mavis were not a good fit, so he began the process of warnings, with a view to bringing her employment with him to an end. This became quite complicated, as Mavis had been studying the process required to sack an employee. Bobby had been very active in setting out the rights of an employee (and the responsibilities of an employer) in terminating a person's job.

As it turned out, Bobby went through a long, convoluted, and exhausting process before he was finally able to rid himself of Mavis. We were greatly amused by the irony of a leftie MP being attacked from the left by a proud Joh Bjelke-Petersen supporter.

Bringing Everything Under One Roof

Ridges is a prominent national law firm. Over the years, it has built up from mergers of a number of smaller, specialist firms, into quite a significant firm with a wide variety of legal work.

As a result of the mergers, they were left with the remnants of a number of leases of various small premises around Melbourne. The logistics of managing all the premises, people, merging the different operating systems and fostering 'togetherness' must have driven them crazy.

As the various leases were wound up, they negotiated a new, long term lease in one of the best buildings in Melbourne's legal precinct.

At the same time, Ridges was also implementing a new management structure, with a more professional team of managers taking over the reins from the 'old guard' lawyers who had each largely run their own practices until this time.

I have often observed that very few lawyers make good managers. The qualities that make a good lawyer are generally very different from those possessed by quality management. In most law firms these days, the firm engages personnel with management expertise to run the firm, freeing up the lawyers to use their legal skills to best advantage.

So, management had a huge undertaking to implement new structures and systems, and relocate everyone into the new premises. After securing the new premises, and having them fitted out, with new IT and other systems, it was now time to have everyone relocate. This was planned to take place over one weekend.

The planning for this had been undertaken for months, with military precision, and a firm of removalists was contracted to do the physical moving of the items to be moved.

A few weeks before the moving weekend, a group of partners decided to take a hand in the move, and to ensure it was done 'properly'. They came to management to tell them that they were taking over and would manage things from there on. Never underestimate the size of a lawyer's ego!

One of my former workmates was at that time working in Ridges's management. It was hilarious listening to his description of the eyeball to eyeball confrontation between the two groups.

On the one hand, management had been thoroughly planning the move for months and had all the details worked out. On the other hand, a group of the owners of the firm had determined that only they had the means and wherewithal to ensure that the job was adequately done.

Management did not flinch. Their response was straightforward: "With the greatest of respect, gentlemen, you have employed us to run the non-legal parts of the practice, so you can put your time to best advantage in running your files. Now we have organised all this, all the steps are in place. All you need to do is go back and look after your clients. We'll do the rest. Just keep out of the way and let us get on with it."

After a few minutes reflection, the partners decided to follow the principles of delegation. They backed off, muttering that the move had better go according to plan, otherwise there may be consequences. With little grace, they vacated the battlefield, and left management to do its job.

In the event, the move went smoothly, and everyone was happy with it. Plus, the old partners learned a useful lesson.

Sorting Out the Firm Structure

Several law firms have run into problems as a result of not having their partnership properly documented, or from having unwritten understandings between them. Lawyers can sometimes be very prickly where their own interests are concerned, and some are not above taking advantage of a lack of proper documentation for their own benefit.

Where there is a verbal agreement only, you can be sure that the parties to the agreement will have differing recollections as to what the precise agreement was. As lawyers can also be very litigious beasts, they can finish up in court fighting matters out to the death - at great expense, of course.

Phillips Case and Service Trusts

Many law firms (and other professional services firms) are set up in accordance with the structure that was given the green light in the leading case of *Phillips v Federal Commissioner of Taxation (Phillips Case)* in 1978.

Typically, the firm is owned by the partners, who divide the profits between them in accordance with the terms of their partnership agreement. In the absence of some other structure, there is no way they can spread the profits to family members and thereby save tax.

This problem is dealt with by having a service entity (generally a company which is trustee of a unit trust) which provides a whole range of support services to the firm - at a price.

In a law firm, all the legally qualified employees are employed directly by the firm, but all other staff are provided by the service entity, as well as the office premises, plant, furniture and equipment, etc. The cost of these services is the passed on to the firm, at a mark-up.

Generally, the units in the unit trust are owned by the family trusts of the partners, in the same proportions as their share in the partnership. The profits in the family trust are distributed to family members with the aim that the tax paid overall is reduced.

This structure also serves another purpose. As well as saving tax, it enables the partners of professional services firms to protect their personal assets. Generally, the partner will have no (or very few) assets in their own name. Accordingly, if the firm strikes financial trouble, the creditors have no access to the personal assets. Matthew, a typical law firm partner, used to note that the only thing that he owned was a key to his wife's house.

In *Phillips Case,* the Federal Court held that it was legitimate to structure a business in this way, so long as the mark-ups were paid at commercial rates. A loading of 6 - 8% was permissible on such items as plant, furniture and equipment, and 50% on the salaries paid to staff (this was in line with rates charged by office personnel hire companies at the time). If what a firm is paying is in line with commercial rates at arms length for the same services, it does not matter that the services are provided by a related entity.

The critical point is for the firm to pay a reasonable market rate for such services. If it is marking staff expenses up by 100% (from its own service trust) when it could acquire them at an add on of 30% in the market place, it would not pass the *Phillips Case* test.

This became relevant a few years ago when the Australian Taxation Office (ATO) announced a proposal to review the way in which firms were claiming these expenses. This produced an outcry from a few law firms, who squealed that the ATO was trying to re-write the law.

Sober analysis indicated that, in fact, it was proposing to merely *enforce* the law, not change it. It was those seeking to *extend* the scope of the law who were trying to change it, not the ATO!

It is all very well to say that the ATO has it wrong, when some sections of the tax industry are being overly greedy in their claims. Where a firm is claiming a mark-up of 80% when it could be obtaining the same services at a mark-up of 35%, it is abusing the system. The 80% add-on in those circumstances is not protected by *Phillips Case*. It is, instead, in breach of the conclusions reached by the court in that case.

In my view, if you abuse the system, don't come squealing when the authorities point the finger at you!

How *NOT* to Operate a Law Firm

In one firm, there were four partners. For the purposes of the exercise, we'll call them Julius, who held a 40% share, and Brutus, Cassius and Marcus Antonius, who each held 20%. So far, so good (if you believe in unequal equity ownership, that is).

There was also a long-serving law clerk, Magnus, who could not be a partner of the firm as he had never qualified as a lawyer.

The building in which they conducted the practice was owned by a unit trust, with the family trusts of Julius, Brutus, Cassius, Marcus Antonius and Magnus each owning 20% of the units. This was intended to compensate Magnus for the fact that he could not share directly in the firm's income.

Now this might have worked if the firm had been managed properly, or paid a proper and commercial rent for its occupancy of the building - but it did not! In fact it had not paid any rent for several years, or even determined what an appropriate rent was. None of the lawyers seemed to have any interest in, or regard for, proper administration and management of their practice - a fact that would cost them all dearly.

This was foolish for a number of reasons. For example, by paying rent to the trust, the partners of the firm can legitimately reduce the income of the firm (and thus their own taxable income) and increase that of family members, who would be paying tax at a lower rate. This can mean a considerable tax saving. See the discussion of *Phillips case* above.

In this case, the failure to pay rent worked in Julius's favour, as the firm income was higher and he made more money. However, it was a huge disadvantage to the others, particularly Magnus, who missed out in a big way through the non-payment of rent.

It might not surprise you to hear that the firm became quite dysfunctional over a number of years, with very little direction, planning or co-ordination of its activities and client services. Partner meetings just didn't happen, no decisions were made, and each lawyer was effectively running their own practice - meaning that they were doing the same type of work (sometimes in competition with each other), and not developing better skills and specialties.

So, there was no sense of unity or shared purpose, and the practice (which should have thrived and grown) stagnated and atrophied. The partners were their own worst enemies.

After a while, Julius began to be resented by some of the others, who decided to take their own steps to remedy the inequality for which they felt that he was responsible. You might imagine that they'd call a meeting to discuss the problem, and work out a sensible resolution. But with these characters, you'd be wrong!

Thus began a pattern of deception and dishonesty, with files being run outside the firm's system. A whole shadow firm arose. Bills were not rendered, clients were asked for payment in cash, and an entire underground practice developed.

Over a period of time, very significant amounts of money were diverted away from the firm's proper accounts, and distributed in cash, none of which found its way to Julius.

Julius, however, was not the only victim. The Tax Office was not receiving the income tax that should have been paid, and of course, the GST on the amounts paid was never remitted.

Ultimately, something like this cannot last. Julius eventually became aware of it, the legal practice authorities became involved, and then the Tax Office weighed in. Several criminal offences had been committed, the firm fell apart, and some of the partners suffered criminal convictions, as well as losing their practising certificates.

For people who had been well regarded as lawyers, such a result was the ultimate folly - not to mention disaster!!

Lawyers are supposed to be highly principled and trusted advisors to their clients. How can they look after their clients' affairs, when they can't look after their own?

A Bonus Story

Ivan, a sole proprietor of his firm (but with a couple of employee lawyers), ran an excellent practice, and had a strong client following.

Some years ago, Ivan had a very profitable year. On the basis that the whole firm should benefit, he paid all staff a truly generous bonus.

What he had not foreseen was that a number of the staff retired and went off to travel the world. He now had to find and train replacements for them all.

Another Bonus Problem

Ivan's was not the only law firm to run into a problem over bonuses. Another firm, after a very good year, paid nice bonuses to all its employees.

A couple of months later, the firm treated all the staff (and their spouses) to a slap-up dinner at a very swish restaurant.

At the dinner, the senior partner addressed the gathering, thanking all for their contribution and hard work over the previous year. He spoke about what a record year it had been, and how the firm had paid huge bonuses to all the fee earners.

At this stage, a number of spouses began exclaiming "What.. what bonuses?" This was the first that some of them had heard of the bonuses.

Oh oh - disaster! Some of the fee earners - and indeed the firm - paid a heavy price for this!

CHAPTER 12

MORE LAWYERS AND
A LITTLE FUNNY BUSINESS

Thomas Byrne

Tommy Byrne was one of the great characters of the legal profession, and the founder of the great Ballarat firm that became known as Byrne Jones & Torney (later BJT Legal).

In his early days, Tommy was representing a young person who had sustained an injury as a result of another party's negligence. The other party had an insurer, which made a good offer of settlement. Tommy's client and their family were happy to accept the offer, but, because the plaintiff was under age, it had to be approved by the court.

The action had been taken under the Wrongs Act, which was the legislation that enabled a person in the plaintiff's situation to lodge a claim.

In approving the settlement, the judge gave a brief outline of the background, and how the case came to court. Included in his outline was the statement that Mr Byrne had issued the proceedings under the Wrongs Act.

As often happens in country towns, there was a newspaper reporter in the court, noting all this down. Unfortunately, the reporter made a simple, but serious, mistake in transcribing the story. The paper actually quoted the judge as saying that Mr Byrne had issued the proceedings under the *wrong* act. Oops! Apparently minor mistake, but serious consequences.

This actually turned out well for Tommy in the long run, with the newspaper paying out a tidy sum in damages, as well as publishing an apology.

Big John

I worked with Big John for about a year, but we kept in touch for many years after he left.

John was a large man who had a personality to match. He loved a party, and never lacked for friends. People gravitated to him easily, and he was popular with clients. He was the kind of lawyer you would use in your marketing (a Finder), and he would bring in lots of work. The only problem was that you'd need other lawyers in the back office (the Grinders) to make sure it got done properly.

John knew just enough law to be dangerous, but not enough to be successful. He would have no difficulty finding new jobs, but he would move on (or be moved on) when his new employer worked him out.

For many years after he left where I was, John would call me on a regular basis, generally with a question about something quite fundamental. I'd generally be able to point him in the right direction within about five minutes, but he was not a fast learner.

Once, John was boasting to me that he had had 30 years in practice. In John's case, I could have responded that he had one year's practice 30 times!

In one of my calls from John, he told me about a client who had a problem with the preparation of a mortgage. In the course of the conversation it became apparent that he didn't know who was the mortgagor and who was the mortgagee - a real problem when you're trying to run a mortgage practice!

The next time I heard from John, he'd moved on again, and was setting up his own practice. His new office was in an area with a large retired population. He was very excited about establishing a substantial practice based on deceased estates. He liked the idea of setting up wills with testamentary trusts. I was concerned that this might be a little out of John's league, and cause him more problems than he could handle.

The last I heard, he was still there, so I might have been wrong. I hope I was.

Barnet Rockman

Barnet (Barney) Rockman was a regular speaker at legal conferences and seminars. A real character and a great raconteur, Barney kept his audiences enthralled.

One of his specialties was the mother-in-law joke. A couple of his favourites:

- "she's got a job at the airport - kick starting jumbo jets."
- "I worship the ground she's coming to."

Barney called himself a sole practitioner. While he had no partners, he seemed to always have a good array of employee lawyers churning out the work. He had a highly organised practice, where he was the finder, as well as, to a large extent the minder, with several grinders toiling away in the background.

Barney's time was well before computers analysed everything that happened in a law office, but he had amazing systems in place, allowing him to keep a very close eye on every file. He had a code for everything. Plus, he had a very advanced computer - his own incredibly sharp mind. Nothing escaped him!

As well as running his practice, and regular seminars taking up his time, Barney often wrote scripts for TV comedy programs. He noted that the TV channels paid modestly for his services, but gave it away after a (then) prominent show rejected one of his scripts, then later used it without payment or attribution.

I asked Barney if he took any action against the program, but he shrugged "Not worth the time and trouble. I've got a practice to run! I just didn't send them any more scripts."

Bob the Steam Train Fanatic

Bob Hatch practised in Maffra, in Gippsland, for many years, some as a sole practitioner, and several in partnership with Peter Anderson and others.

Bob was an authority on many obscure and arcane ares of law. He wrote many articles and books, including on property and deceased estate laws. Rocky used to laugh that if you had a problem with the laws against perpetuities, Bob was your man.

Bob served for two years as president of the Gippsland Law Association, part of which involved regular attendance at Law Institute Council meetings in Melbourne.

At the end of his term, Bob sold his practice, and became a full-time employee of the Law Institute, helping it to provide services to its members, the lawyers of Victoria.

So ended Bob's colourful and respected tenure in Maffra. One of his idiosyncrasies was his love of steam trains. Bob and a few friends would travel many miles to inspect steam trains, and take photos and videos in great number.

Bob made a point of having an expensive stereo system set up in his office. At least twice every day, the office would shake as the sound of a steam train commenced, apparently in the distance, from one side. It would swell and roar through the office over about 30 seconds, before fading slowly out the other side.

Sonny and His 'Family' Clientele

Since the Second World War, Australia has benefited from immigration from scores of different countries and cultures. Some groups have retained contact with their families and relatives, and many of the children and grandchildren have gone on to hold important positions here.

Sonny was a son of an immigrant family. He built up a successful legal practice, and became a leader in his community. Hundreds of families regarded him as one of their own, and trusted him to look after their affairs.

Mick, who had been one of my articled clerks, came to me a couple of years later on behalf of his mate Marco. Marco's parents had a problem with Sonny, but didn't want to get him into any trouble.

Marco's parents had bought their original home under an old terms contract from the Housing Commission. They paid it off over many years, and then bought another house (with a bank loan) and moved into it. They asked Sonny to transfer the title of their original house into their names.

As they had heard nothing for some years, they assumed that Sonny had done what they asked. By the time Marco graduated from university, he began to suspect that Sonny was not all he seemed to be. Marco searched the title, which showed that the property was registered in Sonny's name, with a large bank mortgage against it. About 18 months previously, about the time the mortgage was registered, Sonny had spent up big on his daughter's wedding and European honeymoon.

What to do without calling in the authorities? Sonny deserved to have the bucket tipped on him, but that wasn't my call. I suggested that Marco or the family go and talk to Sonny, without telling him all they knew, and merely say they wanted to raise money for their children, and needed to collect their title.

They did this, and were given various excuses, but they politely insisted. Over some months, Sonny admitted that he had transferred the title into his own name, but told them that he did this under a trust for their benefit.

This could only have been complete and utter nonsense. It would have been an offence to mortgage the property unless the money raised was for their benefit. In any event, there were no documents establishing any trust, they derived no benefit under the 'trust', and he could not have created a trust in respect of their property without their knowledge.

I told Mick that it would not be necessary to make any threats to refer Sonny to the authorities, as he would be aware that he would be in serious trouble if his actions were revealed. So, they continued to be pleasant and polite to him, as they gently but firmly insisted on him providing their title to them.

Sonny's next step was to write them a letter confirming that he was having the title transferred back to them, but that there were issues with stamp duty. I confirmed to them that stamp duty would be payable on Sonny's transfer to them, but that was for him to pay, as he should not have had it in his name in the first place.

Over a period of about six months (presumably to allow Sonny to pay off or refinance his bank debt), the necessary steps were taken, and ultimately Marco's parents received their unencumbered title.

Sonny is still in practice, and still positions himself as a leader of his community. I hope he hasn't done the same thing with anyone else's title.

My own view was that Sonny deserved to lose his certificate, and spend some time in jail. I felt, however, that I owed an obligation to Marco and his family, and it was their call, not mine

Darby and the Bank

While Seamus was a controversial, larger than life personality in his regional town, Darby was his equivalent in another area. Very different people, but some similar megamaniacal tendencies.

Darby was the senior partner in his own law firm, and had a very high (and not always justified) opinion of his own abilities and legal expertise.

My colleague Rita was acting for a bank who instructed her to commence recovery proceedings against Darby for failure to make any repayments on a number of mortgage loans. He seems to have adopted the view that he need not ever make a repayment - and would vigorously contest any attempt to recover the money or sell up the mortgaged property.

In discussing Darby, we would laughingly say that we had all been searching (without success) for the interest-free, non repayable loan, whereas Darby was sure he had the secret.

Darby was at least creative in his arguments as to why he shouldn't have to repay the loans (or even the interest). He fought every single issue to the death, but lost heavily each time. The only success he had was in delaying the bank's action while he fought on, but the court continued to award very heavy legal fees against him - and the interest was accruing on it all at penalty rates.

To secure his loans, Darby had provided the bank with mortgages over his office building, his substantial home and a coastal property. In the process, his accountant prepared and certified statements of his income (and that of his business interests) over several years. Darby signed statutory declarations confirming that the statements were complete and accurate in all respects.

So now, here was Darby, in the witness box, with his hand on his heart, swearing that the accountant's figures, and his own statutory declarations, were false - and it was all the bank's fault!

The judge was very sceptical about Darby's claims. How could a court accept what Darby now said (was the response) when that would mean that he had committed perjury in his statutory declarations when lodging the loan application? Not a good basis for allowing his defence!

So, having lost at every stage of the court process, Darby still resisted, as the bank proceeded to enforce its judgements. Eventually, we were able to have the court issue a warrant for the sheriff to obtain possession so the bank could sell the properties as mortgagee. He still tried every trick in the book, but was unable to stop the process, only to delay it.

Eventually, on the day when the sheriff was about to change the locks on his house, Darby came up with the money to pay out all the loans. I don't know who his new lender was, but worried that they'd later find themselves selling him up also.

While he may have delayed the inevitable, the cost to Darby was considerable. In addition to the money he borrowed, he finished up paying over $200,000 extra in penalty interest and costs. Not to mention his own side. He had used his own barrister Jake almost full time to fight every issue - and a barrister in the Supreme Court is a very expensive commodity!

Darby and the Olympics

Just as the bank's case against Darby was coming to its inevitable conclusion, my good friend Geoff was starting to get after him in another big fight.

In early 1998, Darby was the driving force in a company offering a fantastic advertising opportunity for the Sydney 2000 Olympics. He secured a contract with a major company (Geoff's client) for advertising on a blimp which would be floating over the Olympic precinct for the two weeks of the games, and a week either side for good measure.

The deal was that Geoff's client company would have its corporate logo on display to the world for a mere two million Aussie dollars. All was signed up and the company paid a deposit of $500,000.

Darby had explained that this was needed upfront to pay the USA manufacturer that would construct the blimp.

Once completed, Darby's company would bring it out, set it up with the advertising, and launch it well before the games began. What an opportunity for an enterprising company to promote its products and services to the world!

Geoff's client immediately wrote the $500,000 cheque and waited for the blimp to be delivered...and waited...and waited.

Darby now became very difficult to contact, not returning phone calls or other messages. There was no information about the progress of the construction, or when the blimp would be delivered.

Quite simply, there was no communication at all from Darby or his company, and, come the Olympics, there was no advertising blimp carrying Geoff's client's colours floating above Homebush (or anywhere else for that matter).

As you'd expect, the disappointed corporation sent Darby a demand requesting a refund of the deposit it had paid. Definitely not, was the response, it was a non-refundable deposit (this made me wonder - was it perhaps related to the concept of the non-repayable loan?).

Geoff had a very close read through the contract - nothing in it to say that the deposit was non-repayable! So they litigated, and on and on it went.

They sued Darby's company and Darby and his co-director personally (they anticipated that otherwise the company might prove to have been stripped of its assets and be nothing more than an empty shell). Jake again represented Darby, and again they fought every point, every inch of the way.

Before the case got to the hearing, Geoff's client made an 'off-the-record' offer that it would accept $500,000 in full settlement, and waive its claim to interest and costs. Darby rejected the offer with a derisive snort. Halfway through the trial, it made another offer - to take $350,000 in full settlement. Darby's response was the same - no dice, this is a fight to the finish!

Darby and Jake continued to argue that the deposit was not refundable (an optimistic argument given that their company provided absolutely nothing, and the contract gave them no way out). Darby fought particularly hard to avoid being held personally liable, but the judge ruled that, given his personal involvement in the discussions, and the assurances and warranties he had made, he could not avoid being personally liable.

The case was duly published in the law reports, and the judgement makes interesting reading. The judge was very scathing about Darby, describing him as a most unimpressive witness (in the normally restrained style of 'judgespeak' such strong criticism of a witness or a party is quite unusual).

Once again, Darby lost on every argument, and was ordered to pay the $500,000, together with interest and costs, an all up total of over $750,000. Eventually, after threats of bankruptcy, Geoff's client got its money.

One of the lessons I had learnt as a young lawyer was the importance of quickly assessing your (or your client's) case. If it's a loser, get the hell out of it as quickly and as cheaply as you can. Darby must never have learnt that one. To finish up $400,000 worse than you could have settled for is almost, well, criminal.

The other old maxim that Darby seems to ignore is that the lawyer who acts for himself has a fool for a client.

One final footnote - last I heard, Jake was suing Darby for his fees. Poor Jake! Darby would have been a very difficult client to represent. To then not get paid (or eventually receive your money only after suing) would be the final insult!

Geoff the Traveller

Not long after finalising his client's case against Darby, Geoff took his family on an overdue holiday to Italy. They had a lovely time checking out Rome, Florence, Milan and some lovely rural areas.

After nearly four weeks of blissful time, they were due to come home. Only problem was, Geoff had developed a serious case of deep vein thrombosis.

So, the rest of the family came home. Geoff, however, had to remain, living in a villa in Tuscany, for another two weeks, until he could get a clearance to fly home.

How sad for Geoff, having to while away the time in Tuscany while the rest of us were toiling away at home!

Peter

Peter was another pillar of the Catholic Church in his town, and spoke often of his strong religious values. He was a tall and confident man, a real entertainer, and projected himself and his voice well in any situation.

Tony was Peter's best friend of many years. Peter and his wife Emma were very close to Tony and his wife Maureen.

Tony began confiding in Peter about Maureen. He was sure she was having an affair, but did not know who the man was. Peter was duly supportive and gave plenty of friendly advice to Tony about how to handle the problem, but the other man's identity was a complete mystery.

Eventually the true story came out - the other man was no less than Peter! This led to two divorces and the end of a long friendship.

The postscript to all this was that Peter and Maureen later married. The Catholic priest in the town would not allow them to marry in his church, so the ceremony took place in the local Anglican church!

Coop

Of the many lawyers I dealt with over the years, Coop was probably the tightest. Unlike Charlie, he didn't rip anyone off. He was just very careful with his money. Once you understood this, he was fine.

Coop was the same with his clients' money. He was difficult to deal with as he looked after his clients' money as if it was his own. He would negotiate hard (and almost always finish with the right result). Many a lawyer who came across Coop for the first time would think they'd quickly pull a fast one here - only to be put through the wringer and finally cough up about what Coop had estimated in the first place.

Tight with his money, Coop was nevertheless generous with his time. He'd always do what he could to help his friends.

Coop fancied himself as an amateur mechanic. He liked to save money by servicing his and his wife's cars, and doing his own mechanical work. He maintained that he got better fuel economy by doing it himself.

He also helped others less mechanically minded. One day Greg asked his opinion on a small mechanical matter. Next weekend, Coop was at Greg's place with his sleeves rolled up, looking under the bonnet of Greg's car.

After a few minutes, Coop called out "I think I might have found it, Greg. Can you hand me a shifter?" "No worries, mate" responded Greg, only to come back after a minute or so with "Err, what's a shifter look like, mate?" Coop patiently shook his head and produced a shifter from his own toolkit, and proceeded to fix Greg's car.

He wouldn't accept payment for his trouble, but was prepared to have a couple of cold beers with Greg.

Coop also tinkered with his wife Sue's elderly Holden. He had problems with its manual gearbox, which he pulled to pieces and put back together. Problem was, first gear caused it to reverse, and reverse made it go forward. He couldn't undo this, so he left it as it was. So long as the driver knew the story, no problem.

As it happened, Sue was a nurse. One night, when she was working night duty at the local hospital, she heard a car revving loudly in the area of the car park. She looked out of an upstairs window, to see her car up to its axles in a flower bed, and two youths haring away on foot.

Well done, Coop - great work, mate!!

Kathy

Kathy was an attractive young woman with a big smile and a happy outlook on life. She was quite a capable lawyer, but was not a morning person. She found it difficult to arrive at work before about 9.45 am or later.

This was a problem with some of her clients, who liked to get their working day moving first thing in the morning. A couple of senior people spoke to Kathy about this, but she couldn't seem to get the message. Each morning she'd arrive, smiling to everyone, between 9.45 and 10.00 am.

Over a few months, Kathy's personal life seemed to be out of control, and her hours became more unpredictable. On a couple of occasions, she was at work at 6.00 am, and her hours became more unusual than ever.

The lawyers in the firm had dinner at a restaurant the night before Christmas Eve. Kathy came along and enjoyed a few drinks. At about 10.30 pm, she used the restaurant phone to make a call. A few minutes later, a car pulled up outside, she got in and it drove away.

The next day (Christmas Eve) the arrangement was that we'd work until 1.00 pm, then gather in the conference room for lunch (finger food and drinks), Kris Kringle and socialising, before everyone went off to celebrate with their families.

Many of the lawyers were there well before 7.00 am. Everyone else arrived well before 9.00. But, no sign of Kathy. The clock ticked past 10.00, and then 10.30. Concerns grew, and one of her colleagues rang her home phone. Her flatmate told him that Kathy had not been home that night. When he said he'd ring her on her mobile, she told him not to bother, as Kathy had lost it the previous weekend.

There were a few jobs that Kathy was due to complete that day, so a couple of her colleagues finished them up for her. Then at about 12.30 pm, Kathy waltzed in, full of smiles as though nothing was wrong. Fifteen minutes later, she was heading into the conference room for lunch, chatting happily with whomever happened to be around.

Early the next year the firm had had enough and Kathy was shown the door. I remained in touch with her for some time. She found another job with a good firm, but continued to have the same issues.

Then she broke up with her then boyfriend, who spitefully sent a number of terrible, obscene photos of Kathy to every person listed in her mobile phone contacts. This was reported to the police, who took statements from many people (including me).

I don't know how this ended up, and I haven't heard from Kathy since then. The last I heard was that she had gone overseas to get away from it all.

Jerker

One of the great privileges of my many years in the law was to work with Jerker, a wonderful lawyer and a fantastic person.

Jerker is a range of contradictions, but a man who, when you get to know him, is a tremendous package of surprising quality.

On first meeting Jerker, you could easily get the impression that he is a typical, serious, blue-blood lawyer, born with a silver spoon in his mouth. Then you'd have to adjust to his knockabout approach to life, and the fact that he'll wear his 'Metallica' T-shirt to the big wrestling show whenever it comes to town.

Jerker is a man who is very easy to talk to, about the law, life generally, and particularly about sport (from his beloved but tragic Demons, to the Victory, to the Storm, to the Australian cricket team, to any kind of sport, anywhere).

You might expect Jerker to like a smooth single-malt Scotch, but you'd be wrong. He's strictly a VB man. The only time he'll drink another beer is when taking a client to the Australian Open, where Heineken is the only beer available. On such an occasion, he's been prepared to swallow a goodly number of Heinekens. Just to be hospitable, of course.

Jerker takes a strict and conservative view of the law, his two pet hates being former High Court Justice Michael Kirby, and Dr. (former Senator) Bob Brown. Someone suggested that might be because they are both gay - but Jerker (happily married with two teenage children) cheerfully stands in the outer with a couple of gay mates, loudly supporting his team.

Outside the law, his major hate is reserved for the Collingwood Magpies. In the AFL, he supports Melbourne and whoever is playing the 'Pies.

In our team meetings, a few of our lawyers were fans of Justice Kirby, and admired his strong (often dissenting) judgments. If a meeting needed a little livening up, a mere mention of Justice Kirby would get Jerker going and debate would flow.

I fear that my little portrait of Jerker fails to do him justice. As a lawyer, a man and a friend, there is none better. Solid gold quality all the way.

Brad - the Phantom

In some of my stories, I mention a few of the different types and personalities of lawyers who make up our profession.

Brad has always been an amazing "Finder' of legal work. You simply send him off somewhere/anywhere and he'll come back with a number of jobs (for the Minders to look after and the Grinders to plough through).

In his youth, Brad was a keen footballer, but could never string many games together. He had a real knack for sustaining an injury (even if the play was up the other end of the ground). Once, he was carrying an injury, so was acting as the team runner, when he twisted his knee.

Brad was also a champion at spilling drinks, food, ink, anything on his shirt. Eventually, his wife banned him from wearing any white or light coloured shirts.

As a result of his remarkable ability to sustain injury, Brad's sporting pursuits were quickly limited to golf. The firm supported his golfing activities, and his membership of his local golf club. He was even encouraged to take a half-day each week to play golf with clients or prospective clients. We began to describe the golf course as his 'office'.

Brad was so effective in obtaining work through his golf days that his attendances at the real office became less common. He would, however be on the phone and the internet, with details of the jobs required, and follow-up discussions as to how the legal services were delivered.

It was therefore only a matter of time before he became known as the 'Phantom'.

About the same time, he suffered another injury - reaching over to turn on his home computer, he suffered a spasm in one of the discs in his lower spine. For nearly two weeks, he was in severe pain, and could barely walk.

Sure enough, the Phantom was quickly dubbed 'The Ghost Who Limps'.

Alex

I worked with Alex for a few years. He became a good friend, and had a ribald sense of humour. Most of Alex's work was looking after the interests of a substantial banking and finance client, with whom he enjoyed an occasional long lunch. Sacrificing his health for the client relationship, he always claimed.

While Alex was an excellent lawyer, he presented as a real knockabout bloke, who loved to stand in the outer at the footy with a couple of his mates, have several beers, and loudly support his team.

Alex and his wife had four young boys in quick succession. The boys shared Alex's energetic nature and disdain of authority, and were a real handful.

Anyway, Alex and his wife bought a house in a nice quiet court in a good suburb, and moved in. Some of the neighbours, including one older woman who lived alone, did not appreciate the liveliness of the new arrivals, or the noise they sometimes made playing outside.

One quiet Saturday, Alex and his boys were playing in the court, when the old lady came by. Alex smiled his usual sunny hello, but the lady was not impressed "Why don't you go back to Frankston" she sniffed, then paused... "Where you belong!"

Alex was very tickled by this, and proudly told everyone about it. "Why don't you go back to Frankston....... where you belong" became part of our language.

Will's Employee Lawyer

As the reader will have gathered, lawyers, like most sections of the community, come in all sizes - and behaviours.

One of Will's employees was a case in point. He and his wife both dressed out of the op shop, and Will felt inclined to remind him that there was a standard of dress required for the office. Not to mention the standards required when representing a client in court.

Next thing Will knew, he had a call from the local police station. The lawyer had been arrested for shoplifting.

As you might expect, that employment relationship did not last long.

Gazza the Turncoat

Gazza joined our firm to replace Julian, one of his surfing mates who went off for a couple of years overseas. He was a lively, funny young lawyer who kept us all entertained, and could find something amusing in any situation.

Gazza was a very capable young commercial lawyer and showed great aptitude in coming to terms with all aspects of complex transactions.

One of our major clients was involved in setting up a number of large shopping centres in different parts of Europe, and needed to have a very capable lawyer, based in London, bringing together the whole show. The job required a very smart lawyer who understood their business model, and knew the key people back here.

They were impressed with Gazza and asked if he would go to London for six months to co-ordinate the work they were doing. He would be dealing with local lawyers, and would be more of a project manager than a lawyer for the purposes of the exercise.

Now Gazza was engaged to be married about ten months later, so he needed to clear the deal with his fiancee Gloria. After some negotiations, and tossing some more money into the pot, off he went. Gloria knew that she'd have to do ninety-five per cent of the wedding arrangements by herself, but bravely agreed.

So Gazza flew off and ran the roll-out in masterful fashion. The client was over the moon with his performance. Gazza gave them their pound of flesh, often getting little sleep, as he dealt with myriad issues in Europe as well as people back home at all hours of the day and night.

So successful was the project that the client rolled out another few developments, which continued on for longer than had originally been planned. This caused a little concern for Gloria, as the date for Gazza's return home was extended a couple of times.

Gazza gave the client a final date by which he must be home. The client wondered why a wedding was so important, until Gazza clarified that it was **his own** wedding. Oh, OK, they couldn't talk him out of that.

The long-suffering Gloria was finally mollified, the happy wedding took place, and Gazza didn't return to London.

After everything settled down, Gazza found it hard to resume his previous career as a lawyer. Less than twelve months later, he accepted an offer from another of our clients to go and work with them full time, not specifically as a lawyer, but managing significant development projects (but with no overseas commitment).

The irony of Gazza the client soon became apparent. As a client, he became incredibly demanding, in terms of performance, turnaround times and costs. Those who look after Gazza's work no longer love him in the way they used to. He actually became the client from hell. He is, however, kicking huge goals for his new employer.

Long lunches

When I was a young lawyer, there were some who regularly enjoyed a long (and often liquid) lunch. I never had the privilege (or drawback) of working under a long lunch regime. The practice later almost disappeared after changes to fringe benefits taxes in the late 1980s.

My good friend Alex was always on the lookout for a lunch opportunity, but most of us worked a much stricter regime.

At one firm where I worked, a few of us would occasionally go to a nearby hotel for a quick lunch on someone's birthday, or if a team member was leaving. We did not have a long lunch culture. On such occasions, we would each pay cash for our own meal, and be back at work well within the hour.

We were all surprised one day when Denny, one of the accounts supervisors, took a call in the middle of the afternoon from that hotel, chasing up a couple of unpaid bills.

Denny did a quick check and told them that none of us knew anything about the bills. He asked if the hotel staff knew the names of any of the lunchers - they didn't, but the same group went there nearly every day. Could they describe any of them? They told Denny "Hold on, they're still here now." Denny told them it couldn't be any of us, as we were all working away in our offices.

It turned out that these were the three partners of a firm with a name that began with the same letter as ours.

One of our staff had previously worked at that firm. She told us how the level of anxiety at that firm would start to rise substantially by around 3.30 pm, when the partners would normally be returning to the office.

Not recommended as a way to run a legal practice!

Non Existent Assets - the National Safety Council

One of the great (apparent) successes of the Latrobe Valley was the National Safety Council, located at the local airport. Keira, who was the council's in-house lawyer, had done work experience with my firm some years earlier in her student days.

The council made quite a name for itself under a charismatic leader in John Friedrich, who built it rapidly to be Australia's leading search and rescue/safety provider. It had state of the art equipment for all sorts of problems, including treating divers suffering from the 'bends'. Whenever there was an emergency, the council was called in.

Friedrich had commenced working for the council in 1977, and became executive director in 1982. He had an impressive list of *forged* qualifications, and a remarkable public relations presence. He was constantly showing politicians, bankers and business types some of the wonderful equipment the council used. He would also tell them that this is only the tip of the iceberg, with much more spread around the country, ready to be put into use whenever called upon.

Friedrich was awarded an OAM in 1982, in recognition of "... his services to the community, particularly in the area of industrial safety and search and rescue services."

Friedrich had a special talent for charming bankers. He obtained tens of millions of dollars in loans from twenty seven different banks, on very dodgy security. Several high powered bankers were later embarrassed when it became apparent that they had advanced millions on security which consisted of nothing more than forged equipment invoices.

The Council's rapid growth meant that corners were cut, but the escalating borrowings had repayment schedules, which ultimately could not be met. In 1989, the Council finally collapsed like the house of cards that it was, in one of the great business disasters of the era.

Friedrich was charged with ninety two separate instances of obtaining property by deception. He was subsequently found dead on his Sale property, with a shotgun wound to the head. The coroner recorded a verdict of suicide.

The Defence Department was also very embarrassed by the disaster, having given him a security clearance and almost unlimited access to RAAF bases. It turned out that it had made no real effort to check his background or qualifications.

The Fabulous Green Boys

1. Max and More Non Existent Assets

The dodgy business of raising money on the security of non-existent assets was raised to an art form some years later. This time the fraudster was a partner of Aroni Colman, a prominent and well respected Melbourne law firm. I knew a few of the Aroni Colman people, and they were completely blind-sided by what happened.

The first time anyone became aware that there was a problem was when the news media reported that Melbourne lawyer Max Green had been bludgeoned to death in a hotel in Cambodia. Very few people even knew that he was in Cambodia, and even fewer knew what he was actually doing there.

The people at Aroni Colman were shocked that one of their partners was dead, particularly that he had been murdered in a Phnom Penh hotel. The bad news became much, much worse, when it transpired that tens of millions of dollars were missing from the firm's trust account. In all, $42,000,000 had disappeared.

The firm had a 'Who's Who' type list of well-healed (largely Jewish) clients, and a reputation of being a leading tax advice firm. Max worked hard to promote the firm and himself as being in the forefront of the tax minimisation industry.

Max promised the clients that he could significantly reduce their tax bills, by investing in low-cost equipment which was leased to Citylink and used in the construction of Victorian tollways. Like Friedrich, he used forged invoices to obtain the money from the investors. Most of the 'equipment' never existed.

The clients, not unreasonably, trusted Max, and accepted the invoices as legitimate, so they paid their money into Aroni Colman's trust account. From there, Max transferred the money into a separate trust account, in his name only, with another bank. He was the only person who knew of this account, which he then used as his own slush fund.

From there, the trail became very murky, and the money was never recovered. The best that anyone could assess was that Max was involved in some substantial precious gem transactions in Cambodia. It all appears to have gone sour, leading to Max's death in a luxury hotel. And no sign of the money!

For the worthy people at Aroni Colman, their problems were only beginning. As Max's activities were clearly fraudulent, the firm's public liability insurance couldn't be claimed on (its cover was limited to losses caused by negligent acts or omissions, not fraud).

Even though the other partners and the rest of the firm were innocent of any wrongdoing, they were skewered by the principle of joint and several liability. In a partnership, all partners are jointly liable for the actions of any one of them. They had a problem amounting to $42,000,000, plus interest, etc.

The firm was ultimately wound up, a number of the partners were bankrupted, and several of them lost substantial assets. Those who had planned their own asset protection strategies (see the discussion of *Phillips Case* in Chapter 9 above) survived, but all suffered a reputation loss, not to mention the psychological trauma (and a couple of divorces).

Most of the Aroni Colman people found positions with other law firms, and are getting on with their lives and careers, trying to put the pieces back together.

2. Phil and the Babcock & Brown Debacle

Like Max, Phil was a tax accountant and lawyer. He had worked with worldwide accounting firm Arthur Andersen. In 1984 he joined the US-based Babcock & Brown, at that time a relatively small firm specialising in leasing aircraft.

Phil rapidly grew Babcock into a major player in infrastructure and property financing. Many commentators noted that Babcock appeared to be modelled on the very successful Macquarie Bank.

Phil took Babcock public in 2004, listing on the Australian Stock Exchange at $5.00 per share. Under his leadership, its remarkable growth trajectory continued. It became renowned for setting up sophisticated structures for investing in former government assets as they were privatised.

Electricity generators, power stations, railways, airports, toll roads, port terminals and other infrastructure items all felt the magic Phil Green touch. He was a master of parcelling up assets, selling them to the public, and arranging the financing. All the while, Babcock retained management control over the cash flows, and collected a nice fee every time anything happened.

It was not unusual for Babcock to purchase an asset for $1 Billion, using $900 Million of borrowed funds. If there was a small drop in asset values, oops! If the assets didn't return a profit, no income for the investors, oops again! A problem could be disguised for a while by revaluing the asset upwards, but eventually the music will stop, and disaster awaits.

In 2006, Babcock & Brown Wind Power had operating cash flow of $14 Million, but paid $48 Million to shareholders. Sleight of hand tricks helped disguise the problem - like slipping a new Bermuda based company into the mix here, a new trust there, and presto, all was well.

In 2007, Babcock raked in $1 Billion in fees. Half of these fees were paid in bonuses to Phil and his colleagues, on top of the $300 Million they were collecting in salaries.

But eventually, smoke and mirrors will only take you so far. Sooner or later, you have to pay the bill (and the interest). It was only a matter of time before the whole house of cards collapsed.

From a high of $33, shares in Babcock collapsed to practically zero. Over $12 Billion in value was simply wiped out, and many of the infrastructure assets were left with debts much greater than their value.

As for Phil, he lost quite a fortune. Unlike Max, he still has more money than the average punter, and yes, he is still breathing!

As a footnote, Phil and other directors and Babcock's auditors are now being sued by the liquidator for $158 Million, being dividends allegedly paid illegally out of the company's capital.

CHAPTER 13

CRICKET AND OTHER SOCIAL ACTIVITIES

Lawyers v Doctors

In the Latrobe Valley, we would enjoy a social game of cricket annually, on a Sunday, between the local lawyers and our friends in the medical profession.

These were very civilised occasions, with special rules, including:

- Frequent drinks breaks (a nice cold beer went down well on a hot summer afternoon),
- Each bowler could bowl no more than two overs,
- Everyone had to have a bowl (even Sunny who bowled such slow off breaks that, when a batsman missed with a huge heave, and the ball rolled onto his front pad, we agreed that he couldn't be out LBW as the ball probably wouldn't have reached the stumps),
- Batsmen had to retire if they got to thirty, and
- No batsman could be out for a duck (this last rule proved a problem in one case, when we kept getting a batsman out, even when trying to give him a run - we had to become very creative to find a run for him so we could then get him out).

The results were not particularly important. Over a number of years, we generally broke about even.

I had played some cricket, so I always nominated myself as captain of the lawyers' team.

On one occasion, even though I had not bowled for a few years, I decided to take the new ball after the medicos won the toss and decided to bat. My theory was that, without bowling fast, I might get the cherry to swing a bit and pick up a wicket or two.

After the first ball landed about where I aimed, I was feeling optimistic. However the next came out as a slow medium full toss, about shoulder high. The batsman duly belted it for four, one bounce and over the fine leg boundary.

With all the chutzpah I could summon, I pointed to the nearest fielder, Joe (who happened to be fairly new in town as Christopher's articled clerk) and commanded him to "Go and stand where that one landed, and I'll get you a catch".

The fifth ball of the over was (unintentionally) almost exactly the same. The batsman gave it the same treatment. In what seemed like slow motion, the ball sailed unerringly down to fine leg, directly to Joe, who didn't have to move anything, not even his hands. The ball actually struck him in the hand and then (just as I was about to congratulate myself on my inspired captaincy), bounced out and rolled across the boundary for another four runs.

Poor Joe! He was standing there looking stricken, while the rest of us were doubled over laughing. Greg at slip was yelling "Oh Joe. We've set the trap and you let us down". Rocky was almost in tears with laughter "Beautifully planned" he cried, "Trust an articled clerk to drop the ball" and so on.

After a minute or two we made a point of rallying around Joe, and telling him how much we enjoyed the incident and not to feel bad. In fact, his dropping the ball made the day, and gave us a story to talk about for years (as indeed has been the case here).

After completing his articles, Joe moved to another country town, where he carved out a very successful career in the law. I caught up with him many years later. He gave me a wry smile and told me he still had bad memories of that day.

Other Cricket Matches?

Chad, one of the lawyers, wanted to expand on our annual cricket matches. He suggested a game against the local police. This idea had no support from the other lawyers. There were many more coppers than lawyers in the area, and some of them were young, fit, strong and would have been keen to knock our blocks off.

Chad then came up with the idea that we should play a game against the local estate agents. This was considered feasible, so Chad took it upon himself to organise it. He selected a day, and started rounding up the agents.

There was no problem getting a team of lawyers, but he ran into problems with the agents. They held their rivalries very personally, and he fielded a number of calls asking which agents would be playing. After a few times being told "If so-and-so is playing, count me out", he decided it was all too hard.

So, the game against the agents never got off the ground.

Annual Law Conventions

In my first year of practising in Morwell, I was told that I must attend the annual convention of the local law association. It was in Cowes on Phillip Island that year.

Each regional law association has its own convention, which is attended by leaders of the legal profession from the judiciary, the bar and the Law Institute. There are several working/information/update sessions, as well as a major dinner and a few social get togethers. It is also an excellent opportunity to meet fellow practitioners.

So, my wife and I attended the convention, and greatly enjoyed the weekend, particularly the dinner. We were put on a table with a number of other youngish lawyers, some of whom were unpartnered.

Our table was up for a good night, and we were the last to leave when all the formalities were completed. I recall sitting on the pier with my wife, Tom and Will very late with a bottle of port which we'd taken from one of the tables at the dinner. Tom and Will were both from another Gippsland town, and we became good friends. Will in particular has been a very close friend ever since.

At that time, Tom had an E-Type Jaguar. At a very late hour, he announced he was driving home. We could not persuade him otherwise, as he headed off to his car. We found out in the morning that when he started it up, the Jag lurched forward a couple of metres into a ditch and stalled. He could not re-start it again. We were convinced that the car was much smarter than Tom, and in fact saved his life.

Babies and Bets

Over the years, I had a few bets with friends when any of us were expecting a baby. The stake was always six bottles of beer. I'd give odds of ten to one on the date (no-one ever correctly predicted the actual date) and even money on the gender. This was in the days before you knew the baby's sex in advance. There was also some (theoretical) fine print about caesarians and induced births.

My last of these bets was with Will, when his wife was expecting their first child at the same time as my wife was expecting our third. We had two bets - who would be first, and a small game of two-up.

The result was that Will's son was born at about 11.00 pm one evening, and my son arrived at about 1.30 am the following day. So Will won the first bet by less than three hours. In the two-up game, he'd picked odds, so (as we both had boys) I won that one. So, the two bets ultimately cancelled each other out.

CHAPTER 14

A FEW COMMENTS ABOUT ESTATE AGENTS

Most estate agents are fine and honourable people. I have many friends in the real estate industry. There are, however, the few who give the industry a bad name (and are the ones who receive most of the publicity). So, I hope that, in telling a few tales about the bad eggs, I don't offend the decent majority.

There are some fly-by-night types, who seem to suddenly appear in town, and last about three years, one in insurance, one in real estate, and then one selling used cars (sometimes the order varies) - and then they disappear, never to be heard of again. Presumably they turn up in a succession of other towns, repeat the process and move on again.

One estate agency of good repute employed a particular woman as residential property manager. She handled all the residential tenancies. This woman took her job seriously, in that she saw her job as to keep the landlords happy and be very aggressive to the tenants. She would proudly declare "It's my job to be a bitch, and I'm very good at it." No-one who knew her would disagree with that assessment!

There have been a few famous cases of unprincipled agents buying properties in the name of a family member (against the rules) for much less than they were worth, and soon afterwords reselling at a nice profit.

The Footy Tipping Competition

For a couple of years, one estate agents office ran a footy tipping competition in their town. There were plenty of takers, and some thousand of dollars involved. Everything went fine in the first year, but the second year left a very bad smell.

The competition paid out prizemoney for first, second and last at the end of the season. Coincidentally, there were three people working at that agency at the time, two salesmen and the office manager/secretary/receptionist. Remarkably, in that year, all three prizes were won by those three people.

That office closed down shortly afterwards and all three of them left the area.

There was another agent, Saul, who would ring me when any of my clients was buying or selling through him. He would finish up by saying he would send me the "irrelevant details". He never got it when I replied "Don't worry about that, just get me the details of the deal." He was one of those people who could sell ice to Eskimos but couldn't put two words together in writing. I came across several estate agents like that.

Vern and The Very Dodgy Proposition

Vern, an estate agent of my acquaintance, rang me one day to report on a proposition he'd received from a couple of gentlemen who'd come to his office. Apparently one of them was a valuer and the other was in the finance industry.

It was a time when the residential property market was very quiet, and this agency had a number of unsold properties on its books. They told him that they would buy every property he had, at the current asking price. There were, however, a few conditions:

1. The contract of sale would show a sale price that was double the real price, but the vendors would only receive the real price,
2. The two gentlemen would provide the names and addresses of the actual purchasers (different in each case) but the agents would not meet them,
3. The two gentlemen would arrange the finance (eighty per cent of the price shown in the contract) and the valuation (based on the sale price as shown in the contract).

Vern was somewhat suspicious about the proposal. He didn't think it smelled right, but wasn't sure why. When he outlined it to me, I laughed and said "Vern, you're a nice bloke, but I can't promise to come and visit you very often". When I outlined the offences in what was proposed (including fraud) and the possible jail terms, he was glad he had called.

The Standover Man

Over a couple of years, I heard reports about one agent who apparently targeted recently bereaved widows. It was said that he had a few dodgy habits with them, including taking the deceased husband's equipment and tools off their hands, and doing a side deal for an extra commission to him for selling the property (over and above the usual commission to his employer). There were stories also of bullying and standing over the vulnerable ones.

I ask the reader not to assume that I'm just picking on estate agents. As you will note, I'm happy to give lawyers plenty of stick too.

CHAPTER 15

WEDDINGS AND OTHER ROMANTIC DISASTERS

Anne's Wedding

Anne was a word processing operator in my practice. When she was getting married, she asked me to drive (and provide) the wedding car. OK, happy to be of service.

On the big day, I was there nice and early, in a nice clean car, all ribboned up, to take the bride to the church. All OK there, then off to have photos taken. We were away for two and a half hours, while all the other guests went to the pub. It was a very hot, dry dusty day, and I would have killed for a long, cold beer.

After what seemed like the longest three weeks of my life, we made it to the reception - which was dry! Ohh, the agonising, miserable hours of suffering I endured as I smiled through gritted teeth and a severely parched throat. Glasses of soft drink did nothing for my mood or my throat as the reception also seemed to go on forever. I recall the groom making about three separate speeches, all excruciatingly painful…

Another Dry Wedding?

I don't claim to be much of a drinker, but have always believed that a social occasion can sometimes benefit from a little lubrication.

For this reason, I wasn't looking forward to Lynn and Jack's wedding. Lynn's family were non-drinkers, and we'd been told that the big occasion would be dry.

Of course, it was a warm sunny day as we headed off to the big occasion, which was at the bride's family home, in a beautiful garden setting. When we arrived, we were each handed a glass of non-alcoholic apple cider, so I was resigned to this being the best I was going to get all day.

However, Lynn had, at the last minute, persuaded her father that he should provide some champagne for the toasts. He thus ambled in to the local licensed grocer and asked how much bubbly he'd need, just for the toasts. "How many guests?" was the question. "About eighty" he replied. "OK, two crates will do the job".

So, two crates it was. Now, the only drinkers, apart from Lynn and Jack, were four of us, all seated at one table. We didn't quite get through the whole two crates, but we gave it a good shot.

A few glasses of bubbly, lots of dancing, and a really enjoyable wedding, after all!

The Elopement

One of my clients told me about his daughter's wedding. She and her fiancee took off one weekend with another couple who were their best friends.

Without telling anyone else, they had engaged a wedding celebrant in Sydney. They were married under the Harbour Bridge, and then had a fabulous celebratory dinner at one of Sydney's best restaurants.

They phoned the families from the restaurant to deliver the news. My client's wife was a little miffed about missing the wedding, but he was thrilled for them both.

The small wedding party ordered the most expensive food and drinks on the menu, and had a fantastic time. At the end, when they went to pay, the manager waved them away. My client had been on the phone and paid it on his credit card.

His daughter then rang him back and said "Dad, what did you do that for? It was the most expensive meal ever, and you weren't even there." He replied "No worries, you have saved me a fortune on what a big wedding would have cost me."

He was rapt!

Horse Drawn Carriages

At the other end of the scale, there was the story which came out in the NSW Supreme Court. It was all about the bride who had always dreamt of having the big wedding, with horse-drawn carriages.

The groom was delegated the job of hiring the horse-drawn carriages. He duly booked them and paid for them well in advance. The only problem was that, on the day, there was a problem, which resulted in the horse-drawn carriages not being available.

The groom hurriedly hired two stretch limousines for $1,500 and they got through the day, but with a bride who was devastated that her dream was frustrated. In her eyes, the day was ruined!

The couple then sued the horse-drawn carriage company in the local Magistrates' Court for $50,000, which was the limit of the court's jurisdiction at the time. The court awarded them $1,500, for the cost of hiring the limousines, and nothing for the damages they claimed for ruining their lives.

They took the case all the way to the NSW Supreme Court. The (very spoiled and indulged) wife was still upset and could not get over what she saw as a dreadful day of humiliation. She could not forgive her husband for letting her down by failing to arrange the horse-drawn carriages. The poor man was condemned to a life of misery and blame.

The Supreme Court judge had no sympathy for them, effectively telling the couple, and the wife in particular, to "get a life", as he dismissed their appeal.

Ernie the Love Machine

Then there was Ernie, one of Greg's occasional clients. Ernie was the living proof of Sam's observation that there is someone for everyone, so long as you're not too fussy.

Ernie was about fifty-five, short and skinny, with very little hair and no teeth. I can't imagine that any woman could have found him attractive, but he was never without a woman. Mind you, he wasn't fussy either. He'd already been married three times and had quite a few girlfriends.

One day, Greg was walking past the printers when Ernie came out with a box under his arm. He excitedly told Greg about his next upcoming wedding, and showed him the invitations he'd just collected from the printers.

What tickled Greg most was the stipulation at the bottom of the invitations. It read "No presents - cash only".

The Assistants Always Know

I know many lawyers who met their spouse in the office, and spent the rest of their lives together. At first they go to great lengths to keep their affair secret, but this never works. The universal rule in law offices is that "the assistants know everything". Anything that happens, particularly of a romantic nature, spreads faster than wildfire.

Some assistants know in advance when there's to be a fire evacuation drill. A few lawyers I know have avoided the thirty-five level trudge down the stairs by noting the assistants heading down for a 'coffee break'. But back to the story.

One young couple would arrange to meet mid-morning at a nearby coffee shop, and would leave by different doors, much to the amusement of the assistants, who would have it around the office in seconds.

The Receptionist and the Courier

Lulu the receptionist had a big welcoming smile and a friendly personality. She was popular with everyone in the office and was regarded as a real asset.

One day, however, there was a huge ruckus coming from the reception area. A woman whom no-one knew had come in and was screaming abuse at Lulu. As it happened, Lulu had taken up with one of the couriers who made regular deliveries to the firm, and was involved in a torrid relationship with him. This, as it happened, was his wife!

My view has always been that, when a person is unfaithful to their partner, it's not so much the third party who is at fault, although they are frequently blamed. I've always thought that the third party is simply looking after their own interests, whereas it's the unfaithful partner who is in breach of their commitment.

Anyway, this didn't deter the courier's wife. She made a point of embarrassing Lulu and wrecking her day - to the extent that Lulu resigned. She left the firm the same day!

CHAPTER 16

SOME COMMENTS ABOUT CLIENTS

Things That Clients Do (or Say)

We often used to say that the practice of the law would be wonderful if it wasn't for those damned clients!

Clients come in all shapes and sizes, religious and ethnic backgrounds and political views, with an infinite variety of temperaments, weird and irrational behaviours, senses of humour and so on.

They can sometimes be very unpredictable, and that's when lawyers really worry. If you're running a major case, you need to be able to rely on your client not to fall apart when they get into the witness box and the opposition smart-arse starts questioning them.

Many a lawyer has gone into court confident of victory, only to see the client completely unravel in the hands of a skilful cross-examiner. I've seen a few clients completely lose their way and contradict every element of their case in the process of cross-examination.

Some of them then proceed to blame the lawyer for the terrible loss they then suffer - when no lawyer in the world could have overcome the implosion of the client.

And your worries aren't necessarily confined to the courtroom. At one firm, we had a client who would send in an email (addressed to maybe half a dozen of us) at about 3.00 am, and then absolutely crack it if no-one had responded to him by 8.30 am.

Other clients like to ring at, say, 4.30 pm, with a request for a suite of documents - to be back to them by 10.00 that night.

Some firms advertise their services on the basis that their lawyers are available twenty-four hours per day, and require the lawyers to provide their home and mobile phone numbers to clients.

To my mind, this is going too far. If you don't allow young lawyers to have some sort of life, you'll burn them out very quickly, and lose them from the law. Plus, they won't be able to sustain any relationship, and will develop all sorts of problems.

Law already has the highest percentage incidence of depression of any profession. Under the current approach, this is unlikely to change!

When Cash was King

In these highly regulated times, large amounts of cash are much less common in lawyers' offices than they used to be. Much tighter trust account regulations and anti-money-laundering provisions mean the substantial sums of cash do not now materialise in our practices.

In the '70s and '80s, and even into the '90s, payments of substantial cash amounts were, while not exactly everyday, not as rare as you might think.

Over the years, I acted for quite a few people who operated small, retail businesses. These were the typical hoarders of cash (presumably not disclosed to the tax authorities). On a few occasions in the '70s, I was given amounts of $25,000 and $30,000 cash, each as part payment for a business transaction.

In the '80s, this continued. Once I had a Greek client, Dimitrios (who operated a fish and chip shop business) bring in a very smelly bag, containing $40,000 in cash. He had apparently been storing it behind the deep fry vats in his shop. Truly, it stank of very smelly fish!

Then, in the early '90s, Mason wandered into my office clutching a gladstone bag awash with cash. He had just come from the racecourse after a successful day on the punt, and did not trust himself to take it home, as he was sure he'd start splashing it about. He insisted that we open a file for him, for the purchase of a modest house, and hold the money in trust for him till settlement.

So, we opened a file and gave Mason a receipt for the money (counting it out carefully with him). He then left, and walked around the corner to an estate agency. Within a couple of hours, he had signed up to buy a small house. 30 days later, we withdrew the money (by bank cheque this time) and settled the purchase of the house. There was enough left over to pay his stamp duty and buy some furniture.

How About a Smile?

As I've mentioned before, many of my clients operated small retail businesses. Some of them were excellent operators, but there were those who should never have been in retail.

Such businesses often stand or fall on the personality of the operator. Those who can relate to their customers (and if they work hard and use their brains) generally do well.

I have had clients who are prepared for the work, and put a lot of effort into it, but fail in the human relations area.

One of my mantras for retail business is to smile at the customer. Remember, it's the customer who ultimately determines the fate of the business. Surely, when someone comes into your shop (and puts money in your hand), is it too much for you to smile at them?

My niece Monica and her husband Dave operate a small franchise business in a country town. Monica is a great manager, but Dave is a major asset. He has got to know all the regulars. When he sees them crossing the road, or pulling up in their cars, he has their regular order ready for them before they get to the counter.

He engages them in friendly banter, and has quickly become an institution in the town.

On the other hand, in another area of the state, I came across a woman who is the closest I have seen to a female Basil Fawlty on a bad day. We were enjoying a family picnic when the weather turned bad. So, we made our way to a little coffee shop.

Most shopkeepers would be pleased to see 22 people (including six children) come into their shop. Dave would have been in his element. Here was a group who'd spend a couple of hundred dollars (at least) in the shop.

Not this woman. She huffed and puffed and made us feel quite unwelcome. We soldiered on and bought a few coffees and cakes, but she was so hostile (especially to the children, even though they were remarkably well behaved). Her rudeness was breathtaking, calling the children "little shits" (when they were sitting quietly at a table) and snapping at all and sundry.

We got out of there as quickly (and cheaply, as it turned out) as we could - but I reckon she gave us enough material for a couple of episodes!

Big Bill and the Finance Company

Bill was a big man with a big, outgoing personality. He was an account manager with a finance company, and always had the best figures of any of the managers in the state.

Bill was popular around town, and particularly at the local golf club, where he was known for his frequent entertaining and occasionally shouting the bar. He was everyone's friend.

As well as living in a large, modern home, Bill always drove a top of the range four wheel drive, and towed a sleek motor yacht.

What Bill was doing was quite simple. One day, when his finances were tight, he wrote up a loan for a fictitious borrower (this was in the days before a person required 100 points to open a new account). He used the money for himself, but made all the repayments on the dot.

No problem, it was all under control, so he made out another loan, in another name. Every payment was made on time. And this pattern continued for quite a while. All Bill's 'borrowers' had excellent repayment histories!

Bill kept on writing more and more loans, and managing the repayments like clockwork. The company was very pleased with Bill's performance and paid him bonuses, as well as writing to his 'borrowers' with more loan offers - based on their excellent payment records.

Eventually, this led to Bill's undoing. When he was on a nice overseas holiday (having set up all the repayments before he left) one of his colleagues noticed the address on one of the letters going out to one of his 'borrowers'. The colleague knew the people who lived at that address, and that the 'borrower' did not.

A little bit of checking led to the whole scam unravelling - and to Bill having another holiday - this one at public expense. Bankruptcy followed, as well as the loss of the nice home, car and boat.

More Embezzlement

Many years later, Jane was one of my close colleagues at a city law firm. She asked me for my opinion when she received a letter from a prominent law firm on behalf of one of the major banks.

Jane's clients had put up their home, in a very good suburb, for auction. At auction, there had been spirited bidding, and it was sold under the hammer. The successful bidder paid the 10% deposit to the estate agent's trust account by his personal cheque, which duly cleared.

On the basis of the sale being unconditional, the clients then signed up unconditionally to buy another home.

The letter from the bank's lawyers said that the purchaser was an employee of the bank, and had stolen some millions from it. The bank was demanding that the clients repay the deposit to them.

We did our analysis of the bank's claim and our clients' position, and replied, politely telling the bank that the theft was its problem, not our clients'. As our clients had no knowledge that the purchaser had stolen the deposit money (and could not have been aware of it) they had no liability. In addition, our clients were now in a difficult position, as they had an obligation to settle their purchase, with their sale not now able to settle.

Fortunately, our clients were able to negotiate with one of the underbidders from the auction, and avoid a major problem.

After our reply to the bank's lawyers, we heard nothing more from them.

Edgar, Annie and Nicodemus

When my wife and I first moved to Morwell, we rented a two bedroom place not far from the office - I was able to walk to work, which was very handy indeed.

The landlords were Edgar and his wife Annie, possibly the wealthiest people in the town. They lived next door, and we struck up a friendship with them. They became good clients of mine as well. They were also reputed to be quite tight with their money.

Edgar and Annie would have been about sixty or so, and had never been able to have children. Their 'baby' was their huge old cat, Nicodemus.

Nicodemus was about the size of a small horse, and was on a very good paddock. Not only did he have a big frame, he was extremely well fed as well. At this time, he was about seventeen years old, so Edgar and Annie took great care of his health. His ultimate demise would prove to be a true 'death in the family' for them. Anyway, at this time, he was huge but quite healthy.

One long weekend, we stayed with my in-laws in another country area. My mother-in-law's untamed cat had a litter of kittens. Not only were they fiercely wild, they had the most feral look that any cats ever had. They had red, yellow, black, orange and a dirty white colour.

We allowed ourselves to be persuaded to take one of the kittens back with us. We expected that it would eventually get used to us and become reasonably tame. So we took it home and kept it inside, supplying it with plenty of food and water.

After about four days, my wife was coming in the back door, when the kitten flew out the narrowest of gaps and hurtled out the back gate and around the corner, past Edgar and Annie's house. She took off after it and was convinced that it went in underneath the unoccupied house on the other side of Edgar and Annie's.

Ever a resourceful person, my bride opened a tin of the best cat food, found a couple of sleeping pills, crushed them up and stirred them into the tin. She carefully placed it, with a bowl of water, at the spot where she'd seen the kitten disappear under the house.

We never saw the kitten again, but a few hours later, the food was all gone. The tin was empty, so we took it home, along with the water bowl.

A couple of days later, we ran into Edgar and Annie. They were distraught. Nicodemus was suffering from some mystery ailment, and they'd had to take him to the local vet - at great expense. Poor Nicodemus couldn't walk. His hind legs were not working at all. This might be the beginning of the end!

Next time we saw them, a couple of days later, they were much happier. Nicodemus was much better, eating all his food and moving freely. The vet had formed the view that someone must have hit Nicodemus on the lower back with a stick, causing a temporary paralysis. Who would do such a thing?

We were, of course, full of sympathy and concern. Strangely, we never made any mention of the kitten episode, or of our conclusion that greedy-guts Nicodemus had wolfed down the food that we'd put out for the kitten.

I never found out what happened to the kitten, but over the next fifteen years, I reckon I spotted hundreds of cats in the town that had the same wild, feral look and range of colours that it had.

The Tragic Case of the Stubbed Toe That Wasn't

One day, a young man (Brandon) came in to see me, and told me his tale of woe.

Over eighteen months earlier, he'd had a sore toe. It concerned him, as he didn't remember knocking it on anything. So he went to his doctor and had it examined. The doctor had a close look and told him that there was nothing wrong with it, He'd probably stubbed it in the night when he'd got up to go to the toilet.

Happy enough with this diagnosis, Brandon got on with his life. After a while, he began to feel less and less well, but felt reassured by what his doctor had said. Eventually, he felt a swelling in the upper groin, and went to another doctor, who quickly referred him on to a specialist.

This time, the diagnosis was chilling. He had inoperable cancer, and was given less than six months to live. The specialist told him "If only you'd come in about a year earlier..."

Brandon had tears in his eyes when he told me his story.

We quickly commenced proceedings, and the insurer cane up with an offer which Brandon chose to accept, rather than fight on for a larger sum. He wanted to spend his last months at peace with his family.

We could all only ask - "what if..."

Vinnie and the Great Train Robber

One of my clients, Vinnie, operated a business in town, and always had a story to tell.

When the news broke that Ronnie Biggs had been living with his family in the Melbourne suburbs, Vinnie told me that he thought he might have inadvertently aided his disappearance from Australia.

He had been driving on business on the Princes Highway in eastern Victoria, when he picked up a hitch-hiker. They drove for a few hours before their ways parted, and apparently chatted away like old friends. Vinnie was always on for a chat, and his passenger had many interesting stories.

At the time, Vinnie merely noted that the hitch-hiker had an English accent. When it was later reported that Biggs had been living in Melbourne, and had apparently escaped by hitch-hiking around the coastal highway to Queensland, and getting from there to South America, Vinnie became convinced that Ronnie Biggs was his man.

Many years later, I heard Vinnie relating the story in much greater detail (and with much more certainty) on the Sunday morning radio program 'Australia All Over'.

The Surety and the Change of Mind

When a person is arrested on a criminal charge, they are brought before the Magistrates' Court or a bail justice, where the charge is formally put to them, and the case is adjourned to another date for hearing.

In a serious case, the accused may be adjourned in custody. Sometimes the accused is released on bail, or another party provides a surety - a person putting their own money or assets on the line as a form of guarantee that the accused will come before the court when the case is next listed.

We were consulted by a lady who had put up a surety of $25,000 for her brother to be released pending the hearing of a number of charges against him. She had volunteered the surety, as she loved her brother, and trusted him to not flee the jurisdiction.

However, over the next few weeks, she found out more about him than she had previously known. She told me that she was now worried that he would fail to appear, and that she would lose her money.

There is a procedure for just such a problem. We lodged an application with the court, and the magistrate heard it the same day. The lady was released from her surety, and the magistrate immediately issued a new warrant for the arrest of the accused.

"Just Gonna Break His Legs"

Clive, a new client, came to see me, with a worried look on his face. He had run up a number of debts, through gambling and other poor decisions he had made. He was under a lot of pressure to repay the debts, but needed to buy some time.

My first question was about his gambling, as there was no point trying if he was going to continue to gamble. He assured me that he had learned that it was a losing game, and would not go back to it. Surprisingly, he was as good as his word.

However, there was another problem. After we sent out offers to his creditors of payment by instalments, one creditor rang me to say no, he demanded payment in three days. If not paid, he'd break Clive's legs.

In my early days as a young lawyer, I'd done a bit of debt recovery work, but this was a new one on me. I tried a few different tacks with this man, including the suggestion that if Clive turned up with broken legs, he would be the clear suspect. He replied "Don't care, just gonna break his legs".

When I suggested that Clive with broken legs would have no means of then repaying the money, the response was the same - "Don't care, just gonna break his legs." He repeated the same threat over and over.

I told Clive about this, and suggested we call in the police, but he would have none of that. As it turned out, the threat was not carried out, and Clive was able to repay all his creditors in good time - including the 'leg-breaker'.

When the Inmates Are in Charge of the Asylum

Whenever a client company establishes a blanket rule (with no consideration for unusual circumstances) you can bet that a disaster is just around the corner.

This one involved a big client, a major company which operated thousands of business sites around Australia. Many of them were company-operated sites, but there were also many which were sub-let to franchisees.

In this instance, the business was operated by a franchisee, in an inner Melbourne suburb (site 1056). There was a long-term lease, which the landlord regretted entering into. He was looking for a way to bring the lease to an end, so he could proceed with a proposed (and presumably highly profitable) redevelopment of the land.

The lease was for a long term and had been entered into before the introduction of GST in mid 2000. As a result, even in 2003, the landlord was not obliged to provide a tax invoice. Under the GST legislation, the landlord (or their agent) was required to provide a tax invoice for each rental period. The lease in question, being pre-GST, was exempt from this requirement.

It seems that the client's Sydney head office had been taken over by the inmates. An edict was sent out to all administrative sections, telling them that no rent would be paid without a tax invoice. No thought had been given to the pre-GST leases where the landlord was not obliged to provide a tax invoice.

So, early on a Monday morning, I took a call from Henry, the client's manager for the relevant area. He was on the first day of three week's leave, and had been called by the franchisee in a panic. Sorry Henry, better put that holiday on hold!

The franchisee had turned up for work at 6.00 am, to find that the landlord had changed the locks, and brought the lease to an end. What could we do?

We leapt into action preparing affidavits and applying, on the same morning, to the Supreme Court for relief against the 'forfeiture' of the lease.

Ultimately, the court granted relief and re-instated the lease, but only after the rent was paid, as well as all the landlord's costs and expenses, and hefty fees to us and our senior counsel. And a couple of serious undertakings to the court from our client.

An expensive lesson to the bean-counters at head office!

Stacey, the Wombat and the Jockey

Stacey was a young lady from a good local family. She had had an affair with a new man in town (the Wombat*), and had become pregnant as a result. As soon as he became aware of her condition, the Wombat left town, never to be heard of again.

With the support of her family, Stacey had and kept the baby. A couple of years later she met, and subsequently married, a jockey, who was quite well known in the region. He wanted to adopt the child, and they came to me to apply to the County Court for the appropriate adoption order.

We prepared the application and affidavits, setting out the circumstances, and including everything known about the Wombat (in reality not much). and the application was listed for the next sittings of the court.

The cantankerous old judge who turned up for the sittings was not in a working mood when he arrived, and he refused to hear the application. He told us that we needed to give the actual father the opportunity to be heard before he'd make the order. Pity no-one had any idea where the Wombat was - or any contact details.

So, the case was adjourned to the next sittings when a different judge would be on the circuit. In the meantime, we'd sent a letter addressed to the Wombat at his last known address (which we knew he had long departed from). No surprise when it was returned to sender.

At the next sittings, we had a much more vigorous and hard-working judge, who cleaned up the list, and called us into his chambers to discuss the case. It turned out that he followed the races, and knew of the jockey.

The hearing in chambers took about half an hour, of which about twenty seven minutes was taken up with racing talk, before the judge signed the adoption order with barely a glance at the paperwork.

Two different judges, very different approach, very different result!

[* Wombat - Eats roots and leaves. I'll leave the rest of the bad jokes and puns about this story to the reader....]

The House-Warming and the Scary Neighbour

Once, when I was working weekends, a Filipino couple came in on a Saturday afternoon, to discuss some issues with the contract of sale for a house they were about to buy.

We went through the documents, and I explained the clauses that concerned them, and went into general advice, including to measure the land, and the connecting distance from the corner. They knew all about that from their experience in their old country.

They told me about buying a vacant piece of land, alongside other vacant land, and having a new home built on it. All went well, the building was completed, and they had a big house-warming for their family and friends.

After a couple of hours, there was a knock on the door, and they were greeted by some grim-faced armed men in military uniform, who commanded them to come outside. They were thrust into a large limousine, in front of one of the country's leading generals. The general demanded to know what they were doing on his land. My poor clients had not checked carefully enough and had built on the wrong block.

Terrified that they were facing imminent execution, they told him it must be a mistake, and swore that they thought it was their land. The general took pity on them, and agreed they could keep the house, which he would transfer to them, so long as they transferred their block to him and paid the fees.

They hastily agreed, and asked if he would like to join their party. Surprisingly, he agreed, and came in to introduce himself as the new neighbour, and everybody's friend. After their scare, they had a big night!

Give a Relative a Job….

My brother Pat had a similar problem, when he was running a substantial building company.

Against his better judgement, he had been prevailed upon to give a job to his second cousin Wayne, a young man whose confidence way exceeded his abilities. Wayne was a blowhard type, who made himself unpopular with everyone at the company, and blamed others when things went wrong.

One day, Wayne was sent out to measure up and stake out a new home in a relatively new subdivision. The house plan was to go at an angle across the block. Wayne duly reported in that all was done, and the building works commenced a few days later.

When the building was almost completed, Pat received a phone call, telling him there was a serious problem. The new house was sited across the boundary between two blocks!

Pat had a problem all right. His company had to buy both of the blocks of land in question, and find the owners similar blocks (it being a new subdivision, very similar blocks were available a couple of streets away) and pay all the expenses involved. They then had to finish the house in question and sell it for the best they could, on the new 'double block'.

Wayne continued to leave a trail of wreckage before eventually leaving the company. He then set himself up in his own business, doing small building jobs - not very well!

Nelson, the Furniture and the Food Chain

Nelson, a good client of my firm, was a small to medium sized manufacturer and supplier of tables, chairs and various fittings to the restaurant industry.

Nelson came to us to recover a debt of some thousands of dollars he claimed was owed to him by a substantial restaurant chain.

In response to our letter of demand, the chain's lawyers responded, saying that the items which Nelson had provided were of grossly inferior quality, and were worthless. They denied liability for anything.

We responded on Nelson's behalf, asking where the items were. They replied that they were so bad, they had them taken to the tip. We felt that something smelt a little fishy about this, and Nelson instructed us to take the case to court.

The food chain's actions in allegedly disposing of the goods were very suspicious, and we felt that we could make a deal out of that in cross-examination. However, our difficulty was establishing the quality of the product. We arranged a number of witnesses to confirm the quality of Nelson's work.

At this stage we had a lucky break. One of Nelson's employees was returning from interstate, and stopped off at one of the food chain's restaurants in a regional city on his way home. To his great surprise, here was each and every item that Nelson had supplied to the chain. He rang Nelson, who jumped in his car and drove straight there to check it out, and take photos.

When we informed the other side of this development, we were firstly met with a great deal of bluster. However, we suggested that they check with their client. When they did so, they soon came back with an offer to settle.

In the circumstances, the offer was quite insulting. Nelson at that stage wanted blood, and we took a very firm stand. He was keen for the case to proceed, and to invite the media to come along to the hearing. In the end, the other side capitulated, and paid the full amount of the claim, plus interest and costs.

I still to this day remain unimpressed whenever I come across any of the chain's media advertising. Very low behaviour!

The Troubled Nightclub

Billy, one of my colleagues, came to me one day to help him out with one of his clients, a nightclub owner who had run foul of their landlord. They were unhappy that the landlord had been unwilling to contribute to the cost of some structural repairs to the club premises.

So, they decided to teach him a lesson. They stopped paying the rent. Serious mistake!. Non-payment of rent is grounds for the landlord to terminate the lease - which it did by changing the locks and taking possession of the premises.

Why did they not ask us before stopping the rent? We were ultimately able to get them back in, but it cost them heavily to get there.

At around the same time, the club was regularly in the news with reports of violence. They also complained that, with the high rent and other overheads, they were still losing money. They had paid top dollar for the business a couple of years earlier and then spent heavily to refurbish the premises.

Billy and I asked if they expected to move into profit territory in the near future - no, it would take at least another year, perhaps more. Is it conceivable that you'll never get there? Yes, distinctly possible.

Well, why continue to put yourselves through all this? And bear in mind that if the reports of violence continue, the authorities will sooner or later shut you down, and you'll lose everything!

Our very definite advice was to put the business on the market, and be prepared to take a loss, just to get out of it and salvage *something* from the wreckage.

OK, they put the business on the market, and were prepared to take a loss, so long as they could get out of it. There were further incidents of violence, resulting in more adverse publicity, but eventually a purchaser came along, and they accepted his offer.

At this stage the landlord became involved. There was little information about the purchaser, and his financials were very sketchy. Why should the landlord agree to transfer the lease to a person who couldn't show that he could pay the rent?

After months of going back and forth, we eventually convinced the purchaser to put up a bond equivalent to six months rent. The landlord accepted this solution, and we settled the sale as quickly as we could.

Not a moment too soon. The following week there were further incidents at the club, leading the council and the police to both move to shut it down.

Our clients suffered a heavy loss, but at least they recovered some of their money. I felt sorry for the purchaser, who very quickly blew the purchase price plus six months rent, but he must have known that he was taking a substantial risk in stumping up his money.

CHAPTER 17

FROM A DIFFERENT ANGLE

Asbestos

After working in Morwell for several years (and after an acrimonious partnership split), I sold my practice to Slater & Gordon. Part of the deal was the requirement that I remain with them for 12 months, to bed down my clients into their practice. It turned out to be a very enjoyable year, and I worked with some terrific people.

At that time, they were becoming involved in the early stages of asbestos cases. One of the very first was for a former State Electricity Commission of Victoria (SECV) employee who'd been exposed to asbestos many years before when he was working in the construction of a power station.

Proceedings had been issued in the Supreme Court against the SECV, in what was a claim for substantial damages. The man in question was very ill, and there was a concern that he might not survive until the case reached the court.

The problem was dealt with by a process of taking evidence 'on commission'. This involved having the plaintiff giving evidence, on videotape, sitting in a lounge chair at his home.

This was not my file, but the other lawyers in the office were all engaged in other trials, so I turned up at the house, introduced myself to the client, and then introduced the rest of the entourage for the day, including the barristers and the camera people.

Although very ill, the client was quite dignified and gave his evidence clearly, calmly, and in a lot of detail. The mood in the house was very sombre, with a sensitive and respectful cross-examination from the SECV's counsel, Alan McDonald, who was shortly afterwards appointed as a justice of the Victorian Supreme Court.

I felt very privileged to be involved in the client's case, and saddened by his illness. He didn't live to know the outcome, but it was a victory for his family. As far as I know, this was one of the very first damages awards in the country for an asbestos victim.

Slater & Gordon were at that time starting to become very busy with asbestos cases from the Wittenoom area in Western Australia. They were instrumental in many thousands of people obtaining compensation for asbestos related diseases.

Lindy and Michael Chamberlain

OK, I can hear you saying that I would have had no connection with this case, and you're right - I didn't.

Nevertheless, please permit me to make a couple of comments from the perspective of a very humble lawyer looking on from the outside.

After all the publicity about Azaria Chamberlain's disappearance, I was interested to note that Dinny Barrett, a former Victorian magistrate, had been appointed to preside over the inquest.

Dinny was regarded as a practical, no-nonsense magistrate, who was good at sorting out the wheat from the chaff. So when Dinny, after hearing all the evidence, declared he was satisfied that a dingo had taken the baby, I was satisfied with that.

There was, however, a loud (and uninformed) reaction to Dinny's finding. He was pilloried in the media as 'Dingo Dinny' and several commentators declared his finding to be rubbish.

Some years later, I worked with Alex (see above). Alex had been working with the Northern Territory government at the time. His recollection was that "... everyone up there knew she (Lindy) was guilty". In reply to my question as to what evidence they had to prove it, he just laughed "Nothing to do with the evidence, they just knew it."

Anyway, after the production of various items of evidence (which ultimately proved to be much worse than Mickey Mouse quality), Dinny's finding was set aside, and a new inquest established. It decided that Lindy should be sent for trial for murdering Azaria, and Michael for helping her dispose of the body.

And so, the trial took place. My expectation, from afar (and granted that I didn't observe the witnesses first hand) was that, as there were no eye-witnesses, no body, no confession, and no motive, how could a jury possibly convict them?

I was pleased to see that the notable and very highly regarded Victorian barrister, John Phillips QC, was leading the defence.

One of my partners at the time observed that, as some scuttlebutt had declared that the child was sacrificed under some weird religious cult, Lindy's new pregnancy was a masterstroke. "Having her knocked-up" he enthused "was brilliant strategy".

So much for our views. The jury found Lindy guilty of murder, and Michael guilty of being an accessory (helping her dispose of the body). When I heard the news, I concluded that the jury had decided to acquit the dingo, therefore the parents must be guilty!

Eventually, the prosecution case was exposed for the farce that it was (including that the alleged 'blood in the car' was in fact sound-deadening material), and the Chamberlains were ultimately cleared. Too bad that their lives had been destroyed along the way!

In 1984, John Phillips was appointed as a judge of the Supreme Court of Victoria, and in 1991, he was elevated to Chief Justice. He retired from the bench in 2003.

A few years later, he was guest speaker at my then city firm. I asked him about the case. He replied that there was such an intense interest in the case in the territory, and such a strong (albeit uninformed) community conviction that Lindy was guilty, that there was no realistic chance of a fair trial at the time.

Nonetheless, he continued to maintain that, overall, we should continue to have jury trials in murder and other important cases.

The irony was that, in the final wash-up, the decision made by 'Dingo Dinny' was vindicated. His initial finding was ultimately confirmed - nearly 30 years later!

The Masticating Witness

Then there was the unsophisticated country lad who was in the witness box in the Supreme Court. He was, in his laconic manner, standing in the box with his hands in his pockets, chewing gum, recounting his recollection of the relevant events.

After a while, the grizzled old judge leaned over, interrupted the proceedings, and instructed the witness to "Stop masticating!"

"Oh, sorry" the young man replied, as he whipped his hands out of his pockets, carried on chewing his gum and turned to counsel "Now, what were you asking me?"

The Sex, Public Servant, Injury Case

Much more recently, a number of my former work colleagues have followed, in fascination, a workers compensation case brought by a Commonwealth employee.

The facts were quite simple. The lady in question was attending a conference in a country town as part of her employment. She was staying, as arranged by her employer, at a hotel in the town.

One night, a male friend came to visit her in her room. While they were engaging in what was described as 'vigorous sexual activity', a light fitting fell off the wall and landed on her face, causing her an injury.

She claimed compensation, and Comcare (the Commonwealth's workers compensation insurer) contested the claim at every level (including to the NSW Court of Appeal and then the High Court of Australia)

The lady won at every level, up to and including the NSW Court of Appeal - to the disgust of some 'shock jocks' in the media, and a number of my work colleagues. The basis of their objection was that she was having sex at the time. Indeed, this argument was consistently put by Comcare.

In each instance, up to the NSW Court of Appeal, the court declared that the activity was perfectly legal. They each said that it would have been no different if she had been paying cards or chess at the time. Accordingly, as she was there in the course of her employment, the injury occurred in the course of her employment, and she was entitled to compensation.

Every time the case was taken on appeal, a group of 'concerned persons' appeared at my desk asking for further analysis. All I could tell them was that the court had held that:

- the lady was not acting unlawfully while having sex, and
- she was there in the course of her employment.

This approach, however, did not impress the High Court of Australia, which made the final decision on the case. It appears to have agreed with many members of the public, who were saying things like "I don't want my taxes to go to paying this woman for what happened while she was having sex".

The High Court held that the decision to have sex, while clearly not unlawful, was outside the scope of the lady's employment. Since it appears to have caused the light fitting to fall, there is no valid claim for compensation. Simple, sensible approach!

There has been some speculation as to what activity would result in compensation being payable. One view is that, if she had been sitting up in bed, with her lap-top switched on, preparing for the next working session, the connection with her work would exist, so she would be paid compensation.

But, in this case, the sex had no direct connection to her employment, so she was not entitled to workers compensation payments for her injuries.

Enough said! OK gents, back to work now!

Angus Gets His Comeuppance

Occasionally, one gets satisfaction out of a small revenge against someone who deserves it - and it's fine if they don't even know that I've got them. See the reference to the lawyer Serge above.

This time it wasn't a lawyer. Angus was a property/leasing officer with a fast food chain (not the same one that Nelson had a problem with). He was habitually rude to people, and I wondered how he got his job in the first place.

I had come across Angus when acting for a couple of clients. One of them was a leading energy company, which has a number of co-tenanted sites which it shares with various fast food companies.

The other was an operator of outdoor advertising sites. Angus's company had advertising hoardings on a number of such sites.

In almost all of these deals, you have two or more parties, each with its own objectives, and used to wheeling and dealing to achieve what they want. While the negotiations are often conducted robustly, and by strong personalities, there is a professional standard to these transactions.

Generally, the parties are there because each of them wants a particular commercial outcome, and ultimately they have a fair bit in common, so everyone gains largely what they had in mind. Generally, the negotiators find a way to come up with a solution that everyone can work with. There is little personal acrimony - except when dealing with Angus.

In a couple of my dealings with Angus, he was downright abusive, and underhanded. In one case in particular, he was extremely dishonest and deceptive in his conduct. We were aware of what he was doing and made sure that our client had its position protected. The result was more abuse from Angus. He would yell and carry on, and, when he couldn't get his own way, would often hang up in a foul mood.

Next thing I knew, Angus was no longer there. I never found out if he was fired, but wouldn't have been surprised. He certainly deserved the sack, and his company would have been better off without him. I'm sure his attitude cost his company a number of worthwhile deals.

Anyway, I soon afterwards had a visit from a couple of senior executives from my energy company client. One of their best property managers had resigned, and Angus had applied for the vacancy. What did I think?

Well, I was more than happy to tell them what I thought! I noted that the client had a well-deserved reputation for integrity and professionalism in its dealings. Given this, it absolutely did not need such an aggressive rude and impossible person as Angus representing it in significant commercial transactions.

I suspect their other enquiries might have come up with similar views. In any event, Angus did not get the job. I subsequently had many dealings with the person who was appointed to that job. While he was a tough and skilled operator, he was at all times a true gentleman, and a pleasure to work with.

Without doubt, Rocky would have approved!

A Room Full of Lawyers

OK, you must be saying. "A room full of lawyers? Wouldn't that be a great opportunity for a well-placed bomb to do the world a favour?" No, that's not what I'm getting at here.

Most law firms of any size have, amongst other things, a social club or social committee, which organise social events for the staff. This might include a night out at the theatre, the movies, an art gallery, a Sunday trip to the Yarra Valley, anything to create a happy and team-based environment.

Some firms provide a box of fruit a couple of times a week for the staff. One place has recently cancelled its supply of cream biscuits for staff on the grounds of its concerns for their health. The staff are not convinced that this is the real reason. They'd prefer the organisation to be honest and say it's for budgetary reasons.

Anyway, many firms have an occasional trivia quiz, on a weekday evening, with drinks and maybe a supply of pizzas.

You might think a trivia quiz is easy to organise and uncontroversial. You'd be dead wrong! It is difficult to think of anything more competitive and cut-throat than a room full of smart-arse lawyers doing battle.

The people running it need to be very careful when drafting the questions, as there'll be a lot of pedantic, hair-splitting interpretations. Plus, some teams are surprisingly resourceful - not to mention dishonest.

I have to confess to a few times when I've gone up to the organisers, to explain to them (patiently of course) that they've made a mistake. Sometimes I was able to convince them, but not always.

What would you think of a question asking teams to list the top 50 grossing movies of all time? Would you be surprised that one team came up with the correct 50 movies, all in order? Would you believe that they did it honestly, without using any electronic devices to find the answer?

No, I still struggle to believe that, too.....

The Bank Cheque that Bounced

I learned over the years that, in legal practice, you come across many bizzare things. One of these was a bank stopping payment on its own bank cheque.

The law provides particular rules for dealing with dishonoured cheques. If a person (or bank) is sued on a bounced cheque, it is no defence to say that what they received was inadequate or faulty. The only defence that could succeed is if there was a 'total failure of consideration' - that is, that whatever was provided in exchange for the cheque was utterly worthless, of absolutely no value whatever.

Anyway, a client of mine came to me with a bank cheque, drawn on one of our major banks, which had stopped payment on it. The client was in a retail business and had made a sale to his customer, for which he was paid by bank cheque. The customer had offered his personal cheque, which my client declined (he did not trust the customer), and then came back with the bank cheque. The reader might not understand this, but this was in the ancient time before people had credit cards!

My client promptly banked the cheque, but it was returned two days later, marked 'Payment stopped'.

I decided to do the bank a favour and give them a call, rather than write a letter of demand or just issue a claim against them. The manager came on the line when I explained what I was calling about.

He was quite cavalier about it, telling me that the bank had no liability in respect of a bank cheque, as "the customer wasn't happy with what he got." I suggested that, if that was the case, the customer had other options available to him, but that it wasn't the customer's cheque that bounced, it was the bank's. Therefore it was the bank's problem, not the customer's.

His next line was that a bank cheque was merely a statement by the bank that the customer was good for the money. I replied that, if anything, it was a statement by the bank that it (not the customer) was good for the money.

The bank manager remained defiant, continuing to tell me that the bank had no responsibility for its own cheques. So I said to him "Well, my instructions are to sue the bank for bouncing the cheque. I suggest you speak to your legal people, and get back to me by 11.30 am tomorrow (twenty-four hours hence). If I don't hear from you by then, I'll issue immediately, and you can explain to the big boss why you've been responsible for having the bank sued."

At about 11.15 am the next day, a chastened manager called me, saying "Tell your client to re-present the cheque. This time it'll be honoured."

And it was.

Pierre and His Temper

Pierre was an irascible but generally good-natured builder for whom my firm acted in many transactions. Among his interests, he did many commercial constructions.

In this instance, Pierre's company was constructing a new building to be used as residential facility in the aged care industry. Rick and I had been involved with a number of the contractual matters along the way, and there was an agreement for an accredited operator to lease the building when it was ready to go.

In due course, Pierre reported that the building was complete, and that the occupancy permit had been issued. However he complained that he was having problems with the operator, who wanted Pierre to do more work. He had arranged a meeting on site in a couple of days with the operator and a government official, and wanted his lawyer to be present.

So, I turned up at the new facility at the appointed time and met Pierre, his two sons, who worked with him in his business, the government representative and the operator. I asked the operator if his lawyer was coming. He said no, he didn't need his lawyer there, and had no problem with me being there.

Pierre's point of view was that he had obtained the occupancy permit from the building surveyor, and that was all he had to do. He said he'd finished his part, and the rest was up to the operator who was now bound to fit the building out, and should start paying rent immediately.

The operator's view was that Pierre's responsibility (as set out in the documents) was not only to complete the building, but to provide certain fixtures and fit out the facility to a specified level. In the course of the negotiations, this had been made clear, and Rick and I had discussed it with Pierre several times (he later admitted all this, but told me he had forgotten about it).

The government official would not take sides, but merely indicated that the fixtures and fitout would need to be completed before he could certify the facility as ready to open for business.

On the day, Pierre was out of control. When I explained to him that the operator was within his rights, and simply relying on the contractual terms that Pierre had signed up to, he snarled and uttered some very unflattering expressions about the operator.

After a while, and with assistance from Pierre's sons, it appeared that I had calmed him down, so we walked back over to where the operator was standing.

I had just opened my mouth to speak when Pierre rushed at the operator, grabbing him by the throat, yelling abuse, at one stage threatening to kill him, a number of times shouting "I'm going to cut your f...ing throat" and calling him a range of insulting and offensive names.

So there I was, along with the two sons, getting in between Pierre and the operator and trying to haul him off. We eventually got Pierre under control and restored some semblance of peace before everyone left.

Next day, the sons brought in a somewhat chastened Pierre, who apologised for his behaviour and told me he was arranging for the installation of the fixtures and fitout.

I told him he'd better hope that no harm came to the operator, because if it did, he'd be the prime suspect. Pierre laughed and told me that his bark was worse than his bite.

Buying Property for a Child

One of my roles involved providing advice to 'High Net Worth' families on how best to protect and preserve their assets, and to help them establish an asset base for the next generations.

One of our wealthy clients came to us, wanting to know how to go about purchasing a property for one of their children. The parents would be providing the money, but the question was how to document the purchase, given that the child was, legally speaking, an 'infant' (and therefore not able to enter into a contract).

As a complication, the parents (for various good reasons of their own) could not provide the vendor with a guarantee - so we could not name the child as purchaser, with a parental guarantee.

It was also not desirable for a parent to buy the property, and then transfer it to the child, as this would involve double stamp duty.

So, how do we do it?

My solution was for a parent to be shown in the contract as the purchaser. Then, under the 'nomination' provisions in the contract, the parent could nominate the child as substitute purchaser.

As the original purchaser under the contract, the parent would remain personally liable for the performance of the contract, so the vendor would be assured that they would receive their money, and there would be no double stamp duty. And - it did not constitute a 'guarantee'.

At settlement, under the nomination provisions, the vendor would transfer the title to the child. Problem solved!

The clients went ahead on this basis, and acquired the property for the child. Over the next few years, they made similar acquisitions for their other children.

Keiran the Process Server

In my early years, when I was doing debt recovery work, I had a bit to do with Keiran, one of our process servers.

The police generally didn't approve of process servers, and some of them took a set against Keiran, for reasons which I never understood. He was regularly pulled over in his car and given the third degree about what he was doing, where he was going, and then let go without any comment. There seemed to be a campaign of harassment against him.

As with all process servers, Keiran held a number of licences, which were issued by the court, and had to be renewed annually. When an application was lodged with the court, a copy had to be filed with the police as well.

On every one of Keiran's renewal applications, the local police inspector opposed the renewal. So far as I was aware, he never opposed any other process server's renewal application.

So, every year, Keiran would engage me to appear on his behalf before a magistrate, to argue his case for the renewal. The inspector never produced any evidence to support his opposition, but he always expressed a strong view that Keiran should not be permitted to hold the relevant licences.

It was not as though Keiran had a criminal record - he did not! On more than one occasion, the inspector announced to the court that he would not permit Keiran to hold the licences.

Generally, the magistrate, whom a few of us knew as the Chief (see below under 'Know Your Magistrate') would be on the bench for these hearings. When you were dealing with the Chief, you did not tell him how to run his court or exercise his discretion.

Whenever the inspector made the statement that he wouldn't permit Keiran to hold his licences, I would relax. The case was all over. The Chief would proceed to make it very clear to the inspector that, while the police had the right to oppose the application, it was up to the court to make the decision. In the absence of any reason to the contrary, he renewed the licences.

I never found out what the police had against Keiran, but he had his licences renewed every year. Sometimes you could have a quiet chat to the police and find out what their problem was, but not in this instance.

Keiran and the Skin Cancers

As a young man, I played too much cricket and tennis without properly doing the 'slip, slop, slap' routine. The consequence for my pale Celtic skin was an occasional skin cancer in later life. Over the years, I've had quite a few skin cancers cut out from my hands, nose, forehead, neck and cheeks.

On one occasion, there were four small cancers on my face. My doctor cut them out, leaving me with a couple of stitches on each cheek.

Next day, Keiran came to see me about one of his concerns. When he saw me, he enquired what had happened to me. I told him that a man had done this to me with a knife. His expression immediately hardened and he came out with "Do you want me to deal with him?"

I replied "No, it was my doctor, getting rid of a couple of skin cancers." and we both laughed.

I've often reflected on Keiran's response. I'm still not sure what would have happened if it the stitches weren't the result of surgery and if I'd said "Yes".

Russell Mark and Olympic Gold

I can honestly say that I knew Russell before he became famous.

In the course of business, I came to know his father Brian, who had his own real estate business. Brian was a real entertainer, raconteur, storyteller type. In addition to selling property, he entertained thousands at sportsman's nights. He had an inexhaustible supply of jokes, some a little risqué, all of them told with energy and gusto.

Russell qualified as a valuer, but his major talent was as a shooter. His specialty was the double trap, where the shooter must hit two flying clay discs, flung simultaneously at random away from the shooter at high speed. The shooter is permitted only two shots, using a double barrelled shotgun.

In the Barcelona Olympics in1992, Russell finished not far out of the medals. When I next saw him, I congratulated him on doing well. He thanked me, but was disgusted at how badly he'd gone.

At Atlanta in 1996, Russell easily won gold, and was welcomed home a hero. Being the fine, unspoiled man that he is, Russell arranged to bring his medal around for us to see. He generously allowed each of us to hold the gold medal - a wondrous and beautiful thing to behold (and quite heavy).

One of the staff brought in a camera, and took photos of us all holding the medal. Sadly, the camera didn't function, so we missed out on our photos.

In the Sydney Olympics in 2000, Russell was way out in front, and looking certain to win a repeat gold. He lost concentration, and missed a few shots. The British competitor finished strongly, tying the score with his last shot.

The competition went into a shoot-off, which the Briton won. Russell had to content himself with silver, when the gold had looked in the bag.

As Russell was packing up his guns, at a time when he must have felt gutted, a TV reporter rushed up, shoving a camera and microphone in his face. The reporter opened with "Bad day at the office, Russell?"

I imagine that, in Russell's position, many people would have laid the reporter out cold, or at least responded with a snarl and a few angry words. Not Russell! Calmly and politely he drawled "Nah mate. Every day above the ground is a good day!"

How's that for a mature, quality, sensible, rational response?

The Newspaper/Magazine for Lawyers

Some years ago, I noticed an advertisement for a weekly newspaper/magazine for lawyers. The flyer suggested that it would contain inside information on the legal profession in a racy, informative and light-hearted way - with a hint of a little salacious gossip here and there. And what lawyer doesn't like a little salacious gossip?

My interest was sufficiently piqued that I took out a years subscription for the publication. All in all, I was disappointed with the offering. It consisted largely of what appeared to be press releases from a number of the larger firms, and plenty of advertising. Nothing salacious at all. Nothing of any real interest. It took less than two minutes to flick through it.

Curiously, I received four copies of the same thing every week. Two were correctly addressed to me at my home, and the other two showed the same address, but followed by 'Dandenong'. I have never lived anywhere near Dandenong.

This state of affairs continued throughout the year. In the last couple of months, they also sent me invitations to renew my subscription. The renewal forms hit the recycle bin just as fast as all four copies.

When my subscription came to an end, surprise, surprise, four copies continued to turn up each week. After some months, they sent me a letter threatening to sue me for the next subscription.

On receipt of the letter, I rang and spoke to the woman whose name was on the letter. When I pointed out that I had not renewed, she told me that, unless a person cancelled their subscription, they treated it as a renewal, and required payment.

I replied that, as their customers were mainly lawyers, they couldn't realistically expect anyone to fall for that line, and that such an approach was contrary to the laws of contract. I concede that I might have been a little caustic in my comments to her.

The lady then backed off and asked if she should treat my subscription as cancelled. I happily agreed.

So, from then on, I only received two copies each week....

The Hearing Test

One night, when I was living and working in Geelong, I answered the phone at home. The man on the other end called me by name. He told me that his organisation was conducting free hearing tests, under some new program, and asked if I'd like to take the test.

OK, I'll be in that. So I made the appointment, and turned up for the test. It was all done very professionally, by technicians who clearly knew what they were doing, and took about half an hour.

At the end, they told me that I had a hearing impairment of about 5.5% in one ear and about 8.5% in the other.

I wasn't unduly surprised to hear this, and confirmed that there wasn't really any point in trying surgery to improve the position.

At this stage, I was thanking him for the service, and just about to stand up and leave, when he asked if I'd like to sue.

Sure, I'd love to, but who could we sue? Who was to blame for my hearing loss? There were a couple of very loud music venues from years past who might have caused some damage, but I couldn't even recall who and where they were, let alone prove that they'd damaged me.

"Alcoa, of course!" he replied. I was wondering how I could pin it on Alcoa, when the penny finally dropped. What a slow learner I was!

It was all about drumming up a group of hearing loss claims for Alcoa employees, one of whom has the same name as me. The phone call to me was a simple mistake.

So, no compensation for my hearing loss.…..

Max and the Prince Charles Syndrome

Years ago, I had some dealings with Max, a property developer, who'd been in the business for many years. He was nearing his 89th birthday and still going strong.

I had a meeting with him about one of his subdivisions, and went to his office. He was there with another man, who was quite a few years older than me, and looked to be mid 60s at least.

Max introduced the man as his son, and added "He'll be taking over the business when I retire." It was clear, however, that Max was running the show.

The problem was that Max was in fine shape and didn't look like handing over for many years yet. I felt sorry for the son, waiting forever to take over the business and having to cool his heels until he was an old man before getting his chance.

Keeping Control of the Family Business

Another client was a company run by a close-knit family. The directors were four brothers who had come to Australia after the Second World War, had worked hard, and built up a portfolio of commercial buildings.

I was acting for them in some leasing matters, including one when they evicted a tenant for not paying the rent. By this stage, all four brothers were in their eighties, but very much in charge.

Occasionally, I would speak to one or other of their children, who were in their fifties, and some of whom were successfully operating their own businesses. They had the view that the four directors should consider handing over some control, or at least delegating some tasks to younger family members.

My dealings with the company were mostly with two of the directors, who were very clear and very particular in their instructions.

We would sometimes discuss their portfolio, and their overall business strategy. Sometimes the future would come under discussion. On one occasion, they asked me if there was anything I would advise in relation to the future.

I mentioned a couple of my thoughts, and wondered if they had any thoughts on when it might be the time to gradually bring the next generation into the picture. This might enable them to put their skills and energy to work, to get them involved in supporting the directors.

They were horrified at the idea. Oh no, the whole idea was not acceptable. Their children were way too young and inexperienced. To give them even the most minor role would be a disaster!

Cattle On the Road

Anyone who has ever driven a car on a country road has had to stop or slow down when a farmer is moving moving farm animals along or across the road.

Well, in one case, the movement of farm animals gave rise to a case in the Supreme Court, and to a curious change in the law.

It all began when a well-to-do couple from one of Melbourne's more exclusive suburbs decided to buy themselves a holiday shack for weekend tree-change visits. They searched for a while, and found and bought a little place in the Otway Ranges, a nice little house on a few acres. The local farmer who sold it to them owned a substantial amount of land next to it, as well as over the road.

Naturally, they spent a few dollars smartening up the place, and enjoyed travelling down regularly on weekends.

On one occasion, they drove down on a Saturday morning, only to find the farmer moving cattle from his property on one side of the road out the gate, about a hundred metres up the road, and into his property on the other side of the road. They were outraged that they had to wait about forty minutes before they could reach their little weekender.

So incensed were they that they went to their lawyer, who issued proceedings in the Magistrates Court, claiming damages from the farmer for depriving them of access to their property.

A few of us who followed the case were surprised that the magistrate found in their favour. The farmer appealed, and the Supreme Court upheld the appeal. The court pointed out that, when someone buys a property in a farming area, they should not be surprised when farming activities are carried out. And moving cattle up or across the road is very much a normal farming activity.

That's where it finished up - or should have! However, a busy public servant must also have been following the case. The result was an amendment to the *Sale of Land Act*.

So now, in every sale of real estate in Victoria, it is mandatory for the vendor, in their disclosure to prospective purchasers, to provide a curious statement. It must be set out that, if the property being sold is within a commercial agricultural area, the purchaser should be aware that sometimes, commercial agricultural activities might be expected to take place.

This rule applies, even if the subject property is a penthouse in one of our tallest buildings.

When we saw the amendment, some of us merely shook our heads in amazement! Good God, have they nothing better to do?

Clients and Their Limitations

A lawyer can easily make the mistake of expecting a client to understand what the lawyer is saying, when the client actually has no idea what is going on.

An old adage used in the entertainment industry goes along the lines of "You'll never go broke underestimating the intelligence of the consuming public". Lawyers should take heed, but many do not, and persist in using jargon which is a completely foreign language to the lay person.

Some lawyers delight in using Latin expressions. It might make them sound important and knowledgeable, but it's an effective way to lose the client.

A wiser approach is to consider it this way: We are in the business of communication. If the people we are addressing can't understand what we are saying, we have failed! See the reference to Keith in Chapter 8.

So, stick to the KISS principle - keep it simple, stupid!

At one time I was acting for a woman who, when I wrote her a letter, would bring it in and say she needed to discuss it with me. This happened a couple of times, and then the penny dropped - she couldn't read!

I had known she wasn't highly educated, but it had not occurred to me that she couldn't read. Once I twigged, I was able to adjust the way I related to her. I never mentioned that I knew, and she never admitted it to me.

We were able to complete the matter in which she had consulted me, without further difficulty.

A little later, I became aware of the very difficult circumstances in which she was born and raised. With her disadvantages, she did well to become a productive member of society.

Her brother had greater difficulty, committing his first burglary at age five, and regularly being in trouble with the law from then on.

Of course, the communication boot can sometimes be on the other foot. In my early days in the Latrobe Valley, I asked a client for his occupation. I was none the wiser when he replied "TA for JT at W". Asked for a translation, he explained that he was a trades assistant for John Thomsons, one of the construction contractors at the Yallourn W power station.

Felix and Jan

Here was a family business, in which Felix spent a lot of time on the road, and Jan did the paperwork, invoicing, banking, etc.

Jan was a hard-nosed businesswoman, who didn't mind the rough and tumble of business, and often didn't pay her bills until the last possible minute.

Back in the days before the banks were all computerised (yes, there was a time like that once!) Jan had worked for one of the major banks and had her own little bank stamp, which she kept when she left the bank. A couple of years later, she opened a savings account with the same bank and deposited a small amount into it.

From then on, and without letting Felix know what she was doing, Jan would handwrite a 'deposit' in the passbook, and apply her stamp to it. Over some months, this built up until it showed over $40,000. She then presented it at the bank, with a signed withdrawal form, and attempted to withdraw $35,000.

The bank officer smelt a rat, and spoke to the manager, who refused to pay Jan. She came rushing to me, saying that the bank was trying to defraud her out of her money. When I had a look at the passbook and spoke to the bank, it was obvious that Jan was in the wrong, and had been forging the passbook entries.

The best result we could achieve for Jan was for the bank not to refer the case to the police. When Felix found out, he apologised to the bank for what he called Jan's "Mickey Mouse" behaviour.

My next encounter with them resulted in a plea in the Magistrates' Court for Felix on a speeding charge. He had been clocked at just over 170 kph. We had very serious concerns about his licence but, with some exceptional circumstances, and as his licence was essential to his business, the magistrate allowed him to retain it. Felix was over the moon about this, and very grateful.

Unfortunately, Felix's gratitude failed to impress Jan. She was slow to pay my bills, as well as those of others. This time, she was even slower than usual. Eventually, I took payment out of some money that came in when she and Felix sold an asset. Jan made a real fuss about it, and they moved on to another lawyer. He was welcome to them by that time.

Brenda and Paul and Their Landlord - A Lesson in How Not To Negotiate

This was a couple who ran a cafe in a small arcade. They had a lease for five years, and were about one year into it, when the landlord came to them, wanting to move their business.

These days, shopping centre leases have provisions which entitle the landlord to relocate a tenant in certain circumstances, and subject to reasonable safeguards. At that time, there was nothing in Brenda and Paul's lease that would entitle the landlord to relocate them without their consent.

The landlord, Basil, had received an offer from a substantial company to lease more than half the arcade, which included their shop. He proposed to move them to a smaller shop a few doors down.

Brenda and Paul were not happy with the proposed alternative, which they viewed as too small. They told me that it would have left them with not enough room for their oven, display and customer areas. They doubted their business could be profitable there. We had a stalemate.

Basil proposed a meeting to sort things out. Brenda and Paul asked me to come along with them. Basil was accompanied by his son, an estate agent.

We met for about an hour, with Basil doing all he could to convince Brenda and Paul to accept his offer. However he couldn't offer them anything better than the one small shop for their business. I pointed out that, if Basil could not provide an acceptable alternative, he might have to buy their business out.

All the while, Brenda and Paul held fast. After some time, Basil became exasperated and starting yelling at them, and continued on and on with a number of threats to destroy them. They sat in stunned silence, and I simply addressed myself to the son, saying "This is not helpful."

The meeting then broke up, and we walked back to my office. Brenda and Paul were a little shaken, and unsure what to make of what had happened. I told them not to worry, that Basil's outburst was a sign of weakness, not of strength, and that I was confident of their position.

A couple of days later, Basil's son rang me, with an offer to buy the business. We were able to negotiate a price which Brenda and Paul were happy with. In next to no time they were out of the business and looking around for their next one.

Since that time, whenever I've been in a negotiation, I would recall Basil as a shining example of how not to behave.

The Nose Bleed Story

One of my most embarrassing moments as a lawyer happened several years ago, when I had a nose bleed while in a meeting with a female client. I had never previously had a nose bleed. The blood was flowing and I had no idea how to stop it.

Tissues, cold packs on the nose, cold packs on the back of the neck, nothing worked. We finished the meeting and the client left. Eventually, the blood flow slowed and then stopped.

The next day, I rang the client to apologise, and tell her how embarrassed I felt about it. She told me she hadn't worried about it, but she had a suggestion. It just happened that she was doing a first aid course, and went to her class after leaving my office.

At the first aid course, she asked about nose bleeds, and told me there is a simple answer - wrap a rubber band (reasonably tightly) around the top joint of the little finger of the left hand. Apparently there's a pressure point there.

The next time I had a nose bleed, my wife and I were sitting in the top deck of a double decker bus in London. Of course, in a woman's cavernous hand-bag, there was a rubber band. I hastily wrapped it around the joint, and presto, bleeding stopped! - followed by a huge sigh of relief. It actually worked.

A couple of years later, I had a family (including a few young children) in my office discussing a proposed purchase of a business. As I was explaining the documents to the parents, one of the children came up with a nose bleed.

No problem. Quick as a flash, I whipped out a rubber band and had it around the little finger, stopping the bleeding, in no time. The parents were astounded, as I laughingly told them that, well, we don't just provide legal services here...

Did I Do a Drive-off?

A couple of years ago, I was recovering at home after a minor operation when the phone rang.

The caller was a policewoman, enquiring if I was the owner of motor vehicle registered number [xxx xxx] When I confirmed I was, she informed me that they had a report of it filling up with petrol on a Tuesday two weeks before, in the Geelong area, and driving off without paying.

I told her that I had lived in Geelong some years before, but had been at work in the city on the day in question - and that the car had spent a long day at my station down bayside that day.

The policewoman was polite, but sceptical. I told her that I had a couple of dozen (at least) workmates with impeccable credentials, who could confirm that I was in my city office all day that day. It would not have been possible for me to slip out, get my car, drive to Geelong, fill up, drive off and return to work without being missed.

The caller allowed that the complainant had not been certain about the actual registration number. I asked her what time the offence happened. "Around lunchtime", she said.

I told her that, on the day in question, I had chaired a lunchtime meeting of my section, so all attendees could verify that.

The caller was still dubious, and told me she'd make further enquiries.

She called me back the next day, to say I was in the clear, and not to worry about it.

I told her I had never been worried, as I knew it wasn't me.

CHAPTER 18

FAMILY RELATIONSHIPS AND WILLS

There is nothing more likely to fracture family relationships than an argument about the contents of a will. Very few lawyers have not had such a case, on at least one occasion. Some make a specialty of it and do quite nicely out of family disputes.

Stan and His Mother's Will

Some years ago Stan, a new client, came to see me, with his mother's will. He told me that he wasn't happy with it, and I readied myself for the usual diatribe about how he'd been dudded by someone else in the family.

But no, this was the other way around. Stan told me that he had five brothers, and that the family had always been close. The parents had always been strong on treating all the children the same. It had been made clear, during the father's lifetime, that when one of the parents died, all would be left to the other, and when the survivor died, it was to go equally between the brothers. Stock, standard type will.

Apparently, after the father died, the mother became somewhat cantankerous in her old age. She would pick a fight, for no good reason, with her daughters-in-law, one by one, and would change her will each time.

By the time she died, Stan's wife was the only one the mother hadn't picked a fight with. The result was that she left everything she had to Stan.

Stan wasn't having a bar of that. He insisted that everything be equally divided between the brothers. His attitude was that his relationships with his brothers were more important than mum's will - or the money.

The only real value in the estate was the mother's home. We went through the stages of obtaining probate and selling the house. At my suggestion (and for my protection) Stan gave me written instructions directing me to draw six equal cheques and post them out to each of the brothers.

Of course, not everyone would have been as honourable as Stan.

Fergus's Solution

Fergus took a slightly different approach to most people when preparing his will. His wife had died previously, and he wanted his children to benefit equally. However he did not have a high opinion of them, and was sure that they would fight out every issue on his death.

He did not accept my view that many families sort out all the personal possessions between themselves. He knew that they could not agree.

Fergus's solution was for his will to appoint an independent executor, and direct that everything he owned (absolutely everything) be put up for auction, including the useless items that no-one would want. He specified that each of the children could bid at auction for whatever they wanted.

He was sure that some of them would bid far more than some items were worth, but was content that the proceeds would go into the pool and they would all benefit from that. This way, no one could complain that they missed out on something they wanted or felt entitled to.

"What about stuff that no one bids for?" I asked. "Easy", he said "They can go to the op shop. If it doesn't want them, off to the tip!"

So, we prepared Fergus's will accordingly. When he died, many years later, everything went very much as he had predicted. Although there was some muttering from his children, they all accepted the position, and absolutely everything went under the hammer.

Frank and His Father's Will

Frank was a good client, who had a problem when his father died. Dad and mum had lived together in a small terrace house since they were married, over 60 years before. At the time they bought the house, it was common to put it in the husband's name only (thank goodness that custom has changed!).

In preparing his will, the father had apparently assumed that his wife would have died before him. Curiously, he had made no provision for her at all. He appointed Frank and one of his siblings as executors and directed them to sell up the house, and divide the proceeds between the children.

Frank and the other children were happy to retain the house for their mother, except for one of Franks' sisters. She took the very simplistic (some would say unreasonable) view that they should give effect to what dad's wishes were, as set out in the will - namely sell the house and divide the proceeds between the children.

The fact that this would have left their elderly mother out on the street seems not to have concerned her in the least.

What followed was a very unseemly, bitter and expensive battle between family members in the Supreme Court. The executors were divided (needing separate representation) and mum had to have her own lawyers, as she (with the support of most of her children) had to dispute the will.

Ultimately mum was successful as, clearly, her husband had an obligation to provide for her and had failed to do so. The sad thing was that the whole process wasted so much time, money and angst within the family.

Brett Whiteley and the Notorious Home Made Will

I have never been a fan of home made wills. You may well say "Of course you wouldn't, you're a lawyer, and lawyers make money out of wills". That may be so, but lawyers actually make more money out of home made wills, or where there is no will at all. Let me give you a couple of examples

Brett Whiteley was a very famous Australian artist who hated lawyers. He was involved in more litigation than was good for anyone, and paid several fortunes to lawyers. He had made a few wills through lawyers - and because of his complicated domestic circumstances the wills were complex and expensive.

So, when he decided to change his will again, he chose to do it himself. He wrote his new will by hand, and taped it under a drawer in his kitchen. When the hiding place was discovered a little while after his death, the actual will had been removed.

Despite this, the court was eventually able to decide that the will had existed, and was his final will. There was enough evidence to confirm that the will had existed, and what it said. Unusually, the court granted probate of a will that did not physically exist at the time of the proceedings before it.

Ironically, the home made will finished up costing hundreds of thousands of dollars in legal fees. All as a result of saving a much smaller fee in making the will.

Viktor and Another Home Made Will

One of my good clients was Viktor, a small business operator who came to Australia with his family after World War II, from one of the Baltic states.

Viktor had a close friend called Romy, who came from the same area, but was about fifteen years older. Romy was a single man, and told everyone that he was leaving everything he had to his close mate Viktor when he died.

So, when Romy died, Viktor went through Romy's papers and found a home made will, which had been made on a printed form that was available from any newsagency. In the will, Romy appointed Viktor as executor, but failed to complete the section which indicated who was to receive his assets.

The only information we had was that:

- Romy's parents were long deceased,
- His only siblings were two brothers who disappeared when the Soviet Union invaded his country before the war, and were believed to have died at that time,
- He was married but there were no children, and his wife had divorced him in the1930's and gone to Sweden. Nothing had been heard of her since then, and
- He had not formed any domestic relationship in Australia.

Given that there was a possible intestacy (where no-one is entitled to the estate) we were obliged to notify the State of Victoria, which would take the assets if intestacy was confirmed.

We issued the necessary proceedings, and briefed a senior barrister (who had written the text book on deceased estates). However, two days before the hearing, his clerk called to say he was jammed (meaning he was involved in another case which was running overtime) and he would not be available.

The clerk added that Gavan Griffith was available. Gavan was an outstanding barrister who was soon to take silk, and would later be appointed as Solicitor-General for the Commonwealth of Australia. I readily agreed that he should take the brief.

Long story short, Gavan was able to convince the court that the will entitled Viktor to the assets in Romy's estate.

Once again, the proper result was achieved, but Romy would have been horrified at what the home made will finally cost his estate.

The Long Running Estate

One of my pet hates when making a will was people who wanted to keep control of everything from the grave.

I lost count of the times when someone told me that, once they were gone, they didn't trust their partner to provide for their children. They'd say "He (she) will be off with the first floosie (stud) who comes along. You know what men (women) are like. And my kids will miss out." It was staggering to hear how poorly some people viewed the character of their life partner, and how little trust there was between them.

These people would suggest some complicated structure in their will that would tie up their assets for many years in ways that would frustrate everybody, including their children. Sometimes I was able to achieve a more manageable outcome, but not always.

Once I inherited a file handling the administration of a will where the testator (the person who made the will) had died about fifty years before. It was truly horrendous, and I grew to hate this man, who had died years before I was born.

The will had left a substantial estate, with a number of assets to be distributed between a number of beneficiaries (this was done at the time). There was a grand home, in one of Melbourne's best suburbs, and some other property, left to his widow for her life, or until she remarried (she didn't). The old man was one of those who had all the assets in his name and did not trust her after his death.

When the widow eventually died, after about twenty years, some of the other property was distributed, and a new life estate came into effect for his unmarried daughter, in respect of the home and a few other assets.

By the time I came into it, the daughter was quite elderly and ill, and needed admission into an aged care facility. This situation had not been contemplated in the will, so I had lengthy discussions with the trustees of the estate (who were in fact the third set of trustees, as the first two lots were also deceased by then).

Almost all of the original beneficiaries had also died by then, and in some cases we were onto the third generation of beneficiaries, so it was a mess.

The trustees found a facility for the daughter, and we then set about tracking down the beneficiaries, of whom there were many by then.

As the will did not make any provision for the sale of the home until after the daughter's death, we were left to contemplate how to achieve that result. One way was to apply to the court, the other was to obtain the written consent of all the beneficiaries. Fortunately, they were all adult and in command of their faculties, otherwise this option would not have been available.

We decided to try both options at the same time. So, we prepared and lodged the application in the Supreme Court, and at the same time wrote to each beneficiary, explaining the position and providing a consent form for them to sign if they so desired.

We weren't confident about having all the consents signed, so we tried to push forward the application to the court. However it was delayed in the list for a considerable time. As it turned out, we received all the consents before the court was ready to hear our application. So, we were in the process of selling the house to cover the daughter's expenses, when she died.

It was then a relatively straightforward matter to finalise the sale and make a final distribution to the beneficiaries.

Since that time, whenever anyone wanted to include life estates in a will, I would do my level best (sometimes quoting that story) to talk them out of it.

Martin and His Sense of 'Entitlement'

My firm did a lot of varied advice work for a number of accounting firms. We received many instructions on all sorts of matters from accountants. One of these, Alby, called me on behalf of one of his clients, an elderly (and quite wealthy) widow, Martha.

On her husband's death, Martha became the sole owner of a large share portfolio and a number of properties. She had two children, both male, and both successful professionals, who would equally inherit the lot on her death.

One of the problems seemed to be that Martha, although well into her eighties, was in rude good health, and very much on the ball.

One of the sons, Martin, was a prominent lawyer, and a partner in a major law firm. His brother, Marshall, was a leading orthodontist. Alby told me that both sons had annual incomes of several hundred thousand dollars. Unfortunately, they (and their wives) liked to spend more than they earned.

Martin liked to drive a new Ferrari, and traded up on a regular basis. By co-incidence, his car park, in our tall city building, was adjacent to those of a couple of our partners, who delighted in parking their old, beaten-up jalopies next to the Ferrari.

Both Martin and Marshall, in addition to their own earnings, received about $250,000 from Martha's funds. Even this was not enough for these boys! They embarked on a campaign of harassment of their mother, seeking an additional $500,000 per year each.

Hey Alby, you're joking aren't you? No, Alby was deadly serious. Martha was getting very upset about this. From having been (justifiably) very proud of them and their significant achievements, she was starting to despair of their now revealed character (or more accurately, their lack of character). She wanted to preserve the bulk of her husband's money during her lifetime. What the boys did after her death would be their problem.

So, I had a number of discussions with Martha, who was very well and clear in her mind. She was disappointed in how Martin and Marshall were treating her (bullying and demanding, not at all respectful or polite), and feared they had lost touch with the realities of life.

Martha ultimately concluded that she would agree to their request, but would try to give them a modest reminder of what life was like - by asking them both to mortgage their homes to her as security, letting them know that she was lending them the money, not making a gift to them.

After this discussion, and giving Martha and Alby some advice, I left them to do what needed to be done. I didn't hear how it worked out, but I hoped that, for Martin and Marshall's sake, Martha could bring them briefly into the real world!

More on the Sense of 'Entitlement'

Another 'entitlement' claim has very recently concluded in the NSW Supreme Court. In that case, a wealthy landowner left $5.5 Million to his daughter, and nothing directly to his two grandsons.

The boys had been educated at an expensive private school, but did nothing to obtain gainful employment. They simply expected the grandfather to leave all his estate to them (and completely bypass their mother). When he did not, they sued their mother, claiming the whole estate for themselves.

The judge gave them no joy. He described their evidence as 'unimpressive', and declared that their "unhealthy sense of entitlement" might have led them not to bother looking for employment.

Their conduct, he pointed out, resulted in "…unquantifiable family discord, substantial cost and considerable hardship." He noted that, in their greed and impatience, they had given "… virtually no consideration to what should happen to their mother."

One of the boys ultimately settled his claim against the mother, but the other fought it all the way. In the end, he was awarded a minimal amount.

What a disgraceful way to behave - and what a remarkable lack of self-respect? Not to mention disdain for their mother.

The rub, in the end, was that the greedy son got what he deserved (precious little) and was then cut out of his mother's will.

Yes!!! Serves you right, you lazy sod!

CHAPTER 19

A FEW ISSUES WITH MORTGAGES

A Mortgagee Selling to a Lawyer?

My colleague Rita was consulted by Colin, a young lawyer who had purchased a property from a bank (selling as mortgagee) when he had been employed by another law firm. His firm had acted for the bank in securing possession of the property (he had worked on that file), and then in proceeding with the auction.

The bank had obtained two sworn valuations as to what the property was worth. Colin enquired from his firm if it would be possible for him to put in an offer to buy it. The firm considered his position and, after taking some external advice, told him it would be OK.

With about three weeks to go before the auction, and before most of the bank's sales and marketing campaign had taken place, Colin put in an offer, at about the higher end of the valuation range. The bank accepted the offer and the sale was finalised.

The bank's customer was unhappy with the outcome, and claimed that the property was worth about $70,000 more than the bank sold it for. She sued the bank, and called very strong valuation evidence supporting her claim. She won a verdict against the bank for failing to take proper steps to obtain a true market price for the property.

We were surprised that Colin's old firm had given him the go-ahead in the manner it did. In that position, our advice would have been very different. Colin could still have gone for the property, but only at auction, with full disclosure from the auctioneer that he (in his position) was intending to bid. In addition, he would need to be represented by a different (and independent) lawyer.

As I have often said to my young lawyers, so much of what lawyers do is all about complete disclosure. If you act openly and above the table, you are much less likely to find yourself in trouble!

I have also encouraged, when faced with a dilemma (sometimes between what the client wanted them to do and what their conscience was saying) to ask themselves the simple question "What will you say when you're in the witness box and some smart-arse barrister is asking you all the tricky questions about this?". Thinking about an issue in this context generally gives a deal of perspective and leads to a sensible outcome.

An Unusual Mortgage and the Problems It Caused

Terry was a tank manufacturer in a country town. He made good tanks, but was a poor businessman.

Terry's wife Maria was a teacher. She and Terry had a small mortgage debt on their home, and she was very averse to having any additional debt.

Terry was having some cash-flow problems in his business, and decided to raise a loan for $150,000. One day, over a few drinks at the local pub, he told his mate Eddie about his plans. Eddie noted that Maria wouldn't have a bar of any more debt, but Terry assured him that Maria wouldn't find out about it.

Terry applied for a loan, and asked Clive, a local lawyer, to act for him. He hadn't had a lawyer before that, and chose Clive who had been acting for one of Terry's creditors.

The bank duly sent the loan and mortgage documents to Clive, who called Terry. Terry told Clive that Maria was very ill with cancer, and couldn't come to Clive's office. He told Clive that he'd collect the documents, have them signed before a Justice of the Peace, and return them to Clive.

Terry then forged Maria's signature and took the documents to a local JP. He told the JP that Maria was too ill to come, but that she had signed. The JP saw Terry sign, and 'witnessed' their signatures. The new loan went ahead and Terry spent up the money.

Sadly, Terry died unexpectedly within eighteen months. When Maria found out she was livid (Eddie expressed the opinion that it was just as well for Terry that he had died, as Maria would have killed him anyway).

Maria engaged a law firm and issued a claim, but not against the bank, as it had no notice of the forgery. She sued the lawyer and the JP. The court found that the lawyer should have at least phoned Maria to verify what Terry had claimed, and that the JP should not have 'witnessed' a signature he had not seen.

The court held the lawyer liable for 60% and the JP for 40% of the amount of the loan. They were both negligent, so they shared the pain.

Mick and the Troublesome Borrower

When a bank sells a property as mortgagee, it has a serious responsibility to obtain the best price it can. Generally it does this by engaging a competent estate agent, running a good marketing/advertising campaign and putting the property up for public auction.

The auction process is how, in the great majority of cases, the bank establishes the market price. If it sells otherwise than by a well-organised auction, it has to provide a good explanation as to why.

My colleague Mick had a case where the borrower was very difficult and volatile. Even after the bank took possession of the property, he did everything he could to disrupt its plans. Each time the agents put an advertising hoarding on the property, he knocked it down. He harassed, threatened and abused anyone who came to inspect the property, and generally made it very difficult for the bank and its agents to conduct the sales/marketing campaign.

Then, on the auction day, he came along, again threatening and abusing all and sundry, and was so disruptive that the auction was called off. The agents knew who the interested parties were, and later conducted an informal auction-type process by phone, resulting in the sale of the property, for a price that was in line with the valuations the bank had obtained.

The borrower then had the effrontery to go to court and challenge the sale, on the grounds that the bank was negligent in not selling the property by auction. The court showed him no sympathy. It told him that, as the bank had done everything it possibly could, and attempted to have an orderly auction, and he had disrupted it with his dreadful conduct, he had no basis to complain.

Geordie and the Ghostbusters

When I was a young fellow first going out in a regional town, the place to go on Saturday night was the local dance hall. The music was provided by Geordie and the Ghostbusters, who reigned there for many years.

Many relationships began there, and blossomed under the swing and rock music provided by Geordie and his band.

After leaving the area, I heard nothing of Geordie for many years. Then my colleague Rita, who was acting for one of our banking clients, was telling me about this crazy person who burned his house down, just when the bank was about to take possession.

When I had a look at the file, sure enough - it was Geordie (as a much older man). It turned out that his wife had left him, and he was a long way behind in his mortgage payments. His solution - torch the place.

The locals concluded that he burned the house down so his wife wouldn't get any money from a property settlement, but there was no equity anyway, even before the fire.

It was common knowledge that Geordie's next door neighbour was keen to buy the property, which was set on a few acres in a nice area. Geordie apparently hoped that the fire would prevent this from happening. He seemed to hate the neighbour as much as he hated his wife and the bank.

Ultimately, the neighbour bought the property at the mortgagee auction, leaving the bank partially out of pocket, and with nothing left over for Geordie or his wife.

Ghostbusters indeed!

CHAPTER 20

MORE ABOUT LAWYERS

Norm and PT

One of my early employers was Norm, a strong and determined character. He had set up his office in a regional town, where he and the town's leading established lawyer (known as PT) promptly locked horns.

Norm quickly built up his practice, but he and PT spent plenty of time conducting their own private war. They engaged in a fierce and personal correspondence, sometimes with several letters being hand delivered between them in the one day (at that time, electronic communications were decades away).

Their rivalry spread far beyond the mere practice of the law, into local government (they both became involved with the local council, automatically opposing anything put up by the other) and even racehorses. When one of them had a racehorse that won the local cup, the other could not rest until he did the same. They were often like two boys battling it out in the schoolyard.

Norm and His 'Wayward' Daughter

As a prominent Catholic, Norm fathered a number of children, and ruled them all very strictly. He would not tolerate any variation from his strict standards of 'Catholic' behaviour.

Therese, one of Norm's daughters, had a strong independent streak, and would not conform to his ideas as to how she should behave. At age 18, she declared that she was no longer subject to his authority, and ran off with her boyfriend.

Norm would not stand for this insurrection. He hired a private detective, who soon reported back that Therese and the boyfriend were renting a house on Phillip Island.

Norm then co-opted a local police officer, and, along with the private eye, they raided the house in the middle of the night, seized Therese, and sped off into the night.

Therese was admitted to a small private hospital, where she was 'treated' with Sodium Amytal, a sleep-inducing barbiturate, and ultimately returned home where she was kept under strict conditions for some months. Norm made it clear to her that he would again not hesitate to track her down and bring her home if she ran off again.

Sean, Who Couldn't Share a Good Client

From time to time, we had good lawyers come to work with our firm, and bring a good client or two with them. This could be a blessing, but it could also cause many problems.

Sean was one who acted for a major client, and brought it with him when he joined the firm. During the several years he spent there, he continued to personally attend to all the work for that client - and scarcely had a chance to do anything else.

By doing it this way, he made it impossible for himself to develop any kind of specialty (he was effectively a sole practitioner for that client, performing a wide range of general work) and also ruled out the possibility of increasing his own client base.

Lawyers who operate this way are probably insecure about their abilities. If they were prepared to 'share' the client workload (while still being the focal point) they could build a bigger practice, increase their skills and use the particular client recognition to market themselves to other potential clients.

Yes, there is some risk of losing control of the client, but if you handle the sharing properly, there are huge benefits for the individual lawyer and for the firm.

After a few years, Sean moved on, taking the client with him, and there was almost a sense that he had never been there at all. His involvement in what had been happening at the firm had been minimal and was barely missed.

Kim's Approach

Kim was another who brought his own significant client, personally performed all the work for that client, and some years later left and took the client with him.

Kim refused to delegate any of the client contact, but he liked to delegate the menial tasks.

From time to time, as firms grow and develop, they undergo restructures and reorganisations. This often involves re-shuffling offices. When this happens, most lawyers physically move their files and personal belongings themselves, with some help from an assistant. Not Kim! His practice was to leave the office for a few hours, and only return when his assistant had done it all for him.

When he left us, Kim and a couple of his mates set up their own firm. Maybe it was the extra stress and burden that he now carried, maybe there were other things going on in his life, but Kim became a different person. No longer the cheeky, funny, happy person that he was when with us. No, he became very cranky, bad-tempered and abusive, particularly to his staff - and likely to erupt at any time and for no apparent reason.

Any lawyers and support staff who joined Kim's firm soon moved on. He lost a few friends that way.

Andy

Andy Silver spent a couple of years working with us. Like Sean (see above) he brought a large commercial client with him. Ruth, Andy's fiancee, was the daughter of one of the co-owners of a substantial retail network business with many outlets, so Andy brought plenty of work with him.

Andy was smart enough to know that he wasn't capable of personally doing all the wide variety of legal work. His approach was to range around the office, picking someone's brain here and there, posing a 'hypothetical' question to almost any lawyer he came across.

For work that was too far outside his area of expertise, Andy would make up a file (ensuring that he controlled what was done and what was billed) and get others to do the necessary work.

Ruth and Andy's wedding was amazingly huge, outrageous and expensive, and several of our lawyers (and their spouses of course) were invited. No expense was spared at this extravaganza.

While marvelling at the magnificence of the celebrations, a couple of the firm's partners drily observed that they'd have been happier not to have been invited, so long as Andy's father-in-law paid the firm's fees a little quicker and with less argument. They also noted that Andy had developed a practice (not approved by the firm) of heavily discounting fees charged to the father-in-law.

Not long afterwards, Andy left the firm, and established his own practice. While wishing him well, and maintaining the friendship, may of us were relieved at his departure. He then set up a practice with his father-in-law's interests as 90% of his clientele - and in premises rented from the father-in-law.

Hooks and His Firm

I first met Hooks when we were both law students. He was a couple of years ahead of me, and was always known as Hooks, although no-one ever explained why. He was always smiling and cheerful, and loved life.

After graduating, Hooks found a job as an articled clerk with his sister's husband Cliff in a regional town. He returned to the city every weekend to party with his mates. On one occasion, after a very heavy weekend with very little sleep, he drove back to work early on the Monday morning. He just made it to work in time for his 9.00 am appointment.

The clients were a married couple who had come in to make new wills. After some brief small talk, they began telling Hooks what they had in mind. A minute later, they looked up to see him slumped over the desk, snoring away.

Hooks was able to overcome this setback, and a couple of years later Cliff made him a partner in the firm.

Not long afterwards, Warren decided he'd like to move to the area. He saw an advertisement for a job with a sole practitioner nearby, and duly lodged an application. He drove down for an interview, which he felt went well. A couple of days later, the lawyer called him to say "Without prejudice, you've got the job!"

Warren puzzled over what this meant, and decided he didn't need to work with that lawyer. He shortly afterwards finished up with Hooks's firm, which was growing fast.

Soon afterwards, Cliff disgraced himself on the conference room table with one of the female employees. He left town (and the firm) shortly after.

Following Cliff's departure, Black Jack arrived at the firm, and was soon followed by my good mate Rocky.

Black Jack cut a dashing figure around town. Although married, he was popular with many ladies, including a few of those at the office. It wasn't long before he was found *en flagrante* on the (same) conference room table with one of the staff.

This led to Black Jack's departure, but not before his wife came wailing to Rocky's wife Gail about what a bastard he was, at the same time as the young employee was crying her heart out to Rocky.

So, at this time, the partners of the firm were Hooks, Warren and Rocky. Their wives decided that their conference room was out of bounds, so they moved to new offices - and sold the old table! As equal partners, their offices were all exactly the same - except that Hooks, being the senior man, insisted that his office chair be an inch higher than those of the other two.

Hooks also served the local law association for several years, including two as its president. During his tenure, the association was famous for its social activities and socialising.

Hooks later left the firm and the area. Last I heard, he was a candidate for election to Racing Victoria.

Moons and His Mortgage Practice

I have mentioned Seamus above, in a number of contexts. It was generally believed that, after the decline in personal injury cases, he was only able to survive in practice through his wealthy clients who had money to lend to borrowers who did not meet bank lending guidelines.

Many law firms, particularly in country towns, had their own mortgage fund, with investors happy to lend out their money to other clients of the firm. The interest return was generally more than they could recover by investing the money elsewhere.

Moons was a contemporary of mine in my student days. A couple of years after completing his articles, he bought a small practice in a country town from a sole practitioner, running a general practice for a standard mix of largely rural clients.

In his practice, Moons ran his own standard mortgage fund, looking after both investor and borrower clients. However, he added his own new wrinkle to it. Not unlike Big Bill's approach with the finance company (see above, in Chapter 16), Moons decided to make the system work for himself.

As a trusted adviser, Moons (as with all law firms) held a safe full of wills, deeds, securities and titles on behalf of his clients. So, when his investor clients had money to lend, and if he did not have a borrower client with needs to match, Moons came up with an easy solution.

Quite simply, Moons would select a title from his safe, and prepare loan and security documents between himself, as trustee for client A (as lender) and client B as borrower, using client B's title as security.

Client B never saw the money, and was not aware that his title was being used. As far as he was concerned, his title was clear and merely left with Moons for safe custody.

The transaction was fully documented, and the mortgage registered. The loan repayments were always paid on time. If there was a problem at any time, this was covered by a new loan being taken out, and the snowball grew.

The problem came to the surface through the sharp eye of Theresa, who was an accountant in a neighbouring town, and was also the auditor of Moons' trust account. As auditor, she satisfied herself that all the loans were fully documented, and all repayments duly made.

In Theresa's accounting practice, she lodged tax returns for many clients, including one of those whose title was being used as client B (the borrower). In going through client B's tax details one year, she commented that client B should be claiming the interest he was paying on his mortgage loan. Client B responded that he had had no borrowings for years, and no interest payments to claim.

Oops! This led to the collapse of the whole house of cards, and a fully paid holiday for Moons, as well as to the loss of his practising certificate.

Problems with Solicitors' Mortgage Practices

Over the years, it became more and more difficult to operate a lawyer's mortgage practice. Given that they were often used a a lender of last resort, the chances were that there would be a higher percentage of bad loans. As most of the funds were relatively small, it was never easy to keep the fund's loan portfolio balanced.

One country firm's fund fell over disastrously when almost all of its lending was invested in one apartment development project in suburban Melbourne. When construction costs ran out of control, the fund collapsed, with losses approaching $25 Million.

Add to this the occasional dishonesty by a lawyer in running their fund. This led to moves to tighten up the lending approvals and administration processes. The market moved a little, to what became known as SMICs (Solicitors Mortgage Investment Companies), with much tighter regulation by the law societies in each state.

Still, problems continued to persist, and eventually, the Australian government, through the Australian Securities and Investments Commission (ASIC) introduced a whole new level of compliance and administrative requirements.

Any person or company wanting to operate in financial services now requires a licence from ASIC. Conditions attached to the licence are very stringent in terms of capital adequacy, liquidity, reporting and so on.

The compliance obligations have meant that it is now uneconomic for most law firms to operate their own funds. My last firm opted out, and sold its mortgage fund to a much larger fund. In the early 2000s, the number of SMICs in Victoria fell from over 1000 to less than thirty.

The few that survived were large enough to have their own specialist managers and sufficient funds to keep their operation profitable. In some situations, there were mergers between six or more funds in different parts of the state.

Even after the consolidation, the profit margins of the funds were nothing to be excited about. One of the larger funds had a meeting with a group of senior managers at one of the banks. The fund lawyers made a pitch to the bank that it should buy their fund, and that it would make a good fit with the bank's wholly owned trustee company. They offered the fund to the bank for $40 Million.

The bank did its own assessment, and noted that the fund had too many retail offices, and that its overheads were out of all proportion to its size and profitability. It offered to take the fund off their hands for a mere $500,000. No deal!

Crunch Time

In the difficult financial climate following the global financial crisis, life became a real problem for the mortgage funds.

A typical fund would raise money from its investors by issuing debentures to them (the longer the term, the higher the interest rate) and then on-lending the money to borrowers at a higher rate again, thus providing a profit for the fund. There would also be costs on the mortgage documentation, helping the bottom line of the relevant firm.

When financial times are tough, borrowers (particularly those who borrow from lenders of last resort) are more likely to fall behind on their repayments. That's when these funds can hit the wall. Defaulting loans suddenly amount to over 20% of the total loan book, and there's not enough money being repaid to pay the investors when their debentures mature.

So, during 2012, some of the major funds, including Banksia and Southern, had liquidity problems, leading to repayments on their debentures being suspended. Banksia went into receivership. Its investors have, over nearly two years, received up to 65% of the money they invested. The receivers have indicated that investors might ultimately receive between eighty and eighty-five cents in the dollar.

Following the appointment of receivers to Banksia, Southern had its debenture repayments suspended. After a few weeks, it was able to sell its business to Bendigo & Adelaide Bank, with the result that all debenture obligations were paid in full.

In 2013, Gippsland Secured Investments (one of the very oldest and most solid funds) had similar liquidity problems, again with a suspension of repayments to its investors. Late in the year, the investors received 15% of their money, and the receivers have estimated that they will ultimately pay out a total of eighty - ninety per cent over a period of time.

A group of GSI investors made serious efforts to buy out the fund, but eventually were unable to complete the rescue. This led to a plethora of mortgagee auctions around the Gippsland lakes area.

The investors in these funds had regarded them as equivalent to a bank (even though they did not have the same government guarantee support that the banks had).

ASIC has come in for criticism, on the basis that it recommends that these funds have a minimum liquidity of 8% of its total funds, but does not enforce the recommendation. Lack of supervision and enforcement allowed the liquidity ratio to drop to less that 2% in some instances.

My own view is that the time is coming when continuing regulatory tightening and the nature of financial markets will ring the death knell for these funds. They have become an anachronism in these times, and ultimately I expect them to become absorbed into the larger financial system.

CHAPTER 21

HOW COULD YOU BE SO STUPID?

From time to time, you come across a lawyer or a client who does something so silly that you find it difficult not to laugh at them, or to burst out with "You did what?" or "How could you have been that stupid?" I can recall biting my tongue a few times, and muttering sympathetically about how unfortunate the poor person was.

Fast Fred was one of these. Refer back to his encounter with "The Axe" in Chapter 3, as an example of a lawyer risking his whole career for a client, something a lawyer should never do!

The following are a few examples.

Snorkel and His Twin Brother

In my early years in practice, personal injuries cases were a major part of a small firm's business. Lawyers would earn good fees out of a claim for damages where another party had negligently caused an injury.

In motor accident cases, there was always an insurance company behind the negligent driver, so you knew you'd get your money. Once you had established negligence, the question was - how much money was proper compensation?

Insurance companies, of course, would not always take this lying down. If they could establish contributory negligence (if the injured party contributed to the incident by their own negligence) the damages payout might be significantly reduced.

There was also the question of how serious the injury was. The injured party would be examined by the insurer's doctors, who would take a hard and sceptical look at the alleged injury. The trial might sometimes be largely contest between the medical experts on each side.

Insurers would (and still do) often hire investigators who might stake out the injured party and video their activities. They liked to show that the frail-looking person who has to be helped into court was in fact carrying on a robust and healthy life.

Which brings us to Snorkel (he had a huge nose and apparently a snore to match). He was a big, heavy man in his forties at the time, well and truly overweight, and suffered injuries in a car accident. Snorkel operated his own landscaping business, working outdoors, and using some heavy equipment. He told us that his injuries meant that he could no longer perform many of the physical tasks involved in the business.

The insurance company sent an investigator to check Snorkel out. They came back with videos and photos showing a busy and active man doing all the normal heavy physical work which the business entailed. Sure looked like our man!

Grimly, we put all this to Snorkel, who laughed derisively. "The dickheads!" he exclaimed "They've been following my identical twin brother. He told me about them." "You have a twin brother?" We asked. "Sure do" he grinned "Had him all my life". Next day, he brought in a copy of his and his brother's birth certificates. Yes indeed. Twins!

Thus encouraged, we pushed ahead and prepared the case for trial. We told Snorkel we'd need to talk to his brother, as he (the brother) would be required to give evidence that the images were of him, not of Snorkel. "Sure" he replied, and brought his brother in a couple of days later. Oh dear!

Yes, Snorkel had a twin brother, and yes, they had been identical - once! BUT, as they grew older, Snorkel had put on a lot of weight and his twin had not. One was like a whale, and the other was a slim, athletic type.

All of a sudden, the case had collapsed. The man the insurance investigator had checked out was clearly Snorkel, not his twin. We beat him about the head with the reality of the situation, and quickly settled for a very modest amount, not the fortune he had expected.

How he'd thought he could get away with it, I'll never know. Surely he didn't look at the whale in the mirror and see himself as his lithe twin brother?

And …lucky we found this out before we got him in front of a jury!

Ross - the Forgetful (Slack) Accountant

Over several years as a commercial lawyer, I had a fair bit to do with Ross, who had an accounting practice nearby. Ross had been in practice for many years and had several loyal, long-standing clients.

One of Ross's best clients was a family group, who had a number of assets and a couple of businesses, some of them in a particular family company. The group relied on Ross to look after many administrative matters for the company, including its tax returns and company returns to the Australian Securities and Investments Commission (ASIC).

In his latter years, Ross became busier and busier, and began to take some short-cuts. For some years, he failed to lodge the company returns. The result was that, eventually, ASIC deregistered the company.

For the next few years, the family carried on the company business, blithely unaware that the company no longer existed.

214 • KEVIN O'DONNELL

Sooner or later, however, the problem was bound to rise up and bite Ross. And so it did!

The family had a piece of real estate, which was in the name of the company. They decided to sell, called in the estate agents, produced a copy of the certificate of title (showing the company as the owner) and presto, it was sold.

As a matter of course, the purchaser's lawyer obtained both a title search and a company search. Oops, the company didn't exist, so how could it contract to sell the property?

When a company still has assets but becomes deregistered (and yes, it does occasionally happen) the assets vest in ASIC, so that's where the property's ownership lay.

Ross came rushing around to see me in a serious panic (and with his ears still ringing from the call from his unhappy client). What could we do to sort out his problem and rescue the sale? No point asking ASIC to confirm the deal - they weren't interested in Ross's problem. The only answer was an urgent application to the court to have the company re-instated.

OK, we dropped everything, lodged the application, prepared affidavits and had them sworn and filed, briefed a barrister, paid fees, etc. We were able to have the company re-instated (ASIC in such circumstances simply accepts the decision of the court), so the transaction could proceed.

The sale was settled, albeit a couple of weeks late. The relieved family group breathed again and pocketed the proceeds.

As for Ross, it cost him a good client and some thousands of dollars in fees. He took this case as a cue to sell up his practice and hang up his abacus.

Eric the Gullible Punter

In my days as a law student, a few of us would have an occasional punt on the horses. Most of us fairly quickly concluded that it was a mug's game and gave it away.

One thing we investigated (with more enthusiasm than our formal studies) was the theory that you could make a profit by backing several horses in the one race (even every horse in a race). The plan was that you could calculate the amount of each bet so that, no matter which horse won, your winnings would exceed your outlay.

It took no time for us to work out that this was just another way to lose. The bookies and totes always had the odds in their favour - to the extent of 110% or more, so that it was impossible to win by using that method. In short, we quickly gave up on that theory.

Fast forward many years, and there's Eric in my office wanting to sue a Queensland (of course) company for misleading him into buying a computerised gambling program, based on the same principles. He had been conned into parting with about $40,000 to buy this program, which was guaranteed to make him money by telling him which horses (several of them) to back (and for how much) in specified races. After forking out his hard earned, all he had to show for it was a string of losses.

When Eric was telling me his tale of woe, I was chewing hard on my tongue, to help me keep a straight face and talk sympathetically to him, rather than to start laughing and say "You did what? You blithering idiot? Did you ever stop and ask yourself why they'd be looking for suckers like you if the system really worked? No way, they'd keep it to themselves!"

While sympathising, I didn't hold much hope for recovering Eric's money. Yes, he had been misled, and under the then *Trade Practices Act,* he'd easily enough obtain a judgement against the company, and possibly its promoters. However such promoters operate on a fly-by-night basis, leaving no assets behind for creditors.

And so it was here. The company that had conned Eric was already delisted and the trail was cold. To chase the individuals down every burrow would cost a lot of money, with no real prospect of success. The people he had dealt with would have no assets in their own name, and all he would do would spend more money on another gamble (and again a very risky one) that he'd be able to recover anything.

Poor Eric! It was a salutary (and expensive) lesson. He left the office a sadder (and hopefully wiser) man.

Saul the Finance Broker

After working in real estate for some time, Saul took out a finance broker's licence, and started selling loans. He also sold insurance, so, at the same time he was organising loans, he'd sign up the borrowers for a range of insurance products as well. "By the way, would you like a car with that? Got a great deal for you!" He was a natural salesman. In fact he sold himself. Once he gained the borrower's confidence, he then sold them a package.

One of Saul's problems was that he was hopeless at paperwork. His records were a mess, and he ignored many of his regulatory obligations. He was incapable of getting the details in proper order or properly documenting a transaction.

For Saul, there was always an angle, where he would be obtaining some extra benefit for himself. Thus, he constantly ran into trouble.

He would often ring to tell me what deal he was putting together for a borrower (or sometimes for himself). In most cases, the deal made no sense. I'd ask him what he was trying to achieve. When he told me, I'd respond that his plan would not achieve it, but if we went down this track instead, we'd get the result he wanted. "OK" he'd say, "Let's do that then." Remember the old adage - "Keep it simple stupid!"

Whenever Saul ran into a problem, he'd come to me to sort it out for him. But he wouldn't always listen to good advice.

On one occasion, he was being investigated for breaches of the *Finance Brokers Act*. He readily agreed to an interview with two investigating officers. Against my advice, and with supreme (and badly misplaced) confidence in his own ability and intelligence, Saul gave them all the information they needed (and which they could not otherwise have obtained).

The result was an open and shut prosecution for several breaches, and the loss of his licence. Sheer arrogant stupidity.

A year or so later, a woman, Andrea, came to my firm with instructions to act for her in the purchase of a small take-away food business. She had the financials for the business, had a loan organised, and was ready to go ahead. It turned out that Saul was arranging the loan for her (and clipping the ticket a few times on the way through).

When we had a close look at the numbers and the details, a few problems became apparent:

1. Andrea had no security for the loan, apart from the business (and such a business is notoriously poor security - for instance, if business is bad and she couldn't pay the rent, the landlord would change the locks - game over!),
2. She was relying on her pensioner mother to mortgage her house as collateral for the loan (an absolute no-no), and
3. There was only the remotest chance that she could reach break-even on the business, let alone make a profit. The whole transaction was a dead-set loser.

We put it into writing that Andrea should not go ahead with the transaction, but she insisted that all would be well. I suspect that Saul had filled her with false confidence, and she would not listen to us. In the end, we refused to act for her. I don't know if she went ahead with the purchase, but we refused to have anything to do with it.

Many years later, when I was with Keith's firm, a client mentioned to me a strange and complicated transaction in which he was a bit player. The transaction had such a weird aroma that was quite familiar. I asked him who had put it together. Sure enough, it was Saul.

Simply incapable of running a straightforward transaction.

Derryn Hinch

No, I've never met or had anything to do with Derryn, but his pattern of behaviour qualifies him for a mention in this section.

Derryn is an old hand at appearing before the courts on charges of contempt. He is renowned for his strong and fearless campaign against child abusers. This is entirely to his credit.

His problem has been that he has sometimes broadcast information about upcoming cases, disregarding court orders against such publication.

In exercising his passion and outrage (and yes, his ego), Derryn has been guilty of (and found guilty of) contempt of court for interfering in the administration of justice. The irony has been that he has more than once jeopardised the trials of the perpetrators of these horrible crimes.

In 1985, Derryn was fined $10,000 and served a term of ten days jail for publishing the prior convictions of a paedophile priest before the priest's trial.

Again, in 2011, he was convicted of contempt of court for naming two sex offenders in breach of a suppression order. He was seriously ill at the time, so, instead of a prison term, he was sentenced to five months home detention.

In 2013, Derryn was again convicted of contempt of court for publishing details of the criminal history of Jill Meagher's murderer before his trial, again in breach of suppression orders.

The judge was scathing in his criticism of Derryn's conduct. He declared that, given his history, Derryn should have been well aware that his conduct was prohibited, and that he was a serial offender. He fined Derryn $100,000, in default a jail term of fifty days, if the fine was not paid within ninety days.

In the end, Derryn has decided to make his point by serving the fifty days porridge rather than pay the fine. That's his choice, but you can only admire him for sticking to his principles.

Derryn has an unswerving belief that he knows better than the courts and that he is entitled to say whatever he likes, in his campaign against paedophilia. It is ironic that he, like the criminals he campaigns against, thinks he is outside or above the law.

Fifty days - that's a penalty!

One of Derryn's favourite sayings is "You can't legislate against stupidity." Well, Derry, put your ego aside for a minute and have a good look in the mirror!

Me?

"What about you?" I hear the reader ask. "Have you never done something stupid?"

Well, yes. I can think of a number of things that qualify. Some in my private life (and not within the range of these ramblings) and some in my professional life.

There are too many to detail here, but two in particular that, in retrospect (always easier), I look back on as stupid:

1. Blithely going into partnership with persons whom I should never have trusted to behave honestly and honourably, and
2. Putting up with Saul as a client for as long as I did.

I later came to regret these examples of stupidity. If I had been a little wiser at the time, I'd be better off now.

I must say, however, that my years as a lawyer have been tremendously satisfying and rewarding, and that the great majority of my colleagues have been wonderful people, as well as excellent practitioners.

CHAPTER 22

THE BENCH AND
THEIR HELPERS

Justices of the Peace

Long ago, when I was a young lawyer, it was common for a Justice of the Peace to hear relatively minor prosecutions in the Magistrates' Court. These were (almost) exclusively male, and were generally business-people or farmers, and stalwarts of the community. They would also hear applications for bail at odd hours, and did all this in an honorary capacity.

In court, sometimes they might sit with a magistrate, and on some occasions one of them, or two sitting together, would constitute the court.

One day, I was appearing for a young man on a relatively minor charge. He pleaded guilty to the charge, and gave evidence as to how he regretted his transgression. He was from a very good family, and we had excellent character evidence.

The two sitting JsP agreed not to record a conviction, and then embarked upon a few very rare minutes extolling the accused's character, and saying what a wonderful young man he was.

As we left the court, I commented that, at one stage I thought they were going to award him a medal instead of a penalty. Even he was bemused about how much they had praised him.

Then there was a much tougher JP, known locally as Hanging Harry. Harry believed that maximum penalties were laid down in legislation for a reason, and should be imposed on a regular basis.

On one occasion, a local man was up on a very minor charge. At that time the maximum penalty for the specific offence was a fine of $60 in default imprisonment for six days. In those days, it was rare for a court to impose a penalty of more than $10 or one day for such an offence.

Harry misread the penalty provisions and imposed a fine of $600, in default sixty days. The clerk of courts hastily jumped to his feet and pointed out the problem, whereupon Harry ungraciously revised the penalty to $60 or six days. He was heard to mutter that the penalty was woefully inadequate.

There were two Justices of the Peace who had held their positions for over sixty years, and had a healthy disregard for anything that happened after 1950. They had not long retired from the local council. As well as occasionally sitting in the court, they were on a couple of committees around town.

The problem with this was that they refused to recognise daylight saving time. So, whenever the court, or a meeting, was due to commence, they would turn up an hour late. They had made a considerable contribution in their time, but this was just farcical - they outlived their usefulness by at least a generation!

The Small Claims Tribunal

Way back in the 1970's the Victorian government of the time introduced an alternative to the courts for resolving consumer complaints. It introduced a new service, called the Small Claims Tribunal (SCT).

Some years later, VCAT was established, and the SCT was incorporated into it, but that was later. My tale relates to the early days of the SCT.

A client came to see me about a debt he was claiming from a customer, who was being difficult, and refusing to pay his bill. He told me that the customer told him he was going to complain to the SCT. The client had no idea what that meant, but wanted to pursue his money.

I knew of the SCT, not through any dealings with it, but other lawyers had told me they believed it had a bias in favour of the consumer. They said that their small business clients felt they had not received a fair hearing at the SCT. If my client had a better chance in the Magistrates' Court, that's where we wanted to be!

I knew that once proceedings had been issued in the SCT, the courts had no jurisdiction. Likewise, if we issued in the courts first, the SCT had no jurisdiction. In other words, it was a question of who got in first.

So, I quickly prepared a Magistrates Court summons and had it issued and served on the customer. As it happened, the SCT issued its claim the next day. Tactical victory - we were in first!

I had been told that the SCT registrar was an empire-building type, but had previously had nothing to do with him. I still remember his name well, but won't include it here (not even as a *'nom-de-plume'* as I have with many others).

Anyway, the erstwhile registrar rang a few days later. He had apparently been informed that we issued first, and he was furious. When he called, it happened that I was in the mens room (something in me must have felt moved in advance).

My telephonist told me that he was unbelievably rude and aggressive, would not accept that I was not in my office, kept demanding that she put him through to me, and would not stop yelling at her. She described him as a 'real nasty little Hitler' and already hated him fiercely.

So, I called him back. It was quite an extraordinary conversation, and I seriously wondered about his sanity. He ranted and raved and yelled that I had to withdraw the Magistrate Court proceedings. I tried to explain that I couldn't do that without my client's instructions, which I doubted I'd receive - and anyway, why should I withdraw it?

"So we can hear the case at the SCT" he screamed. I asked what was the point of that, as the parties would receive a fair hearing in the court. If the customer had a case, let him come and present it to the magistrate. He continued to rant and yell, but had well and truly found my stubborn streak. In any event, it was no longer my call - and I knew what my client's position was.

When it became apparent that he could not bulldoze (bully?) me into submission, he eventually hung up in a huff.

I expected to soon receive a defence to my summons, but it never arrived. As soon as time for a defence expired, we entered judgement, and not long afterwards, we received payment of the bill and costs.

I concluded that the customer's complaint could not have had much merit, as he wasn't prepared to run it before the magistrate. I also, for quite some time, harboured reservations about the SCT.

Some time later, the registrar moved on, and then the SCT was subsumed into VCAT. In my experience since that time, VCAT does a wonderful job, in all its various jurisdictions, and has an excellent reputation.

I don't know what became of the original SCT registrar, and wouldn't waste my time thinking about him.

Know Your Magistrate

It could never have been easy to be a judge or magistrate. Sometimes there would be two strong but opposing cases put to the court, with excellent advocates, and fine points of law. The magistrates courts hear over 90% of the legal cases heard, and cover an enormous variety of cases, with great success.

The position of judge or magistrate requires remarkable legal knowledge, patience, consistency and the most uncommon quality, common sense. A sharp (and sometimes suspicious) mind is invaluable - see my earlier references to the 'Axe' in reference to Fast Fred.

The 'Chief'

One of the strong magistrates of my early days was a man known to a few of us as the 'Chief'. Greg coined the phrase as in 'the chief justice of the high court of Gippsland'.

There was no doubt that the Chief was in complete control of his court. From time to time, we would see a bumptious barrister come down, determined to teach the locals a lesson - only to be sent back with their tail between their legs. Some magistrates were occasionally overawed by a confident barrister - not the Chief! He was always in charge, and if you went into battle with him, he always had the last word.

I recall one day when I was appearing for a widow and her (mildly intellectually disabled) son. After hearing all the evidence, the Chief announced that he preferred my clients' version. The opposing barrister challenged him and blustered on for some time, arguing strongly that the son's evidence was unreliable. The Chief declared that he accepted that the son was incapable of twisting the truth.

As my opponent went on, I simply kept my head down, and soon received a favourable decision, and a nice costs order.

With the Chief, we learned very quickly not to waste his time, especially when there was a busy list to get through. If you had a drink driving case, with a blood alcohol reading not much over .05%, the last thing you would do was make a lengthy plea.

In one such case, the defence lawyer stood up as soon as the police case was closed, only to be met with "What are you concerned about, Mr X?" He replied "Might I assume from your worship's question that you don't intend to interfere with my client's licence?" "Yes" replied the Chief, so the lawyer immediately sat down.

Greg had a case before the Chief one hot Friday, where he was opposed to a visiting barrister. Greg's client was being sued in circumstances where her dog had bitten the complainant in a park.

It was the last case in the day's list, and the clock was ticking towards lunch-time. The barrister had been proceeding painfully slowly and the Chief had given a couple of hints (not picked up by the barrister) that things should be moving faster. Greg felt that the Chief would appreciate not having to resume the day's work after lunch.

About this time, the barrister announced that the complainant's case was completed. Greg stood up and (optimistically) submitted that, on the evidence, his client had no case to answer.

The Chief jumped in very quickly. "I couldn't agree more Mr S" he declared. "The doctrine of 'Scienter' obviously applies here. To succeed, the complainant must establish that the defendant was aware that the dog had a propensity to violence. There is no such evidence before the court. The complainant's case is therefore dismissed with costs."

Before the visiting barrister knew what had hit him, the Chief fixed Greg's costs in no time, adjourned the court for the day, and headed off for what was presumably a relaxed, pleasant lunch.

Those of us who regularly appeared before the Chief generally subscribed to the 'Know Your Magistrate' school. We found ourselves laughing at his jokes, limiting our cross-examination and submissions to the essentials, and recognising his encyclopaedic knowledge of the law. Those who failed to do so were generally less successful.

One of the his heroes was Sir Stanley Burbury, who was promoted from being a magistrate in Tasmania to its Supreme Court, eventually being appointed as the state's Chief Justice, and ultimately its Governor. The Chief regularly quoted Sir Stanley, so we also made a point of doing so. On one social occasion, Greg and I made him laugh when we asked about his plans to reach the Victorian Supreme Court and Government House.

Christopher was one who found it difficult to appear before the Chief. His response to a joke from the bench was to tilt his head to the side, raise an eyebrow and look puzzled. This did not help him when some of us were almost doubled over with laughter.

Nevertheless, Christopher eventually came to an accommodation with the Chief. At a law association dinner he introduced the Chief as "One of the most learned magistrates currently sitting in Gippsland". The Chief roared his appreciation of the joke.

The 'Snail'

Another of our magistrates was known affectionately as the 'Snail'. He was extremely thorough, and pondered longer over his verdicts than did the Chief. The result was that he got through fewer cases in a day, so that cases were adjourned over to the next hearing day.

The Snail was, however, not without a sense of humour. One day, he fined a local man, who was a fellow local Rotary club member, on a minor traffic matter. It just happened that the defendant was the 'sergeant-at-arms' in the Rotary club. At the next Rotary club meeting, the 'sergeant-at-arms' repaid the favour by fining the magistrate $1.

In one case, I was appearing before the Snail and opposed to Christopher in a civil dispute. The parties had unsuccessfully held an informal mediation session at one stage at a local greengrocer shop.

The way the case was proceeding was somewhat dull, and at one stage I ventured that the mediation attempt had been 'fruitless'. After the case was done and dusted, we were chatting away in the clerk's office when the Snail suggested he should have found me in contempt of court for such a dreadful pun!

Tom and Jerry

Tom was an experienced magistrate who was quick to sort out those who appeared before him, and to learn who could be trusted and who were less reliable.

Jerry was a long-standing policeman who never attained much seniority in the force (apart from years of service, that is). One of his occasional duties was to be the officer on the door at the local court. When a person was required, he'd call out their name. If no-one responded, he'd announce "No appearance Yerp (his abbreviation for 'your worship')".

I was in court one day when Jerry gave his evidence against a person whom he'd charged with speeding. His evidence was that he'd been siting in his police car, parked at the kerb, when he saw a car speeding through an intersection about 150 metres away. He estimated that it was travelling at over eighty clicks in a sixty zone.

Jerry went on that he reversed out of his park, and took off after the car, doing a right hand turn at the intersection, and pulling it over about 400 metres down that street.

As soon as Jerry finished his case, Tom immediately dismissed the charge. When Jerry protested, Tom told him that, if he accepted the evidence, Jerry must have exceeded 300 KPH to have reversed out, proceeded to the corner, completed a turn and pulled over the defendant as he alleged - and he doubted that the police car was capable of such a speed!

Jerry's next episode with Tom was to do with a charge he laid against a driver for failing to stop at a railway crossing when the red lights (sometimes call 'wig-wags') were operating. This happened on a country road, where the speed limit was eighty KPH.

"How far from the level crossing was the defendant's car when the lights came on?" enquired Tom. "Approximately ten metres, your worship" replied Jerry. "And what was his approximate speed?" asked Tom. "Just under eighty Ks." responded Jerry.

Tom quickly concluded that it would not have possible for the defendant to have completely stopped from eighty KPH within ten metres, and dismissed the case.

Another one of Jerry's cases was a charge of failing to stop at a red light. The evidence (uncontested) was that the driver had not actually driven through the red light. He had, just before the intersection, executed a perfectly legal left-hand turn on a piece of road not governed by any lights. There was no other traffic around at the time.

The driver then drove a short distance down the cross road, did a (perfectly legal) U-Turn, returned towards the intersection, and executed another (again perfectly legal) left-hand turn.

In short, the driver had avoided (gone around) the red lights without going through them. Hence, no actual breach of any law.

Tom benignly commented on Jerry's enthusiasm, and again dismissed the charge.

Leo the Terrier

Leo was a small, slim, bald magistrate who occasionally came on circuit to relieve backlogs, or when a regular magistrate was on leave. He'd often be seen out on a vigorous walk around town early in the mornings. He was a terrier in so many ways.

Leo made a point of getting through a prodigious amount of work, and sometimes completed the day's work ahead of time. He prided himself on his efficiency in court. He would then pressure whichever practitioners were around to accompany him to a local pub.

This was dangerous, as Leo had three drinking rules (also based on efficiency principles):

- you don't sit at tables, you stand at the bar (eliminates waste of time going back and forth),
- you drink from the largest glasses in the pub (more efficient and better value than small ones), and
- you don't sip your beer, you pour it down.

Many a next morning would see an unwell lawyer appearing in court in a dazed state, and a fit looking Leo looking very smug on the bench after a long early morning walk.

Whenever a drink driver came before him in court, Leo would come down hard. "No-one likes a beer more than I do" he'd growl, "BUT......YOU DON'T DRINK AND DRIVE!" And he'd proceed to deal severely with them.

Leo also had a way of cutting through, to make sure that people understood his message. On one occasion, a little immigrant lady from Yallourn North was up before him on a shoplifting charge. She was unrepresented, and was accused of stealing a small item valued at about $2.50.

Leo asked her if she was guilty. When she didn't reply, he asked "Did you steal from the shop?" She stammered a very shaky "Yes", in heavily accented English.

He then asked what her husband thought of this, and quickly divined that she hadn't told him about it. He then growled "What will he think when he comes home for dinner tonight.... AND YOU'RE NOT THERE?"

The poor woman dissolved into a sobbing, blubbering mess. Leo let her absorb the message for a minute or so, then let her go on a bond to be of good behaviour for a year. He added that if she came back before him, he'd lock her up and throw away the key.

She shuffled off in mortal fear of Leo and the law. Everyone else in court had a quiet chuckle. We all knew from the start how it would end up, but admired Leo's style of getting the message through.

Dasher

The Magistrates' Court bench has had many characters over the years. Dasher was one of them, and would often look for ways to brighten up a dull period in court.

One day, Dasher was hearing a police prosecution of a man whose dog had bitten a girl. The young lady was in the witness box, describing what had happened.

As she was quite attractive, Dasher paid close attention to her evidence. He enquired solicitously "So where did the dog bite you, Ms X?" She blushed, and replied "On the leg, your worship."

Dasher enquired if she'd show him where on the leg. She shyly lifted her skirt, and pointed to a spot on her upper thigh, close to the hip. Dasher looked for as long as he decently could, then turned to the police prosecutor and commented "Gee Sergeant, I'd bite that myself!"

Dasher, Henry and the Paternity Case

Many years ago, when Henry Jolson (see more about Henry below under 'Barristers') was a young barrister, he was briefed by a local lawyer to come down to the Morwell Magistrates Court. His brief was to represent a young local man who was facing a paternity suit (this was long before DNA testing became available).

The young lady in question was seeking a maintenance order against his client. The young man's defence was that other men had also had sex with her, at about the same time, so he should not be singled out to pay up.

Henry drove down with his young wife, for a day in the country (and so she could see him perform).

As the parties took their seats in court, the clerk announced that the case was to be heard 'in camera' (this meant that the court was to be closed to the public). He asked all persons not involved in the case to leave the court.

Henry stood up and addressed Dasher "Excuse me, Your Worship, I am embarrassed. My wife has come all the way from Melbourne with me."

An innocent looking Dasher surveyed the court and responded "Wife? I cannot see your wife, but if that lady there would come and sit at the bar table, she can be your instructor."

So, Henry's wife sat at the bar table and looked vitally interested in the case.

Henry's first witness was a local police officer who gave evidence that he had had sex with the lady. To this, Dasher leaned over and politely enquired "So, you think you might be the father?" The officer suddenly had some doubts about where and when the encounter had taken place.

As it turned out, Henry's client lost the case. The evidence indicated that the baby bore a striking resemblance to him.

Stuart, Squash, and the Brawny Footballer

As well as the magistrates being characters in their own way, the clerks of the courts had their own eccentric ways and personalities. They could be very entertaining, sometimes frustrating, but always good for a story or two.

Stuart was a chubby little fellow, but a very good squash player, who was proud of his skill on the squash court. He would describe his victories in some detail, especially boasting about his tactical acumen.

As befits a person who worked in the law, Stuart could quote all the rules of squash, and used them to his advantage. He particularly enjoyed being in the front position on the court, and playing the ball down the wall. The rules allowed him, having done this, to remain exactly where he was.

If his opponent's shot hit him, Stuart would win the point. Most players would politely move a short distance towards the centre of the court, and give their opponent some room to play their shot. Not Stuart. He stayed put and won the point - it was all about winning! Fancy anyone in the law having that attitude?

On this occasion, Stuart was playing against Craig, a powerful sportsman who had recently finished a successful league football career with Hawthorn (in the period when they were known as 'Kennedy's Kommandos'). Stuart and Craig had never played each other before.

As usual, Stuart employed his 'down the wall' strategy against Craig. It worked the first couple of times, causing Craig to mutter

232 • Kevin O'Donnell

to himself in frustration. The third time it happened, Craig, using every ounce of his enormous power, drilled the ball into the right cheek of Stuart's rear end. It almost disappeared as it went about five centimetres into his flesh.

Craig was most apologetic - "Sorry mate - your point" he declared. Stuart bravely tried to carry on, but was obliged to forfeit the match. The bruise took a long time to come out, and it was over a week before he could walk properly again.

The Confused Jury - How Much is 'X'?

In a personal injury case, sometimes the jury is required to decide how much compensation the plaintiff should receive for the injuries they have suffered.

The compensation can be calculated for a number of categories, which might include:

- medical and hospital charges,
- damages for pain and suffering,
- loss of income to date,
- loss of earning capacity,
- ongoing medical and care expenses, and
- loss of enjoyment of life.

In one famous case, the judge went to great pains, over some hours, summarising the evidence and instructing the jury on the different heads of damage they should consider.

He dwelt for some time on how they should consider the concept of damages for pain and suffering. He told them that, when they had calculated that amount, they should set it aside, while they then went on to consider the other categories. They could regard the pain and suffering amount as 'X' and bring it back in when they had worked out the other amounts.

The jury listened solemnly to all of this, and then went out to consider its verdict. A few hours later, they came back in and announced that they awarded the plaintiff $35,000 plus 'X'.

The judge and the lawyers in court just put their heads in their hands and groaned.

Judge Cairns Villeneuve-Smith

Possibly the most sensational and divisive case in South Australia in the 1950's was the murder charge against the indigenous man Rupert Max Stuart. The local newspaper, the *News,* led by a young Rupert Murdoch, ran a very strong campaign against what it claimed was a racially biased prosecution of Mr Stuart. This led to the then Playford government setting up a Royal Commission into the way the case was run.

The Royal Commission was very critical of many aspects of the police case, and the position taken by the prosecution, but overall supported the conviction. The result was a major schism in the legal profession in the state.

After the Royal Commission, a number of leading South Australian barristers were so disillusioned that they quit the state and moved to Victoria. James David O'Sullivan, who had appeared for Stuart, was one of them. Cairns Villeneuve-Smith was another one.

Tragically, O'Sullivan was killed in a motor vehicle accident in Western Victoria only a few years later. Cairns Villeneuve Smith built up an excellent practice at the Victorian bar, and later as a County Court judge.

I was an articled clerk when I first came across Cairns. My firm briefed him regularly, especially in cases where strong, fearless and impassioned advocacy was called for. He had a brilliant, cutting turn of phrase. I can still recall sitting opposite him, as the 'instructor', trying but failing to keep a straight face as he tore apart an opposing argument or made a self important witness look ridiculous.

On one occasion, we briefed him to represent an eighteen year old boy who was charged in the County Court with 'unlawful carnal knowledge' of a fifteen year old girl. The outraged old judge was determined to impose a term of imprisonment on the boy, even though the evidence showed that the girl was more experienced than the boy, and that she instigated the encounter. Cairns fought and fought for his client with an amazing fierce determination. In the end, and after persuading the judge to consider the position overnight, he won the client's freedom.

I often thought that, if my liberty was ever at stake, I'd love to have someone like Cairns fighting like that for me.

Some years later, after Cairns had taken silk, he was appearing at another Royal Commission - investigating police corruption in the abortion 'industry', following allegations involving Dr Bertram Wainer, who had set up an abortion clinic. Cairns was counsel assisting the Royal Commissioner, Barry Beach QC, who soon afterwards was appointed to the Supreme Court.

Cairns was devastating in his cross-examination of some of the allegedly corrupt police officers. One of the highlights involved asking one squirming officer about a number of red marks showing in a photo of the face of a person after a police 'interview'.

After some indecisive answers from the officer, Cairns put to him "You're not suggesting that those marks are blushes of embarrassment after he called Sergeant X 'Four eyes', are you?".

Cairns's cross-examination of the police broke down a number of them, and led to the Royal Commission recommending many changes to police procedures, and to some police resentment of both Cairns and Barry Beach.

When Cairns was later appointed to the County Court and Beach to the Supreme Court, the police attitude was very negative to both of them. Soon, however, it transformed into a grudging respect for two fine, fearless and independently minded lawyers who applied their talents to whatever task they were given.

Judge Gordon Lewis - A Man For All Seasons

I first came across Gordon when I was an articled clerk and he was a partner in a Hamilton law firm. He had done his articles with the same city firm that I finished up at many years later. After some years working as a solicitor in the city, he moved to Hamilton and soon became a partner there.

Gordon was highly regarded as a quality lawyer who was largely responsible for the Hamilton firm's growth.

After 16 years as a solicitor, Gordon was appointed as Executive Director of the Law Institute of Victoria (LIV). There were some comments about the appointment being from left field, but it turned out to be an inspired move. Gordon was a great success, and really opened up the LIV to its members, allowing it to become a vital part of the Victorian community. Its voice was heard at all levels of government and it became a prominent voice on behalf of many who had not previously been heard.

Six weeks after he started with the LIV, it was rocked by a defalcation (theft) of $11 Million by a Victorian lawyer - the largest to that time. Gordon was responsible for putting steps in place to compensate victims of dishonest lawyers.

The following year, the LIV building was seriously damaged and many of its records lost in a flood. Then in 1978, it was almost completely destroyed in a fire. The major suspect was a lawyer who had just been released from prison, and was apparently seen outside the building with two four gallon drums of petrol and a box of barbecue matches. The suspect was given an alibi by his wife, and was never charged.

Gordon dealt with all these problems in his customary efficient manner, and used them to modernise the Institute and make it the model for other law societies around the country.

At the same time, he was very visible to and supportive of the law associations around the state. He would always attend their conventions, and discuss the various issues which confronted regional lawyers. His understanding of their issues was profound, and his gregarious and approachable nature allowed him to discuss their problems in their own language.

I was secretary of my association for two years and on the executive for many years, and developed a great appreciation for Gordon's support and common sense approach.

The Victorian government at the time became aware of Gordon's capacities and energies, and, in 1986 appointed him as its Commissioner for Corporate Affairs. Fifteen months later, it moved him up to be the Victorian Government Solicitor - the first non-public servant to hold that position.

Then, in 1990, he was appointed as a judge of the County Court, a position he held for nearly fourteen years.

The ABC also appreciated Gordon's talents. For some years he provided legal help in a weekly talk-back session on ABC radio. After his appointment to the court, he gave up that role, but continued with ABC radio as a film reviewer.

After his retirement from the bench in 2004, Gordon's energies and abilities have seen him in a variety of roles, including:

- Cricket Australia's Senior Code of Conduct Commissioner,
- being commissioned in March 2008 to provide Victoria's Racing Integrity Report (delivered in August 2008),
- being appointed in April 2011 as one of Victoria's Corruption Commissioners, and
- being appointed as Victoria's Road Safety Commissioner in December 2011

That these appointments have been made by both Labor and Coalition governments speaks to Gordon's impartiality and clear decision making at the highest levels.

Truly a remarkable man and a wonderful, inspiring life in the law.

Dinner With the Chief Justice

The opening of the legal year is always a big deal. In Melbourne, all the religious groups have their own ceremony, attended by prominent clergy and lawyers of that faith, resplendent in their various coloured robes and wigs. Blessings are given to all parties for the legal fraternity and the administration of justice for the coming year.

In the Supreme Court circuit cities, a similar process takes place. The major religions each take turns, and the visiting judge (or judges) play their part.

One famous year, the Chief Justice came to Sale. As well as attending the religious ceremony, he presided over a splendid opening session of the court, sitting along with the judge who had come to sit for the month's circuit.

Determined to do justice (sorry) to the occasion, the CJ had given notice that he would like to break bread with a good representation of Gippsland's practitioners. So, about forty of us met him for dinner at one of Sale's best restaurants that night.

We all had a lovely dinner and several drinks. Some time after 11.00 pm, I was thinking it was time to head home. However, the CJ surprised us all by indicating that he wanted to bat on. Hooks, who was president of our association at that time, was on the committee of the local mens club. He just happened to have the keys, so we found ourselves in the club, with full access to the bar and the snooker tables.

Our expectation of the CJ was that he was an old style stuffed shirt. Not that night he wasn't! He was just as noisy as anyone else there, drinking hard, telling stories and joining in with the snooker players.

Snooker is often played in a silent and dignified manner, but not here. I recall a lot of noise as Rocky and I played against the CJ and another of the locals. Yells of triumph and frustration were common on all sides as fluke shots and near misses were the order of the night.

I can't remember who won what, but a few of us decided it would be bad manners to leave before the guest of honour, who was clearly enjoying himself and in no hurry to call it a night.

Me, I struggled home at about 4.30 am, and made heavy weather of the next day's work.

Justice Starke and the Ronald Ryan Story

Sir John Erskine Starke (born 1913, died 1994) was a justice of the Victorian Supreme Court from 1964 until his retirement in1985. He was famous for many reasons, but particularly as the judge who pronounced the death sentence on Ronald Ryan, the last person to be hanged in Victoria.

I had the privilege of sitting next to the judge at a dinner towards the end of his years on the bench, as many of us hung on his recollections of the case.

Ronald Ryan and Peter Walker escaped from Pentridge Prison in 1965. In the course of their escape, prison warder George Hodson was shot dead. The circumstances of Hodson's death were fully canvassed at the trial, and many questions were asked about how he died. The jury. however, was sufficiently satisfied that it convicted Ryan of murder.

As the presiding judge, Starke was obliged to impose the death penalty. At the time, the laws of Victoria gave him no option. The death penalty was automatic.

For many years, the Victorian government, as a matter of course, had commuted the death sentence into a term of life imprisonment. The last previous hanging had occurred in 1951. However, this time, the premier, Sir Henry Bolte, was determined that Ryan would hang.

Bolte had attempted a couple of years earlier to have a prisoner hanged, but was frustrated at the very end by the High Court of Australia.

In 1961, Robert Peter Tait was charged with a particularly gruesome murder of an elderly woman at the Hawthorn vicarage.

There was little doubt that he had killed the woman, but serious questions were raised about his mental capacity.

Starke QC was the lead lawyer for the defence in Tait's trial. The jury rejected the insanity defence and convicted Tait of murder. Bolte and his government rejected all pleas to commute the sentence, and the execution date was quickly set. Bolte was in favour of capital punishment for violent crime, and wanted to be seen as a strong leader. In his mind, Tait must hang.

Starke and his legal team refused to give up in the face of Bolte's intransigence. They had very powerful evidence of Tait's insanity. After a number of appeals, and delays of execution, they were able to convince the High Court that Tait was in fact insane, and thus could not be guilty of premeditated murder. The final verdict was not guilty on the grounds of insanity. So, Tait did not hang.

Starke commented "After Bolte was denied with Tait, he simply waited for the next cab off the rank. Poor Ryan happened to be the next cab."

The irony was that Starke, from being defence counsel for Tait, was the judge who was obliged to sentence Ryan to death. Ryan's legal team, with strong public support, campaigned hard for the death penalty to be commuted, but Bolte would have none of it.

There were many attempts to introduce new evidence, and Starke was kept busy hearing all manner of new applications, about new evidence and attempts to delay the execution.

On each occasion when an application was made, Bolte expressed his frustration, But Starke was convinced that each one deserved his consideration. As it transpired each time, on examining the evidence, he concluded that it was insufficient to justify a new trial.

The execution was delayed a number of times. Starke told us of one occasion, when Ryan was to be hanged on a Monday morning. He was on call over the weekend, when, on the Saturday, a fresh application was lodged, based on a claim that there was new evidence as to how Hodson was shot.

The application was lodged late on the Saturday morning, and a police car was despatched to collect Starke from the Mornington racecourse, where he had gone to, hopefully, relax for the day and maybe back a winner.

As the police car was racing him back to the city, its radio was on. He recounted to us the police conversations he overheard, very strongly in favour of the execution. One officer reported that Starke was heading back to the court to hear a fresh application. He noted that the air on the police radio was blue with unfavourable comments about him for even looking at the application.

In the end, after a few delays, all avenues of appeal ran out. Ryan was hanged in the early morning of 3 February 1967.

This was one of the occasions where I remember where I was at the time. It was a bizarre, empty feeling that the state was executing one of its citizens.

The execution led to a change in the Victorian public's view of the death penalty, which was finally abolished in 1973.

The Federal Court and the Untenable Argument

Every now and again, the courts flex their muscles when a party tries to run a line of argument that has no legs. This only happens occasionally, and only when the argument is a complete waste of time - where its chance of success is nil, zero, nada, zilch....

Such an occasion took place in the Federal Court of Australia in early 2013.

The case involved a group action being brought by a group of investors against a large firm of auditors. It followed the collapse of a major company, involving losses of many hundreds of millions of dollars. The investors claimed they would not have invested in the company if they had known the company's true position, which should have been detected by the auditors, and disclosed to the investing public.

The audit firm contested the action all the way, and denied that it was negligent in any way. It argued that it did not have any liability, as the error in question was made by only one of its partners, not by the whole firm - never mind that the audit fees went into the firm's account.

In turn, the partner in charge gave evidence that the error was not his. It was, he said, made by a junior employee in his section, and he couldn't be responsible for everything a junior employee did or failed to do - never mind that the partner set out the audit parameters, delegated the tasks to his underlings, and signed the audit report. (I was always a strong believer in delegation - *but* the rule is that *they who delegate must supervise!*).

It has long been a principle of law that a party is responsible for the actions or inactions of an employee, servant or agent in performing their duly allocated tasks. This is called 'Vicarious Liability', the liability of the organisation for the acts or omissions of a subordinate.

I don't know where the defendant's 'creative' argument came from, but it was represented by one of Australia's biggest law firms and a battalion of silks. Note - expressions like 'creative' and 'novel' in legal proceedings are code for 'junk' or 'you must be joking'.

The case was being presided over by Justice Michelle Gordon, who was distinctly unimpressed by the line being run by the defence, and the court time being taken up by running the argument.

Her Honour listened to the argument for a short while, and then reminded the practitioners that the court would not take kindly to lines of argument that had no merit. She announced that, if practitioners persisted with arguments which wasted the court's time and which had no chance of success, she would have no hesitation in making costs orders against those practitioners *personally*, for the time involved.

The plaintiffs lawyers nodded their agreement, but the defence lawyers expressed their outrage. How could a judge tell them how to run their defence? Her Honour invited them to reflect overnight on what she had said.

The next morning, counsel asked for the case to be stood down while important issues were canvassed by the parties (code for "We're seriously talking settlement").

In quite quick time, the case was settled, and a very substantial payment was made to the investors.

An argument that had no legs should not have been run, and merely wasted everyone's time!

This case reminds me of one of the first lessons I learnt as a young lawyer - assess the merits of your case as early as you can. If it's a loser, get the hell out of there as quickly and cheaply as you can!

CHAPTER 23

BARRISTERS

Never Leave the Barrister Alone With Your Client...

Some barristers should never be left alone with your client. If they can settle a case quickly, they still receive the same brief fee, and then move on to the next brief.

As a very young solicitor many years ago, I was in an interview room at the court with the barrister and the clients. It was a civil dispute, and my clients were suing for money owed to them under a contract. There had been a very low offer of settlement, which they had rejected as nothing like enough.

The registrar interrupted us; there was a phone call for me in his office (this was before the days of mobile phones). I kept the call short, and was away from the clients for no more than five minutes. I was stunned on my return to find that the case had been settled for less than the amount the clients had previously rejected.

The rub was that the barrister then returned happily to his chambers, leaving me to deal with the unhappy client. I never again, no matter what the circumstances, left client and barrister together again without my company - and I drummed that rule into many a young lawyer.

The Art of Cross-Examination

The most commonly quoted adage of cross-examination is to never ask a question if you don't know the answer. I have often observed over-confident barristers (some of whom are famous for their infatuation with their own voice) shoot their own case down in flames by asking one question too many.

In one case, the barrister was running a self-defence argument, on behalf of a man accused of a violent assault causing serious injuries. The accused claimed to be a man of peace who struck the other party in the belief that he himself was about to be assaulted.

The barrister had been quite successful in his cross-examination of a witness, and had established that the 'victim' had been verbally aggressive and insulting to the accused. He finished with a throwaway line "So it (the accused's striking of the 'victim') was quite unexpected?"

"Oh no" replied the witness. "I know how violent and hotheaded (the accused) can be. I could tell he was about to snap." Oops - better to have sat down and not asked that last question!

Then there are those clients who expect their brief to fiercely attack the opposing witnesses at every opportunity - and sometimes to construct that opportunity. This isn't, however, always the best approach.

I have sometimes observed the value of the more subtle style of some top barristers. With a smooth and cheerful manner, some barristers in particular have a talent for engaging the witness in friendly conversation. I have seen this result in some surprising admissions from someone whose testimony had started out in a most hostile fashion.

In one instance, the client was disgusted to see the barrister cosying up to the much hated witness. I had to strongly resist the client's demand to sack the barrister on the spot. The client had entirely missed the great skill of the cross-examination, even though it meant a much better result in the long run.

The common phrase "Trust me" can be of cold comfort to a client when their freedom or their financial welfare is on the line. An important part of the lead-up to the hearing is to instil confidence that the lawyer and the mouthpiece know what they are doing.

How to Settle Your Family Law Case

Over the years, I tried to keep as far away from family law as I could. My friend Linda enjoyed it as much as I disliked it, and particularly liked to be opposed to a barrister if the case was held up in the list.

Her favourite scenario was to be sitting at the court, waiting for the case to be called on. As the morning progressed, she would note the opposing barrister start getting fidgety. Often the opposing solicitor had left their client alone with the barrister (not recommended - see above). She reckoned that they'd be thinking about the paperwork in chambers, or possibly even the golf course, and wanting to get to it.

After a while, they would become much keener to settle, and she sometimes noticed them applying pressure to their clients.

Linda maintained that she received some very favourable settlements by just sitting out the barristers.

The Barrister and His Fee

I crossed swords with one barrister (Duncan) over his claim for a fee in a building dispute case. Duncan ultimately gave the law away for a media career, where he has become quite famous.

I had briefed him to appear in the local sittings of the County Court. On his way down from the city, he stopped off at the site of the dispute and had a look over the building in question. He then became involved in another case, and handed the brief back. I had to quickly engage another barrister to appear.

We then became engaged in negotiations with the other side. Both parties compromised, and we cobbled together a settlement that pleased neither side, but satisfied both.

The next week, I received a bill from Duncan's clerk for some hundreds of dollars, for his 'view' of the building. I rang him to point out that his 'view' was of no benefit to the client as he'd not been able to appear for us. He maintained he was entitled to the fee, and said we should claim it as part of our costs. I told him that we'd finally settled the case for a very skinny settlement, and there was no room for any payment to him.

I thought he was very cheeky in claiming a fee, and told him it would not be paid. He accepted the fact, but quite ungraciously.

Chuck Berry - a Difficult Barrister

I first came across Chuck as a law student. Most of us were fairly knockabout, and quite relaxed about student life. Chuck was from one of the major public schools, and seemed to regard himself as above us all (I hasten to add that the great majority of the public school types I met were good people and got on well with everyone).

Anyway, I felt that, after four years as an undergraduate, Chuck was starting to show a few shreds of humanity. Not to worry, he was soon in the rarified atmosphere of the bar, and it was said that he quickly became even more of a prick than before.

Working as a barrister seemed to agree with some lawyers, who really blossomed in the different atmosphere, but some (including Chuck) became unbelievably rude, boorish and obnoxious.

Chuck was certainly successful at the bar, but he was not a person you'd want to spend time with. It was said that, if you had a client you couldn't stand, you should send them to confer with Chuck, and find an excuse not to be there yourself.

Chuck had a remarkable ability to find himself on the wrong side of people wherever he went. He had a long-running stoush with ASIC, over the way he ran a company. This was eventually settled by his giving an undertaking not to be involved in the management of any company for a period of years.

Chuck's ability was widely recognised, and he also practised interstate, setting up chambers in a few other capital cities. He managed to antagonise other barristers and chamber managers in the process. We would regularly hear stories of abusive slanging matches, non-payment of rent for chambers, and litigation between Chuck and several other parties.

Chuck also found himself offside with members of his own family, with them lined up on one side, all opposed to him, in a dispute over a property in which they all had an interest.

The Indomitable Don Campbell QC

Don Campbell was the only silk I came across who had been a KC (Kings Counsel - he had taken silk in the time of King George V1). By the time I met him, he was very much a grizzled veteran of the bar, and in the twilight of his career.

Always fierce and irascible, Don (known to all as 'Donny') loved nothing better than turning a case into all out war - and for this he didn't have a lot of friends in the law. But if you were on trial, with your back to the wall, Don was the man you wanted in your corner.

Thus it was when he was appearing for Frank Hardy, who was very unusually charged with criminal libel arising from his famous book 'Power Without Glory', published in 1950. Hardy, who was a communist, had written a 'novel' about the famous character, John Wren. He had changed the names of all the main characters, but most were clearly identifiable.

The main character was portrayed very unsympathetically, as a man involved in many serious crimes. In the novel, the man's wife was implicated in an adulterous love affair, resulting in her having an illegitimate child.

The Melbourne establishment was outraged by the publication, and took the very unusual step of having Hardy charged with criminal libel - not the civil suit which is the usual procedure. So, it was the state, not just the injured lady, who was lined up against Hardy.

In Donny Campbell, Hardy had a man who would fight the prosecution every inch of the way, and had his own very caustic views of many establishment figures. Campbell battled every point, including pointing out that, in a novel, each character is developed as a composite of different people, and that Hardy had no malicious intent towards Mrs Wren.

His major argument, though, was that the only way to identify Mrs Wren was as the wife of the central character (in the novel called John West). And the only way he could be identified with John Wren was by conceding that he (Wren) was guilty of all the nefarious activities performed by West in the novel.

Campbell hammered this point over and over. Ultimately the jury accepted it, and acquitted Hardy.

Campbell had been stricken with polio in his youth, and used a walking stick to help him get around. In his latter years, judges would offer him the option of remaining seated when addressing the court, but he would never accept such an offer. He hated to be seen as disadvantaged in any way.

He would sometimes tell a story against himself, arising from a case when he departed from the old rule - never ask a question if you don't know what the answer will be. He was cross-examining a plaintiff's doctor, when this exchange occurred:

Q. How would you describe the plaintiff's pain?
A. Like a red-hot iron being placed against the sole of the foot.
Q. What would you know about a hot iron being placed against the sole of the foot?
A. I was a prisoner of war in Changi!

Oops - better not to have asked that question!

In addition to his work in the general courts, Campbell had a significant practice before the then Liquor Commission. He had a tendency to utter an occasional Spoonerism, which led to some merriment when he was asking a witness about liquor delivery. Unfortunately, it came out as a question about having his liver de-liquored…

Judges and Barristers - Occasional Tensions!

There are many celebrated instances of mutual loathing between certain judges and eminent barristers who appear before them. You have an interesting contest of powerful intellects and egos, each trying to impose their view of the law upon the other.

Many years ago, in the NSW Supreme Court, Evatt QC was appearing before a cantankerous old judge, where it was clear that neither of them could stand the other.

Evatt addressed the judge for about three hours on an obscure point of law, during which the other people in the court found it very difficult to stay awake. When he eventually sat down, the judge addressed him with "Well, Mr Evatt, I've listened to you for three hours now, and I must say I'm none the wiser.

Evatt rose to his full height, paused and casually replied "That may be so, your honour, but I'm sure you're much better informed."

Touche - a point to Evatt. However, advocacy is all about persuasion. He made his point, but he lost the case!

Another famous hatred existed between Sir Garfield Barwick, Chief Justice of the High Court of Australia and Keith Aickin QC of the Victorian bar. Aickin was a brilliant, smooth, silver-tongued barrister from the establishment side, while Barwick was a self-made man with a few rough edges, and a very irascible manner.

For years, Aickin resisted overtures that he take a place on the High Court. He simply could not abide the idea of working with "…. that bastard Barwick".

In 1966, Aickin was appearing before the High Court in the *Marrickville Margarine* case, which dealt with issues relating to interstate trade.

Aickin saw an opportunity here. He addressed the court for hours, in which he constantly pronounced 'margarine', with a hard 'g', as in 'Margaret' (as distinct from 'marje-a-reen', the more common pronunciation). As he expected, this gradually got under Barwick's skin. Eventually, Barwick leaned forward on the bench, and growled "Mr Aickin, why do you insist on pronouncing the word that way, when everyone else pronounces it 'margarine'?" (using the common pronunciation).

Aickin was ready for this. He pulled out his copy of Fowler's *Dictionary of Modern English Usage*, and quoted from it at length. His point was that his pronunciation was the correct one, whereas that favoured by Barwick, while much more common, was in fact incorrect and used generally by the lower classes. Ooh - very brave, but was it wise?

"I see" replied a seething Barwick, as Aickin's arrow found its mark. While many in the court were impressed by Aickin's cool effrontery, they could read Barwick well enough to know that he would find grounds to ensure that Aickin lost the case - no matter what!

Barwick as a barrister had been truly impressive, and had been able to convincingly argue even the most unlikely propositions. In this case, he put together an impeccable judgement - against Aickin's client.

No-one was surprised by this, probably not even Aickin.

Some years later, Aickin eventually took what many regarded as his rightful place on the High Court. What surprised many was that he and Barwick from time to time collaborated in joint judgements.

Barristers on Circuit

In the regional areas of Victoria, the law is administered by the Magistrates Court, while the superior courts visit the main regional centres a number of times a year, on what is called a 'circuit'. Some cynics prefer to use the word 'circus', but that is unkind.

Depending on the level of business in the court list, a circuit may last two weeks, or sometimes up to four weeks. It can be a busy time for firms who do a lot of litigation work, with other parts of the firm being diverted from their normal practice to support the running of the firm's cases.

It was customary for the local law association to hold a dinner nearing the end of the sittings, in honour of the visiting judge and his entourage. Several local lawyers would attend and entertain the judge, together with the barristers who were in town at the time. These dinners were always popular and sometimes went very late. Occasionally, the court's proceedings were conducted somewhat sluggishly the following day.

The Big 'Stick' on Circuit

I had known 'Stick' (as he was universally known) as a law student. He was a smart, outgoing, competitive student and sportsman, and went on to have a long and successful career at the bar. His standing was confirmed by his eventual elevation to the ranks of QC in 1992. He also sat on a number of sporting tribunals, dispensing justice to errant sporting types.

He still works on a part-time basis, and does a lot of work on Harness Racing Victoria's Racing and Appeals Disciplinary Board.

In my early days in Morwell, I had a County Court case which required briefing a good quality (but not too expensive) barrister to represent my client. The young Stick was just the right man for the job.

The case started on the Tuesday, and ran over to the next day. Stick was a very dutiful husband, and drove home to his home (and lovely wife) in Mt Eliza.

Stick's quality as a barrister was quickly apparent and many local lawyers began to brief him. He soon became a regular on circuit, and began to stay overnight, enjoying the very social nature of circuit sittings.

In fairly quick time, it seems that Stick was spending much of his working life on circuit in the region. He became very busy, not only in the County Court, but also in the regular Sale sittings of the Supreme Court.

For some time, there was a regular cabal of barristers who would come on circuit. They became close friends, excoriating each other in court, and then going off together for drinks and dinner, often with the locals.

In his student days, Stick had developed a well-deserved reputation as a man who could hold his liquor. Nothing that happened on circuit did anything to damage that reputation. There were some heroic nights, in which Stick was always one of the last of the men (and women) standing.

During the 1980's, there were some titanic efforts, and very late nights. Bear in mind that these took place mid-week, with court appearances beckoning the next morning - a prospect that did nothing to tone down the excesses of food and drink.

This culminated in a famous dinner at Boisdale House, a grand local venue a few kilometres from Sale. The dinner was attended by many notable locals, as well as the judge, visiting barristers and local solicitors.

After a sumptuous feast, washed down by local wines, several beers, ports, brandies and much more of the same, many of the guilty parties were in very bad shape when the court resumed the next morning. Several cases which were expected to fight to the absolute death were very quickly and quietly settled - and all conversation took place in very hushed tones.

Now, Rocky and his wife Gail had earlier invited Stick and a couple of other barristers to dinner at their home in Sale on the following evening. They arrived on time, but it was clear that they were still quite unwell.

After a very subdued pre-dinner drink, they sat down at the dinner table, and Gail served up one of her specialties, a beautiful lobster bisque.

Stick solemnly surveyed the soup for a good 30 seconds, gagged slightly, then, without a word, he pushed his chair back, slowly stood up, quietly walked to the door and left!

Henry the Peace Loving Barrister

Henry Jolson was a regular visitor to the Latrobe Valley as a young rising barrister, and made many friends there. Sadly, he died in October 2013, well before his time.

As well as his contribution to the law as a barrister (including many years as a QC), and his recognition as a wonderful citizen, Henry was a large part of a remarkable effort to assist the Middle East peace process.

This came about partly because of his connections within the sporting landscape and particularly the Australian Football League (he was a director of the Western Bulldogs Football Club and a Judge/Arbitrator of the court of Arbitration for Sport (Switzerland).

Henry also had contacts with the Peres Centre for Peace, established by the then Israeli President Shimon Peres in 1996. The centre set up many areas of modest co-operation between Israelis and Palestinians, including sport.

In recent years, as part of its promotion of Australian football throughout the world, the AFL has held an international football tournament, with teams from many countries coming to Victoria to compete for the AFL International Cup.

In both 2008 and 2011, the Peace Team flew to Australia to compete for the cup. Sponsored by the Peres Centre, and supported by many worthwhile organisations, the Peace Team comprised 13 Israeli and 13 Palestinian players, coached by former Brownlow medallist, Robert DiPierdomenico.

Henry was an active participant, and official Ambassador of the team. If you measure the team's success by winning matches, you'd be disappointed. But the real success was the blending of the 26 players into a team with shared goals and purposes.

Team sport is a wonderful paradigm for life, with the ethic 'what is best for the team?' being the over-riding consideration. It is impressive to see a player sacrifice their game (and sometimes even their health and safety) for the common cause. In this respect the team has been a great success.

Writing in "The Age", journalist Martin Flanagan reported that, after returning home, one of the Palestinian players invited the Israelis to his wedding in a village described as a 'Hamas hot spot'. Eight of the Israelis attended clandestinely. Photos were taken of them dancing together in their Peace Team jumpers.

Sure, such an effort is merely a drop in the ocean of what needs to be done to bring about peace in the Middle East, but every step, however tiny, is important and necessary.

A few days before his death, Henry received a message from one of the Palestinian players, saying that most of the things in his life were bad, and adding

"...the only positive thing that happened to me is that I am part of the peace team. Through the peace team I realised there is no give up in life and someday you will find the spot of hope if you decide to survive. In Australia I met many people who were very kind with us, showed us love and appreciation and interest in us as Palestinians, these people are as my family....Our feelings, our hearts and our minds are with you Henry and we wish we could be with you and hope to see you asap."

Shalom Henry - Rest in peace!

CHAPTER 24

THE LONG ARM OF THE LAW

'Radar' the Policeman

Occasionally you'll come across a lawyer with a 'God complex', one who believes he can do no wrong. A magistrate like the Chief (see above) liked nothing better than to cut them down to size.

There were also a few coppers who believed they could do no wrong. One of these became known as 'Radar'. His claim was that he didn't need any electronic equipment. He could tell a car's exact speed, even several kilometres away, and each and every variation in speed while he had it under observation.

Under cross examination, Radar would stick to his guns. He would not concede that there was any possibility of an error. Not even by one kilometre per hour. If he said the speed was 117 KPH, it was not possible that the actual speed was 116 or 118. No need for any equipment when you had Radar on board!

What an absurdly fanciful notion!

A few magistrates took what I regarded as the soft option and accepted Radar's evidence uncritically. Others regarded his evidence as arrogant and unacceptable.

On one occasion, a County Court jury rejected the Radar approach, after a skilful cross-examination made him look pompous and ridiculous.

There were some magistrates who would let police get away with behaviour they should not have tolerated. As an example, one policeman, at the end of his evidence, added "I might add, your worship, that the defendant is a well known thief", with no evidence to support the assertion.

This was a disgraceful claim (and the police in fact had no list of prior convictions to allege - and could only do this in any event if the magistrate found the charge proved). What was just as disgraceful was that they were allowed to get away with it. Any self respecting magistrate (e.g. the Chief, Leo or Dasher) would have thrown the book at them!

The Young Champ and the Police

In the early 1970s, a young Morwell man, Rocco (Rocky) Mattioli, started making a name for himself in the boxing world.

One day, he was at a local pub, when a foolish drinker thought he could make a name for himself by belting the youngster. A few seconds later, he was on the floor. One of the staff called the police.

Now there were a few young coppers in the area at that time who fancied themselves as quite useful with their fists. A carload of them was at the pub in no time.

Rather than coming in calmly and talking things through sensibly, they lined up to try out the young Rocco. One by one they were sat on their pants. It wasn't until they co-ordinated their approach that about half a dozen of them were able to gain the upper hand and cart Rocco off to the lockup.

Rocco was convicted of a couple of assault charges, but didn't suffer serious consequences. He learned from the experience, and I never heard of him coming before the court again.

Chad was Rocco's lawyer. I recall acting on the other side of a couple of commercial transactions which Rocco entered into as his success continued and his wealth grew.

Chad was a very jovial, outgoing lawyer with a good reputation. All the same, he wasn't above suggesting, when negotiations hit a hurdle, that he'd send Rocco around to move things along a bit!

The whole area was very proud of Rocco, and celebrated heavily when he won the world junior middleweight title in 1977.

Happy Harry

I first came across Happy Harry when he was giving evidence against a client of mine in the Magistrates Court. We clashed heavily when I cross-examined him, and did not like each other.

Over the next few months, we came across each other several times, and surprisingly became good friends. He was remarkably honest and straightforward, and you always knew where you stood with him.

Happy had his own view of some of his colleagues, and would always stand shoulder to shoulder with the honourable, honest, good cops. He was less sympathetic with those who took short cuts or put their own interests above their duty.

He was very unenthusiastic about one of his superiors who turned a blind eye to a number of serious infractions in favour of enforcing some silly, petty rules. A police officer was not supposed to have any other income than his earnings from the force.

Happy was a cricket fan, and was persuaded to become a cricket umpire in the local area, largely because there was a shortage of umpires. He was paid a pittance for his services, but this aroused the ire of his chief.

I recall many occasions when Happy was umpiring games I played in. He would point out his chief, standing by the fence by himself, and would mutter some unflattering comments about the chief being a hypocrite and not having a life or any friends. Happy enjoyed the umpiring (you certainly wouldn't do it for the money), and seemed to survive the chief's disapproval.

There was one occasion when Happy did a major favour for one of my team-mates. After many hours celebrating a premiership victory, Roddy was involved in a minor accident with another car, which came from his right, after he'd proceeded through a stop sign.

Happy attended the scene and took charge. He told me later that his report made much of the heavy rain at the time, the wet road, the poor lighting at the scene, and Roddy's view being blocked by a vehicle parked close to the intersection. He did not check Roddy's breath reading, and there were no charges laid.

Police and Drink Driving

Police measures against drink drivers are very common these days. Most people are happy to co-operate with these measures, as they work to make the roads safer for the community. So long as everyone is treated the same, the public will generally not complain.

However, when one group is treated differently from the rest, things get way out of kilter. When that group is a specialist police group, this can lead to disaster.

In 1978, the Traffic Operations Group (TOG) had a new chief appointed for the Gippsland region, based in Sale. On 3 May 1978, he invited all Gippsland's TOG members to Sale one morning for a 'meet and greet' session.

At the session, he made a big deal of the evils of drink driving, and how they were to attack it hard. He then invited them back to his place for a BBQ lunch. ***With alcohol. Before they drove home!***

At about 6.30 PM the same day, a group of five students (from what soon afterwards became the Gippsland campus of Monash University) was returning to their homes in Morwell. They came to a set of traffic lights, showing green, and proceeded to cross the Princes Highway.

As they crossed, a police car came from their right, through a red light, at a speed estimated at 130 KPH (in an eighty KPH zone). At the last half-second, the police siren came on.

The police car ploughed into the small car with the five students in it, killing three and seriously injuring the other two.

The Inquest

Christopher and I were consulted to act for the students (and the families of the deceased). We each briefed young barristers with a persistent attitude. Christopher engaged Stuart Stribling, and I briefed John Jordan (who is now a County Court judge).

The police closed ranks to cast a cloud of doubt over the whole exercise. They engaged Oliver, Gippsland's leading criminal lawyer, and spun him a line of lies (which ultimately led Greg to note that Oliver "…had the shits with them!"). If they'd told him the truth, he could have developed a very different strategy, and they would have finished up much better off.

The police appointed their own 'counsel assisting' the coroner, and presented a very sanitised (by which I mean completely fictitious) story of what had happened. This included:

- the three coppers in the car had left the BBQ in Sale at 1.00 pm and spent the rest of the afternoon 'checking stop signs' in Traralgon, before driving to Morwell in the late afternoon;
- they were pursuing a speeding car, a white or light coloured HR Holden Commodore, and had had the siren on for at least thirty seconds before the collision;
- the driver, Constable Peter Grummisch, had not been drinking, but was so upset after the collision that he went to a nearby house where the owner offered him a drink of Dimple whisky to help him to calm down (I knew the young man who lived in the house in question, and the suggestion that he would have Dimple whisky in the house was absurd). This led to Grummisch having a blood alcohol reading just over 0.10%; and

- the traffic lights were showing green when the police car entered the intersection.

The Coroners' Court set aside two days for the inquest, and the police were certain that they would suffer minimal damage only.

The most unpopular policeman in the region (known as 'Fang') did not discriminate in his attentions. He would book anyone, including other police. It was said that he once booked his own mother! Interestingly, he was the only TOG member who didn't attend the BBQ. He was later quoted as saying that the invitation to the boss's BBQ was hypocritical and inappropriate.

Fang, it appears, was not going to be corrupted as some of the others might be. I had had a number of dealings with Fang's younger brother, who was a process server, and had unsuccessfully applied to join the police force (he later became a prison warder, which was a concern). He told me, in the morning just before the inquest began, that the police had the process all wrapped up tight.

As it turned out, the inquest ran for two weeks, not two days. Christopher and I (and our barristers and the clients) spent many hours (often well into the night) tracking down witnesses, following up leads, drawing charts, connecting various dots, and developing our own quasi-prosecution files.

Gradually, the police conspiracy (for that is what it was) began to unravel, and the mood changed. What had started as a cocky, confident group of coppers started to look like a guilty clique, scrambling desperately to cover its tracks, all the while digging itself further into a hole of its own making.

Several witnesses had seen the police trio drinking through the afternoon at a well known hotel in Traralgon (they were slow to come forward, as they worried about the consequences of offending the police), but each little step forward encouraged others to come forward.

Seven witnesses who saw the accident testified that there was no HR Commodore (or any other vehicle for that matter) being pursued, and that they did not hear a police siren until the instant of the crash.

And on it went...

At the same time, I was having a new fence built at my home. One day when I went home for lunch, I was surprised to see Peter Grummisch there, working alongside the fencing contractor. I didn't comment on it, and nothing came of it (I suspect that Grummisch wasn't aware whose house it was). Not surprisingly, Grummisch was on leave from the force at the time.

At the end of the second week, Oliver was disillusioned, frustrated and angry that his clients (and their supporters) had lied to him. The Coroner was scathing about, firstly their behaviour on the day, and even worse, their criminal conspiracy to perjure themselves and to pervert the course of justice.

Grummisch was sent for trial in the County Court on a charge of causing death by culpable driving, and the others on criminal conspiracy and perjury charges.

At his trial, before Judge Leo Lazarus, Grummisch was the beneficiary of a masterful defence run by Jeff Sher, QC, and was eventually acquitted.

His colleagues were not so fortunate. They were convicted by a jury, and Chief County Court Judge Des Whelan sentenced them each to two years in prison.

A few months afterwards, I had a chat with Judge Whelan at a law conference, not long before his untimely death from cancer. His view was that, while committing perjury to get a person off is not quite as serious as perjury to falsely convict someone, it was still a very bad case of perjury (and criminal conspiracy) - from people who were sworn to uphold the law. His sentence was for one quarter of the maximum available, and he felt it was appropriate in the circumstances.

The officers appealed the sentence, but it was upheld.

So ended a very sad episode for the police force - not to mention the innocent students and their families!

The International Police Effort

Senior Detectives Hart and Jellie were institutions in the Latrobe Valley. While Seamus held court in his pub, their 'office' was at the local RSL club, where they and their minions propped up the bar at great length.

Those who were on side with these two had a charmed run, but those who didn't found that life could be very tough. It was said that they operated on a gut instinct. If their gut said that X was guilty, evidence would be produced to confirm that view, and to cast doubt on any contrary view. Sometimes, the evidence made no sense, but they'd forge on, looking for a quick and easy conviction.

Hart and Jellie were not viewed affectionately by the top levels of Victoria's police, and they were never going to be promoted much higher. As police officers, they were good drinkers. They laughed at their own jokes, and ridiculed anyone who disagreed with them. They even went so far as to boast about occasionally 'fitting up' someone they decided they didn't like.

They had a huge stroke of luck one day, when a criminal who had fled Australia was apprehended in England. They had been involved in the early investigations into the crime, and were required to travel to London for two weeks for the extradition proceedings, and bring the miscreant home to face trial.

We shuddered at how they would represent Australian law enforcement, and hoped that they would not cause a rift in our relationship with the mother country. Apparently they were given fierce instructions before they left home. Anyway, all went without incident, and they escorted the accused back for his trial.

The Policeman on Sick Leave

After a colourful career, Senior Detective Jellie became an object of suspicion from higher ranks in the force. He was the subject of a series of complaints from accused persons, some about his methods of obtaining 'voluntary statements' (reports of a boot in the groin were disturbingly common) and a generally cavalier approach to obtaining 'evidence'. While he was being investigated, he took the time honoured course and went on sick leave.

Some months later, while still on sick leave, he was called as a witness in one of his cases, in a County Court trial. His evidence was regarded as critical in the case.

As soon as he was sworn in, a sympathetic Crown Prosecutor noted that he was on sick leave, and suggested that he be permitted to be seated while giving his evidence. Mr Jellie acknowledged that yes, he was ill, and needed to be able to sit down.

So, Mr Jellie gave his evidence in chief from a sedentary position, looking suitably forlorn and frail.

On the same day, the local weekly newspaper appeared. In its sporting pages, it ran a summary of local cricket matches from the previous weekend. One of the reports commented on the slow batting of a certain Mr Jellie, who had occupied the crease for several hours while compiling a painfully slow 27 runs.

A copy of the newspaper magically appeared in the hands of the defence counsel, who had a picnic at poor Mr Jellie's expense. He had a field day pointing out the contrast between the poor pathetic image of the 'sick' man in the witness box, and the cricketer who batted all day. He ridiculed Jellie's honesty and integrity, to the extent that the jury concluded he had no credibility, rejected his evidence and acquitted the accused.

Obtaining a Voluntary Statement

Before the days of Hart and Jellie, there was a very old-fashioned Latrobe Valley policeman (described by Greg as 'Basher Bill').

Basher Bill was famous locally for his announcement of his two pet hates - 'Poofters and Queers'. Greg and I often wondered how he could discern the difference between the two groups, but that didn't worry Bill, who was proud of his technique for getting them to confess to their 'nefarious nature'.

No boot in the groin from Bill, but his suspects generally showed quite a deal of general bruising - apparently from falling over several times in the cells.

Unsurprisingly, Bill didn't stay long in the area. We heard that some 'counselling' had taken place, and the last we heard was that he was assigned to some very remote country town - hopefully well away from those dreaded poofters and queers!

Investigating the 'Wallaby' Story

In the early 1980's, there was a very weird group of people who lived in a 'commune style' area on the outskirts of Moe. They would have had a combined IQ of about 35, and had serious problems.

They came across an injured wallaby, and that's when things started to get seriously strange. Reports indicated that a couple of them had a sexual encounter with it. By that time, its condition was poor, so they decided to warm it up - by putting it in the oven for about 20 minutes.

When they took it out, it looked even worse, so they popped it into their fridge for another half hour. By this stage, its condition was much worse, so arguments developed over what to do next. Take it to a hospital, call a vet, call the police, what to do? One of them called a vet, who took the wallaby in, but was so concerned, he referred their conduct to the police.

What followed was a major investigation that took thousands of hours of police time. The whole sorry saga was investigated to a remarkable degree. Some 'senior' detectives became obsessed with the case, and spent amazing amounts of time on it.

Ultimately, no charges were laid, as the whole picture was so confusing, and the evidence unreliable. It seems to have been decided that there would be great difficulty in establishing just who had done what, and what their state of mind was at the time. Nevertheless, the investigation continued …..

The Wallaby or the Shotgun

Meanwhile, other things were happening, and not receiving attention.

At around the same time, I arrived at work one morning to see that a shotgun had been fired through one of the front windows of the office. There was a jagged hole in the window, and the drapes, while a spent shotgun cartridge lay on the floor.

I immediately rang the police station. A young constable came around quickly, had a look and said "This is a job for CI. I'll get them to come around in a few minutes."

We waited......and waited......and waited. No appearance your honour! They never arrived. We made a couple of calls, and were told they'd be there soon, but they never came.

We called our insurer, and had the plate glass window replaced, but never heard from the police again.

Too busy investigating the major crime about the wallaby. No time to look at a minor matter like a shotgun blast through a law firm's office window!

CHAPTER 25

My Time as a Mentor

For a period of about 12 years, in the latter part of my career, one of my roles was as a mentor/teacher/trainer of articled clerks and young lawyers.

It was almost by accident that I became a mentor in the section where I worked. Ferdi was the official mentor in the section until that time, but he had difficulty relating to female lawyers. He was generally abrupt, rude and unpleasant to them (in a way that was different to his relationships with male lawyers). As a result, Samantha, who was the articled clerk on rotation with my group at that time, kept well clear of him and gravitated to me.

Soon after this time, Ferdi left the firm, and I was appointed (almost by default) as the official mentor for the section.

Samantha was as much responsible for this state of affairs as anyone, as she had adopted me as her mentor instead of Ferdi. By temperament, I was more suited to the role than Ferdi was, and so it came to be.

Samantha was also much more suited by having me, and she flourished in the new environment. As noted above, Randy maintained that Samantha did all my best work.

Samantha and Justin

Justin was a lawyer who had been with the firm for a few years. He was a good-looking young man with an outgoing (and somewhat narcissistic) personality, and was very popular with the ladies. A real Don Juan.

When Samantha completed her articles, her admission day came around. She honoured me by asking me to move her admission to practice, which I was very pleased to do. Shortly after, she and Justin became an item and moved in together.

They were together for nearly two years before Justin moved on, leaving a badly hurt Samantha behind. A few of us had feared that this would happen, but had not wanted to speak up earlier.

Samantha left us and joined another firm, where she progressed very well as a lawyer, and is now a partner. A couple of years later she met a fine (and more suitable) young man, and finished up marrying him. She and I had kept in touch, and she invited me to the wedding.

At the wedding, I was introduced to her grandmother, a lively, feisty lady. The grandmother asked me if Justin was still alive. I replied "Yes, he is. Can I assume that, if you had a shotgun, he wouldn't be?" She guaranteed me that she would have taken care of him once and for all.

Annabelle

Annabelle was another of my articled clerks soon after Samantha. She was a bright, hard working girl who was always destined for high honours - one of those whom I could not have stopped no matter how hard I tried.

Annabelle and I also quickly became strong friends. She was (and still is) a lovely person who is revered by all in the firm.

As everyone recognised her qualities, Annabelle was in demand in every section of the firm. Adrian, who was the mentor in another section, would regularly tell me how he got into trouble with his wife for raving about Annabelle's qualities.

Following her admission, Annabelle stayed in Adrian's section. As expected, she progressed quickly through the firm's structure, and became the first of my articled clerks to graduate to partner.

Annabelle married a few years ago, and now has a gorgeous baby. She manages everything in her life most remarkably, and continues to be one of the strongest performers at the firm.

Julian and Santa

One of the most enjoyable young people I worked with was Julian, a real live wire, full of enthusiasm, energy and goodwill. He was always looking for the funny, or entertaining, aspect of the case.

Julian was one of the organisers of the 'Santa Claus Pub-Crawl'. A fun event, it was fascinating to see scores of people, in Santa costumes, heading from pub to pub, raising money for worthy causes.

The event grew rapidly, and there were some concerns, but Julian converted it into a corporate event, with many safeguards, and rules, so that its charities receive significant funds.

Julian the Surfie

One of Julian's passions, apart from his love of the beautiful Maria, was his surfing. On many weekends, Julian and his mates (including Gazza) would be up very early, and cracking waves wherever the surf was up.

So, when we had a major job for a client involved in the surf industry, and located in a popular surfing area, Julian was delighted to be on the team we sent down to the coast.

Julian duly arrived early in the day, and immediately impressed the locals with his surfboard on his car's roof rack. Great marketing!

Our team spent several days on site, joining the locals in the detailed negotiations involved in the deal, and putting the paperwork together.

Julian was rapt when, one mid morning, one of the locals burst into the 'war room', to announce that the surf was up. The room immediately emptied, as all the locals grabbed their boards and rushed off to grab a wave.

As the ultimate team player, Julian felt obliged to join them!

Sadly for us, Julian moved on a few months later and had two years working in London, where he introduced the Santa pub-crawl to many grateful Brits.

On his return, he took a position as an in-house lawyer with a major brewing company. He kept in touch, and entertained us with stories of his experiences there, including the regular slab which was part of the employment deal.

Julian and the Mega Firm's Charges

Most of the brewing company's legal work went to a high profile mega firm, and he was shocked at the way they charged for their work. He told me of a short telephone query from his office to the firm, asking about an intellectual property issue. The request was for a simple quick yes or no, with no lengthy legal jargon in the response.

What they received was a 48 page analysis of everything possibly related to the question, signed off by one of the firm's partners, and accompanied by an enormous bill.

This incident led to an explosion about snouts in the trough, and then to a substantial review of the relationship. The next financial year, the fees paid to that firm were reduced by about 75%.

Julian and Wholesale Liquor

In recent years, the brewing company split in two. One part continued on as a brewer, and the other became a pure wine company. Julian is now director of the wine company's legal services. He still receives benefits in terms of liquor, and introduced a few of us to its wholesale wine program.

As a friend of Julian, I am now a member of the wine club, and have access to wonderful wines, delivered to the door, at wholesale prices. There are some wonderful deals.

Very beneficial friendship!

Rochelle Reminds Me of My Advice

I recently caught up with Rochelle, nearly 10 years after her days as an articled clerk. She has gone on the great things as a leading tax expert with one of the large accounting firms.

Rochelle generally presented as a very capable, hard-working and confident young woman. However, she now reminded me that, when she first brought her work in to me, she lacked confidence in it. As a matter of course, she would tell me "I know it's not very good."

My response, after this happened a couple of times, was to say, "Well, why are you giving me work that you say is no good? If you believe it's no good, you must have an idea of what you could have done better. So, do it better!"

Rochelle tells me that I went on to say "Don't ever apologise for your work. You do good work. I expect you to do your best and present it honestly, confidently and positively. That doesn't mean I won't change it, but I'll explain why I changed it. And don't forget that I've been doing this for many years."

After this little chat, Rochelle developed more confidence, and became an excellent young lawyer.

There was another time we recalled, from Rochelle's articles rotation with me. I took her along to a mediation on a fairly minor lease dispute. Our client, Shirley, had a number of complaints, and felt she'd been treated badly (and rudely) by the landlord and the agent. An apology would have gone a long way to satisfying her.

At the mediation, Boris, the crusty (and very cranky) old (yes, older than me) male lawyer on the other side did not behave well. After I had summarised our position in a couple of minutes, he droned on for about 40 minutes as though he was addressing the High Court. He then sharply criticised Shirley and us (in an unusually personal way) for having the gall to make her complaint.

The mediator had his hands full that session. After nearly an hour, we finally reached the 'bargaining' stage.

A few days earlier, we'd told Boris that Shirley would accept $20,000 in full settlement of her claim and costs. He had snorted derisively that she'd not get a cent.

After some discussion at the mediation, Shirley indicated that she'd accept $10,000 in full settlement. Boris and his client had a quick chat in another room, and offered $5,000. We had a quick chat and offered to accept $7,000. Boris and his client left the room for another chat.

While they were out, I told Shirley that I expected them to come back and increase their offer to $6,000, and that I'd advise her to accept it, and bring the case to an end. She made a face, but indicated she'd agree.

A minute later, Boris stormed back into the room with his client in tow, grabbed his file off the desk, told us we must be joking, that all offers were withdrawn, and his client would fight the case to the death.

We and the mediator were left open-mouthed. This was not the conduct you expect in a mediation.

As we headed down in the lift with Shirley shortly afterwards, I told Rochelle that she had just witnessed an example of what a lawyer should **never** do. Boris had put his own ego before the interests of his client. In doing so, he had left the client in the position that, no matter what the ultimate outcome, it would cost him much more than he could have got out of it for at the mediation,

Sure enough, the case went on for over two more years. There was a hearing in VCAT, followed by an appeal to a single judge of the Supreme Court of Victoria, and then to the Court of Appeal. All up, the costs ran into several hundreds of thousands of dollars.

In the event, both parties lost big-time. The only winners in that scenario are the lawyers. And given how close we got in the mediation, that's a disgrace!

Melanie and Graham

There are some people who, as soon as you see them, appear to be so well suited that they are destined to spend their lives together. So it was with Melanie and Graham.

They were from different areas and different schools and universities, so they hadn't met until they started with us. After two weeks of orientation into the firm, they were sent into their first rotations, Melanie with me and Graham in the next section.

As it happened, they were seated almost next to each other. In my dealings with Melanie, I noted how they had a great time sledging each other, and what outstanding sledgers (and excellent young lawyers) they both were. I recall saying that they were just like an old married couple.

There was, however, another issue here. Melanie was engaged to Luke, a young barrister, whom she'd met when they were both law students. He was a very personable young man, and they were duly married soon after he moved her admission. They invited me to the wedding, a very happy celebration of two young people.

The problem presented itself soon after. It seems that Luke had a number of substantial debts, and had been much less than honest with Melanie in many respects. Sadly, he proved not to be the man of character and integrity he'd appeared to be. The marriage did not last a year.

Melanie received excellent support through all this, not only from her wonderful family, but also her friends and work colleagues. Not least of these was Graham, whose friendship turned into romance. A couple of years later, they were married.

Graham quickly became an absolute rock at the firm. He threw himself into its social, sporting and cultural activities, in addition to his contributions as a lawyer. Kicking goals in all directions! He became the second of my articled clerks to make partner with the firm.

Melanie has taken time out to have her babies, and is now back working part-time. She is an exceptional lawyer as well as being a wonderful person.

Pepe the Poker Player

One of my happiest articled clerks was a young man called Pepe, who always had a smile on his face. Someone who didn't know him could get the mistaken impression that he didn't take life seriously, but that would be far from the truth. The fact was that his positive attitude kept coming through, and manifesting itself as sheer enjoyment of life.

During his rotation with me, Pepe asked if he could take a week of his annual leave. No problem, he was entitled to it at the time. The reason - to play in a poker tournament!

The reader might be aware of the professional world-wide poker tour, played at casinos, for huge money. The casino in Melbourne was hosting one of these tournaments, with 800 competitors, including some very big names on the poker tour.

Each player paid $10,000 to enter, so there was a nice prize pool. When they heard that the tournament was being held in Melbourne, Pepe and a few of his mates determined that one of them would enter, and that they'd all contribute to the entry fee. Over a period they put a lot of time into the practice and preparation, with Pepe winning the right to represent them.

The tournament was played under 'Texas Hold'em' rules, with generally seven players at a table. Each player is dealt two cards, face down. The dealer then deals three community cards face up (the flop) and then two more cards, one at a time. At every step along the way, the players can place bets.

So Pepe got into the tournament, and away he went. He easily survived the early rounds, and soon was on a table with a former world champion. He looked likely to be eliminated here, when he went 'all up' against the former champ when the odds were very much against him, but he had a stroke of luck and survived.

A few of our people were channelling reports back to us about how he was going. We were hearing that he was down to the last 150, then the last seventy, and all of a sudden, Pepe was on the final table of seven.

My view is that his permanent smile was a great help to him. One look at his happy smiling face might well convince other players that he had a really good hand (perhaps when he didn't). One of the keys to poker is to know when other players are bluffing. It seems that Pepe's bluff was very hard to pick.

Anyway, Pepe was finally eliminated in fourth place (out of 800). For this, he came away with prizemoney of $500,000, a lot of money for a young man on an articled clerk's salary.

When I asked Pepe what he planned to do with the money, he calmly told me that he paid a dividend to his mates (a nice little profit share for them) and gave the rest to his mother. Simple solution!

He then returned to work as if nothing had ever happened.

Olympia

Over the years, I had many articled clerks, and derived great enjoyment from them, their energy and enthusiasm.

One of these was a delightful and elegant Greek girl, Olympia. She was a very bright personality, full of enthusiasm for life, and for everything she did.

Quite often in my work with the articled clerks, rather than provide them with the answers, I would ask them a series of questions, to help them to think the issue through. I reasoned that they would benefit more this way than if I just gave them the answer.

I was going through this procedure one day with Olympia when she burst out with "Oh, you use the Socratic method!" Ah, well...I suppose I do... From then on, she took to addressing me as "Socrates".

The articled clerks were kept busy at the firm, and had a full program of lunch meetings, where senior lawyers from various parts of the firm would discuss recent cases and other developments from their area of expertise.

I was talking to them one day about a case that had recently been filed in the Supreme Court of Victoria. A number of Chinese investors had paid deposits and signed "off the plan" contracts on many of the apartments in a new development under construction in the Docklands area.

The brochures produced to them at the time of the sales program had shown a beautiful gold leaf building. This was critical in the investors' decisions to buy, as gold buildings had great feng shui.

The problem was that, as construction progressed, and settlement approached, there was nothing golden about the building. The investors launched a case against the vendor, seeking to have the contracts set aside, on the consumer law basis of 'misleading or deceptive conduct'.

This discussion with the articled clerks was taking place in one of the meeting rooms of our offices on Level 30 of one of Melbourne's leading buildings, and overlooked the Docklands area. I pointed out the building in question, and they all peered out the window at it.

Olympia was the first to put it into words. "My god" she exclaimed "That's not gold. That's cack brown!"

Such a sweet young thing!

Sandy

Some of my articled clerks had so much going for them that we could all tell that they were destined for success. No matter what I did, I wouldn't have been able to hold them back. While I was happy to bathe in some reflected glory, they were always going to make it.

There were others, however, for whom it was more of a struggle. I soon learnt that they were all different, and that I would need to tailor my approach to their personalities and their balance of abilities. I'm happy to claim more credit for those in this group, as I believe I contributed more to their progress.

Sandy fits into this category. By the time it was his turn for a rotation with me, he'd had a couple of unhappy rotations, and was completely lacking in confidence.

After thinking about how to approach the mentoring task, I started off quite low key, giving him relatively straightforward tasks.

I made a point of being very positive and encouraging, and his response was terrific. I found myself praising his good work, and the difference was amazing.

Sandy advanced through the rotation at a wonderful rate, and never looked back. After admission, he returned to work in my section, and came to be well regarded and highly trusted by one of our best clients. A few years later, he moved on, did a masters degree, and is now working as in-house counsel for a major corporation.

Sandy is one of those young people who continues to live at home with his parents. His mother loves having him at home and makes his life there very comfortable. She does his laundry, and cooks all his meals (including a big cook-up to fill the freezer if she's going away).

For years the only thing Sandy spent any money on was the plasma TV he bought for his bedroom. Whenever he was going out, he'd take his mother's car. He finally paid cash for his own nice new car, but nothing else has changed.

Why indeed would he want to move out?

Lavinia

Lavinia was one of my many favourite articled clerks, with her huge, happy smile. Her ability to relate to people is a huge gift, and her outgoing friendly personality makes her a lovely person to be around. Thanks to Lavinia, I have become close friends with her wonderful parents.

As a law student, she had spent two weeks as a seasonal clerk, doing work experience with Ridges, another significant city firm.

She told us of her experience with Ridges, and the way they handled their employees and their billings. Even though their stint with the firm was for two weeks only, the seasonal clerks were classified as fee earners for the firm, and given a budget to meet.

Then, after lunch every Friday, Ridges would send an email to all fee earners, showing the dollar time recorded by all of them that week. It would then follow up with a please explain to all those who had not met their budget for the week.

All this to someone who had never worked with a law firm before, and was part-way through their law degree!!

Ridges then put pressure on Lavinia to sign up to do her articles with them. Unsurprisingly, she declined and instead chose to come to us.

Kirsten

Kirsten was one of my favourite articled clerks and young lawyers. From the start, she was outstanding, being so much more on the ball than most. She was also a young woman with great personal qualities.

After the customary two weeks of orientation with the firm, Kirsten commenced her first rotation in my section - I was her first mentor. As with some young people, particularly coming into a daunting environment, she was quite hesitant, and kept on putting herself down, and not acknowledging the quality of the work she was producing.

One day, I pulled her up on this, saying "Stop. Before we go any further, I want you to know that I have a very high opinion of you, both as a lawyer and as a person. You have tremendous qualities, so I want you to understand them and conduct yourself accordingly."

This conversation seemed to help Kirsten realise that she was well suited to what she was doing, and to release her from some of her anxiety. She went from strength to strength, and impressed all in our section, and later in the other parts of the firm where she worked.

At the end of her articles year, Kirsten joined my group, and proved to be a real asset. She was also planning a wedding, despite the problems being caused by her prospective mother-in-law. Then, about six weeks before the wedding date, she discovered that her intended was having an affair with another young woman.

The wedding was cancelled, and Kirsten was devastated. With good support from her family and friends, including those of us in her work group, she showed the great depth of her character.

Every couple of weeks, Kirsten and I would go downstairs for a coffee and catch-up, to review her work, and how things were going generally. On one of these occasions, I recall lamenting about how hard life can sometimes be, but noting how the hard times often lead to people doing wonderful, heroic things. Kirsten ruefully agreed that this was true, but added "I wish I didn't have so many opportunities to be heroic."

Heroic, however, was an apt word for Kirsten. She grew from the experience, continued to develop as an excellent lawyer, and rebuilt her personal life. Several months later, she met an excellent young man (far superior to the previous one), whom she married a couple of years later. They now have a baby boy, who is the delight of her life.

I recently had lunch with Kirsten. She agreed with my suggestion that all the pain was worth it, and that in fact, the previous young man had in fact done her a huge favour.

Kristy and Annie

The phenomenon of lovely young women being ditched in the lead-up to their wedding seemed, a few years ago, to be all too common. The same thing happened, in very similar circumstances, to both Kristy and Annie, a couple of years apart.

As with Kirsten, both Kristy and Annie, with family, friend and workmate support, came through the difficult time, and showed their real character. Both later met much better young men and moved on with their lives.

I am proud to call each of Kristy, Annie and Kirsten as my friends.

Skye

I had many 'favourite' articled clerks. Almost without exception they were bright, hard working, enthusiastic and entertaining. It gave me great pleasure to see them, while with me and afterwards, developing into excellent young lawyers. I'm sure that I gained at least as much out of the process as they did.

One of the best was Skye, who had commenced in another profession (this is not uncommon) and switched over to law a few years later. One day we were talking about this, and she told me about doing work experience with a country law firm, when she decided to become a lawyer.

I asked her "Who was it who inspired you to become a lawyer?" She replied "Jenny Orchard was my inspiration. She was the person I worked with when I did my work experience."

I was so pleased to hear this. I had worked with Jenny when she was an articled clerk with Keith's firm about eighteen years before, and again at the branch office. We were good friends, and I had given Jenny a reference when she moved to a different part of country Victoria. She always was a fine person and an excellent lawyer, and it was no surprise that she was inspiring young people to become lawyers.

Skye is now an associate with Jenny's firm, and is proving to be the success that I always expected her to be.

James and Andy

In my role as mentor, I have often suggested to articled clerks and young lawyers that they should talk to me before finalising a decision to move to another firm.- This could help prevent them making a terrible mistake (see under Fast Fred, earlier).

James was one of my articled clerks a very well-spoken and intelligent young man. I have always had a very high opinion of him. James's father Mark is a leading lawyer around town, holding a prominent position within the profession, and was for some years the managing partner of a substantial firm. I had first met Mark when he proudly moved James's admission in the Supreme Court.

I have already mentioned Andy Silver (above) who worked with us before setting up his own practice with his father-in-law as his major client.

A couple of years after completing his articles with us, James resigned from the firm and joined Andy. He had not known Andy in his time with us, as Andy had left before James joined us.

If James had asked me, I would have counselled him against joining Andy - I had always felt that James was destined for a major commercial firm, and time with Andy would not take him in that direction. As it happened, James did not enjoy his time with Andy. He found that Andy, as principal of his own firm, became much as I have earlier described Kim - difficult, disorganised and volatile.

At the same time as James joined Andy, so did one of our assistants, on the offer of a higher salary. She was back with us in less than three months, not because Andy didn't pay the salary offered, but because she found Andy impossible to deal with. Money wasn't everything!

James also left Andy after a few months, and joined a more conventional firm. It wasn't where he had planned to be, but it gave him some breathing space.

At a significant legal gathering a little later, I ran into Mark, and we discussed what had happened. Mark did not know Andy, so he could not have advised him whether the move would work out or not. I mentioned that I have often suggested that young lawyers talk to me before making career decisions. Mark agreed that James should have done so, and doubted that he would make the same mistake again.

Indeed, some months later, I met up with James at another lawyers' function. He told me that he was assessing his future again, and would be applying for a new position soon, and asked me if I'd be a referee for him. Of course I would.

He called me soon after, and I gave him a reference over the phone to a good Melbourne firm who rang me to check on him. A couple of days later, I took a call from the Perth office of one of Australia's mega firms. James received offers from both firms, but opted for the Perth job and is now working hard there on major corporate transactions.

Alan and Suzy

One of the joys of working in a law firm is the fun you have watching the interaction between feisty, funny, lovely young people.

Alan was one of my articled clerks, an impressive young man, and a survivor of cancer at a relatively young age. Very strong and mature, but with a wicked sense of humour.

When I retired from the firm a few years later, he moved into my old office. When I challenged him about the ghosts of previous occupants, he laughed and said, whenever he had a problem, he'd ask himself "What would Kevin do?" I grinned "Easy, Kevin would delegate!", but he was kind enough to insist that thinking about what I might have done helped him to work through the issue.

Then there was Suzy, a very capable young woman who was the assistant for me and a number of other lawyers. Suzy started as an office junior, but quickly impressed with her attitude and abilities. At one stage, she considered going back to university to study law, but there was a lot happening in her life, so she moved on from that.

When Suzy started as an assistant, I teased her about all the work she'd have on her plate, and noted the number of busy lawyers she'd be working for, and called her 'Suzy the slave'. That was a mistake. In no time Suzy was ruling the section (partners and all) with an iron fist. She had a delightful way of cutting through to the issues, and getting people to work together very effectively.

Suzy was also very entertaining and capable of the most ribald language, but managed to keep it in check when dealing with clients and anyone outside the firm.

There was one occasion when I was holidaying in Darwin. Suzy sent me an email on the Blackberry that I had at that time, telling me that a particular client had rung for me. She wanted to know if the matter could wait, or should she ask one of the other lawyers to call the client back.

I replied that I knew what the call was about, and that it could wait till I returned to work. I added "By the way, it's 33 degrees here, sky is the most beautiful blue, I've just been for a swim, opening a cold beer right now. Heading out for a long dinner a bit later. Life's good. How's work?"

Having sent such a provocative email, I was expecting a wicked response. Disappointingly, nothing came through. When I returned to work, I mentioned that I felt let down by the absence of a reply. Suzy told me that she had typed a reply, ready to send, but hit the 'delete' key when she reflected that its very strong language might have led to her dismissal for a serious breach of the firm's email policy!

Anyway, from the day Alan commenced his articled clerk rotation with me, he and Suzy began one of the best sledging contests I've ever seen. They were well matched, and delighted in scoring points off each other. Anyone who didn't know them could have easily (and erroneously) concluded they were the worst of enemies.

Some time after Alan had completed that rotation, he came back to chat to me about a particular issue. Suzy noticed him there, and made a point of coming in and telling him "F... off, you don't belong here any more!"

A little later, Alan returned to work quite close to my office. He and I would have a small wager whenever our football teams played each other (he has the misfortune of being a Collingwood supporter and I'm a proud Geelong fan). The bet would be for $5, or a lotto ticket, and once for buying a ticket on a racehorse (like the lotto tickets, this was also a waste of money).

There was one occasion when Alan suggested that if the Magpies won, I should give him Suzy as his assistant for a day. He'd have great fun, he said, ordering her around.

I pointed out that, for that bet, he'd have to be Suzy's assistant for a day if the Cats won.

That prospect slowed Alan down, particularly when Suzy chimed in about what she'd have him doing if Geelong won. So the bet turned out to be much more boring.

It was just as well for Alan, as the Cats towelled the Pies that weekend. Yes!!

Cynthia

Here we have another outstanding and delightful young woman. Around the time Cynthia was doing her articles rotation with me, she was having some difficulties in her personal life, but very few of us knew it. She showed great character to deal so well with it and get on with her life.

In a later rotation, Cynthia had a big night out with the people from her new section. She turned up for work the next day somewhat second hand, and with a colourful silk top that she'd picked up the previous night (and had no idea whose it was or how she came by it).

Alan and I noted that Cynthia must have been booked to ride the favourite in the third at Cranbourne that day.

A couple of years later, in a casual conversation about charities, Cynthia mentioned to me that she and a close girlfriend had set up their own charity. They actually have! Fully registered and with full tax-deductible status.

Their charity is for supporting two very disadvantaged schools in a remote area of Ethiopia. They have travelled a couple of times to the area at their own expense, and raised enough money to build several classrooms.

As part of their responsibilities, the two young women are directors of the company that holds the assets. As part of all this,

Cynthia has now become an expert in corporate governance and directors duties. They are continuing their hard work, in their own time, and the charity is going from strength to strength.

Thanks to them and their efforts (and networks) hundreds of children now have an opportunity for an education they would not otherwise have had.

Proud to be associated with you, Cynthia!

Rules for Young Players

The most obvious rule in any office today is - take care before hitting 'reply all'. We have had many disasters when an email to 'all users' produces a personal response, which was intended only for the original sender, and goes instead to the whole office. Oops, serious embarrassment!

One thing I drummed into my young lawyers was the expression 'attention to detail'. Several of them were big picture types, who could outline a complicated overall plan, but its value was lost when one found numerous typos and poor finishing. So, they copped another lecture on 'attention to detail'.

In particular, I instigated a new rule for one of my articled clerks a few years ago. He was a bright and capable young man, but his detail work was very ordinary.

To impress upon him the necessary approach, I wouldn't let him into my office unless he solemnly intoned, three times, the expression 'attention to detail'.

It must have worked as he is now a senior associate with a major firm in Sydney.

Make Sure You Ask the Right Question

On quite a regular basis, I'd have an articled clerk who was working in another section, appear at my door with a question they'd been told to ask me. Generally, the bare question would make no sense, so I'd ask what the context was, and what was the nature of the issue under consideration.

Sadly, on almost every occasion, the poor articled clerk had been given nothing more than the bare question, did not know what the file was about, and was completely in the dark. So, I'd send them back with a list of my own questions, including what the context was, and what the original question was designed to find out about.

Invariably, when we knew the background, I could provide a framework for the articled clerk to work through the issue, and we'd jointly come to the correct answer (mostly, we'd first determine what the original question should have been - and this was often very different from what it was).

So, you who work with graduate lawyers, give them some context, and you'll derive two immediate benefits. Firstly, you'll save the firm a lot of time in coming up with the right answer. And you'll also enhance the graduate's learning process and improve the level of satisfaction they get from their work.

Thou Shalt Not Run Out the Managing Partner!

When the graduate lawyers (the current term for the old expression 'articled clerks') start with the firm, they have two very busy weeks of general orientation, to get them familiar with the way the firm works, and many of its contacts, and then go into their first rotation.

Some years back, Dominic was one of these. At the end of his first day in the first rotation, which was in the managing partner Anton's section (and as he had played a little cricket), he was included in the firm's cricket team for a twilight game in the law firm competition.

Anton had played cricket at a high level as a younger man, and was captain of our team. Dominic was batting in the lower order, under instructions to score runs in a hurry, when he called Anton through for a very quick single.

OH NO! Disaster, he's run out Anton.......who was not impressed! Fortunately he got over it quickly and held no grudge.

Dominic later commented that, when he himself was dismissed, he felt like leaving the ground in the opposite direction.

The next day, it was all around the firm, and poor Dominic copped the mirth of the whole firm. 'Terrible career move' and other comments. Surely he could have waited a few days at least before introducing himself so obviously!

Unbelievably, the same thing happened two years later. Adam, just into his first rotation, did exactly the same thing. Again, Anton was the victim (but no-one was prepared to suggest that it was his fault).

Again, Adam bore the brunt of all the wise-cracks the firm could muster. One of the senior partners, keeping a very straight face, told Adam the next day that his name had come up at the partners meeting that morning.

So, from then on, the warning was included in the rules for the new players in their orientation!

CHAPTER 26

MY CONTRIBUTION TO ACADEMIA

In the last phase of my life in the law, I have stumbled across the joys of being a (very occasional) university staff type.

RMIT University did not, until recent years, provide a law degree. It now offers a JD (Doctor of Jurisprudence) as an accelerated course for entry to the legal profession, for persons who have a primary degree in another discipline.

As part of the course, the University decided to introduce a (very limited) practical training program for the students. This is something that universities have always rejected, as being foreign to the concept of a law degree, and beneath their dignity to even think about.

I recall my experience as an articled clerk, when I rocked up to start work. Yes, I had a law degree, but had previously never seen a contract, a statement of claim, a will or a legal document of any nature. And this still happens today!

So, at RMIT, a few of us (senior?) practitioners were called in, for a (very) modest fee, to help with the practical training module. The reader might regard this as quite fundamental, but this was apparently ground-breaking stuff.

What we were engaged to do was try to replicate (very briefly) what the students might experience when they turned up for work at a real law firm. So we had some fun writing a few scenarios to represent some cases they might be given in practice.

My involvement is to attend twice a year, on a Saturday. and have sessions all day, each for an hour, and each with (generally) three students.

In each session, I am notionally the senior partner of a law firm, and the students are supposed to be new graduate lawyers (the term 'articled clerk' is now history). They receive the scenario about half an hour before they come to me.

Occasionally, one will tell me that they haven't studied the point at issue here. My response is generally to ask them if they really want to work at this (fictitious) firm. After all, the principal of the law firm won't be impressed by that line. They'll be told to quickly familiarise themselves with it.

The first question I ask them is "What is the very first thing we look for here?" Most of the students start talking about some case law, or the wording of a particular statute they think might be relevant.

Not so, I tell them, "The first issue is - who is our client?" Is it an individual, a company, its directors, an insurance company, a partnership, the trustee of a trust, the beneficiaries, etc. Often it's obvious who the client is, but experienced lawyers have sometimes been caught out on this point, with great embarrassment, and at great expense.

The next question is - "How do we get paid?" If the firm doesn't get paid, it'll easily go broke, and they'll be out of a job. If the firm works on a 'no win - no fee' basis, I'll ask them for a quick summary of the merits of the client's case, so we can determine whether to take them on.

Once we sort these questions out, we progress to how we will represent the 'client' and what legal avenues are available to us.

I then take them through a process of discussing the scenario, interviewing the 'client' (generally a tutor in the department) and having them express their views on the strengths and weaknesses of the case.

I then give them each a written task, which they have to hand in to their lecturer, who will allocate marks for it. I allocate marks to them for their performance in that hour. It all goes towards their result at the end of the semester.

As I mentioned, this is regarded as ground-breaking. In fact, in early 2012, one of our RMIT people delivered a paper on it at a law teachers conference at Oxford.

How's that for an unlikely way to be famous?

CHAPTER 27

AND FINALLY, A LAWYER'S WISH LIST

As I come to the end of these ramblings, it is time to add the following, in setting out the perspective that a lawyer should bring to their undertakings. This is as follows (please forgive the outdated gender stereotypes):

I wish I had...

A foot large enough to stamp out injustice
A fist big enough to knock out my own self opinion
And a heart big enough to accept true judgement.
A mind broad enough to accept a man as he is...
But a desire to show him a better way.
A tolerant sympathy for the narrow minded
Clear vision to see my own shortcomings
And a simple, unquestioning faith in the unknown.
A heart strong enough to take life as it comes
And a determination to stick with what is right.
Eyes to see the road to self-improvement
Two arms strong enough to hold my sorrows

And an understanding of life's disappointments
To hold my ideals high enough to keep me humble
And strong enough to keep me true.

I am indebted to my good friend and colleague Rowland Hassall for this piece of wisdom. It is his, not mine. I can merely admire his considerable depth as a lawyer.

www.ingramcontent.com/pod-product-compliance
Lightning Source LLC
Chambersburg PA
CBHW031823170526
45157CB00001B/163